Creative Writing Guidebook

11·2008

Creative Writing Guidebook

Edited by Graeme Harper

continuum

Continuum International Publishing Group

The Tower Building	80 Maiden Lane, Suite 704
11 York Road	New York
London SE1 7NX	NY 10038

British Library Cataloguing-in-Publication Data
A catalogue record for this book is available from the British Library.

ISBN: 978-0-8264-9428-3 (Hardback)
        978-0-8264-9429-0 (Paperback)

Library of Congress Cataloging-in-Publication Data
Creative writing guidebook/edited by Graeme Harper.
  p. cm.
  Includes bibliographical references and index.
  ISBN 978-0-8264-9428-3 (hbk.)
  ISBN 978-0-8264-9429-0 (pbk.)
  1. Creative writing–Handbooks, manuals, etc. 2. Authorship–Handbooks, manuals, etc.
  3. English language–Rhetoric–Handbooks, manuals, etc. 4. English language–Composition and
    exercises–Handbooks, manuals, etc. I.
  Harper, Graeme.
PE1408.C7144 2008
808'.042—dc22   2008030734

Typeset by Newgen Imaging Systems Pvt Ltd, Chennai, India
Printed and bound in Great Britain by MPG Books, Cornwall

Contents

Acknowledgements

Sincerest thanks to all the creative writers, from the USA, UK and Australia, who have contributed to this book. The current vibrancy of the field in and around universities and colleges is certainly very well represented! Thank you one and all. Thanks to colleagues at the National Association of Writers in Education (UK), the Association of Writers and Writing Programs (USA) and the Australian Association of Writing Programs (Australia) who have engaged with me in many discussions and contributed notably to how the field has developed, and continues to develop. Excellent! And thanks to those many creative writers who have contributed to *New Writing: The International Journal for the Practice and Theory of Creative Writing* – this has proven a considerable venue for exploration of our field, and it continues to grow. Thanks to those at the International Centre for Creative Writing Research (ICCWR), for the many video links and online discussions, and to those who have attended the *Great Writing* international creative writing conference, now over a dozen years in action. The quality and range of creative and critical work at the conference continues to astound, and to flourish! Thanks to my fiction publishers, who keep the creative fires burning! A sincere and hearty thanks here to Gurdeep Mattu and Colleen Coalter, of Continuum Books, who have made the writing and editing of this work a real pleasure. Thanks also to Sam Rayner, for her assistance with coordination and indexing. Finally, much love and thanks to Louise, Myles and Tyler, to whom my creative and a critical sense of purpose owes a great deal.

Graeme Harper

Notes on Contributors

Ken Dancyger is the author or co-author of seven books on screenwriting, directing, film editing and production. He conducts screenwriting workshops and seminars in North America, Europe, Asia, South Africa and Australia. He is past President of the University Film and Video Association and past Chair of the undergraduate film department at New York University. He is currently Professor of film and television at the Tisch School of the Arts at New York University.

Catherine Zobal Dent is an Assistant Professor of English at Shippensburg University, where she teaches creative writing and advises the undergraduate literary journal, *The Reflector*. Her current project is a collection of linked short stories set on the eastern shore of Maryland. Dent was the winner of the Charles Johnson Student Fiction Award and her stories have been published in *Crab Orchard Review, Louisville Review, Echolocation, MacGuffin, Portland Review* and elsewhere. She lives in Pennsylvania, with writer Silas Dent Zobal and their child Emerson.

Adrianne Finlay received her Ph.D. in English from Binghamton University, where she currently teaches creative writing and literature. Her work has appeared in several journals, including the *Patterson Literary Review* and *The Journal of Popular Culture*. She is the Associate Editor of *Elsewhere: A Journal for the Literature Place*.

Graeme Harper is Professor of Creative Writing, Director of the National Institute for Excellence in the Creative Industries, and Research Director, College of Arts and Humanities, Bangor University (UK). His awards include the National Book Council Award for New Fiction (Australia), among others. A member of the Arts and Humanities Research Council, he is Honorary Professor of Creative Writing in SMAD at the University of Bedfordshire, and Director of the International Centre for Creative Writing Research (www.iccwr.org). Writing as Brooke Biaz, latest works include: *Moon Dance* (Parlor, 2008), *Visiting Japan* (Quasimodo, 2008; www.visitingjapan.info) and *Small Maps of the World* (Parlor, 2006).

Gill James writes fiction and non-fiction for children and young adults. She is a Lecturer in Creative Writing at the University of Salford, UK. She is particularly interested in the Young Adult Novel and Creative Writing in Other Languages. She maintains contact with her readers through an extensive series of school visits and workshops. Her latest book, *The Lombardy Grotto* (Butterfly, Cambridgeshire, UK, February 2008), is a fantasy for 9–11-year-olds. She is currently working on the Creative Café programme, which brings creativity and creative practitioners into cafés.

Jeri Kroll is Program Coordinator of Creative Writing at Flinders University, South Australia, and past President of the Australian Association of Writing Programs. She has published over twenty books for adults and young people, including poetry, picture books (two Children's Book Council Notable Awards), novels and anthologies. *Death as Mr Right* won second prize in the Anne Elder Award for best first poetry book in Australia. Her most recent creative works are *Mickey's Little Book of Letters* (novel) and *The Mother Workshops*, a mixed genre collection adapted for ABC Radio. Her newest critical publication is *Creative Writing Studies: Practice, Research and Pedagogy* (2008), co-edited with Graeme Harper.

Oliver Mayer is Assistant Professor of Dramatic Writing at USC School of Theatre. His plays include Blade to the Heat, Dark Matters, Conjunto, Dias y Flores, Rocio! In Spite of it All, Young Valiant, Joe Louis Blues, Joy of the Desolate, The Road to Los Angeles, Laws of Sympathy, The Righting Moment, Bold as Love and the libretto for America Tropical, a new opera composed by David Conte. 'The Hurt Business: A Critical Portfolio of the Early Works of Oliver Mayer, Plus', is published by Hyperbole Books; 'Oliver Mayer: Collected Plays' is published by NoPassport Press.

Graham Mort is a senior lecturer in Creative Writing at Lancaster University. His BBC radio productions include 'The Red Field', 'The Life of the Bee' and 'Cuba Libre at the Café España'. He is lead consultant for the British Council 'Radiophonics' project in Uganda and Nigeria, developing writing for radio linked to key social debates. 'Visibility: New and Selected Poems' was published by Seren in 2007. Graham has been described as, 'one of contemporary verse's most accomplished practitioners' and 'a master technician' (Sarah Crown, The Guardian). 'Touch', a collection of short fiction, will be published by Seren in 2010.

William S. Penn is the senior prose writer at Michigan State University. The author of seven published books of fiction and non-fiction, he has won an American Book Award (novel), the North American Indian Prose Award (essays), several awards for short fiction and a Distinguished Faculty Award. Currently, he is seeking a publisher for 'Hazing: A Novel in Ten Satires', and a producer for a full-length film script, while completing a literary mystery set in England and a book of essay commentaries titles, 'One Feather, Many Bonnets'. He lives in an emptying nest in East Lansing with his wife and children.

Hazel Smith is a research professor in the Writing and Society Research Group at the University of Western Sydney. She is author of *The Writing Experiment: Strategies for Innovative Creative Writing*, Allen and Unwin, 2005 and *Hyperscapes in the Poetry of Frank O'Hara: Difference, Homosexuality, Topography*, Liverpool University Press, 2000. She is also co-author, with Roger Dean, of *Improvisation, Hypermedia and the Arts Since 1945*, Harwood Academic, 1997. Hazel has published three volumes of poetry, including *The Erotics of Geography* (with CD-ROM), Tinfish Press, 2008. She has also co-authored and published numerous performance and multimedia works and is a member of austraLYSIS, the intermedia arts group: see her web page at www.australysis.com

Silas Dent Zobal was born in Washington and raised in Illinois. He currently teaches at Dickinson College. His short stories have appeared in *The Missouri Review, New Orleans Review, Beloit Fiction Journal, Wisconsin Review, Shenandoah, Glimmer Train* and numerous others. *Iron Horse Literary Review* chose his work for their Discovered Voices Award, and he has recently been awarded a fellowship from the National Endowment for the Arts. He lives in Shippensburg, Pennsylvania, with Catherine Zobal Dent and their 2-year-old son.

Introduction

The *Creative Writing Guidebook* is constructed as a series of dedicated Creative Writing workshops. Workshopping is the primary learning and teaching approach of university and college Creative Writing programs, as well as the principal location of community, informal and school classes. In this book, and in each workshop, the writer/reader can actively explore their genre of choice, or compare and contrast approaches to the writing of different genre. The environment of the workshop emphasizes that Creative Writing is a set of acts and actions, undertaken by writers, a set that is often called Creative Writing 'process' – even if it is important remember that 'processing' Creative Writing often involves fortuitous events, the writer's emotions, reworking, rethinking, sometimes even restarting, events that do not particularly align to the idea, or linear definition of processing.

Each one of the first nine chapters of The *Creative Writing Guidebook* is by a writer who specializes in that particular genre. The last two chapters of the book bridge genre-specifics and consider key concepts such as *style* and *voice* and how these are used more widely in Creative Writing. In doing so, the final two chapters give the writer/reader the opportunity to explore the nature of these concepts, beyond the genre, and to draw from this wider view to inform their specific acts of Creative Writing.

Creative Writing is, of course, both a set of actions and the final product of such actions. That is, if someone says 'I enjoy Creative Writing' they can mean they enjoy the activity of Creative Writing or that they enjoy being the audience for the end-products of the activity of Creative Writing. As Creative Writing is both act/action and end result, it is sometimes thought that the primary critical understanding of creative writers rests in considering the end-products of their endeavours. This, of course, is very far from the truth.

Critical understanding in Creative Writing occurs before, during and after the act of Creative Writing. The creative writer employs an active critical sense in order to be able to construct, review and edit their work. They employ this primarily because it is key part of their survival as creative writers – without a responsive critical understanding, an understanding that can inform and seek to improve their engagement with their own work, and with the work of other creative writers, they would not be able to develop individual projects or to compare and contrast good or bad approaches to the work at hand.

Creative Writing is a distinct way of responding to the world. While it has a relationship with other art forms – such as music, drama, fine art, film-making and architecture – the primary tools of Creative Writing are also the tools of day-to-day human communication, and the application of these tools to the task of creating art is therefore also concerned with how we differentiate the acts and actions of creative writers from other users of words. Not that this is always the case! Indeed, Creative Writing should be one of the most familiar of arts and, in being so, building up skills and the abilities in the field should be a quite natural occurrence. This is not always the case, not least because over the decades quite an aura of mystery has been attached to the act and actions of creative writers. Some of this is justified: not everything undertaken by a creative writer is the result of conscious knowledge, nor is everything undertaken set in motion by planning and orchestration. Often Creative Writing proceeds by way of organized actions combined with fortuitous circumstances. Often it involves the very human activity of making mistakes, and then seeking to correct them; of thinking one way, but finding it impossible to articulate those thoughts in action; of imagining, initially, that a piece of work-in-progress is well structured, well voiced, well pitched, only to decide later that it is none of these things.

The *Creative Writing Guidebook* proceeds on the basis that Creative Writing is an activity based on knowledge and application. This is not, in emphasizing that, solely a 'How To' book. Such books largely fail to explore the nature of knowledge that underpins the acts and actions of creative writers; therefore they are unable to assist the creative writer in moving to a further stage of understanding. While the purely 'How To' book might spark a practical thought or two, it often does not back-up that thought with consideration of the *why* as well as the *how*. Considering *why* assists in grounding acts and actions, and therefore has a deeper and more lasting impact on the learner. Similarly, teachers are frequently enlivened by discussions of this kind because they are built on reason not merely on objectifying an explanation.

The field of Creative Writing in universities and colleges continues to grow and develop. In Schools, too, further work is being undertaken, worldwide, so that Creative Writing increasingly is a subject that can be studied from the earliest days of education to the highest levels of Masters or Doctoral study. What can, and should, be studied at different levels of education continues to produce interesting discussions, and these are yielding considerable results. Similarly, how Creative Writing relates to university and college subjects that are not Creative Writing, but that enjoy a relationship with Creative Writing, is producing many ideas and prospects. These subjects include the study of Literatures (American, English, German, French, Australian, Chinese, Indian, and so on many more), Languages (likewise, those of Europe, Asia, Africa, the Pacific, and so on), Drama, Film and Media, Education, Music, New and Digital Media, Computer Science, Sociology and Psychology, just to name a few. Creative Writing, undertaken in many locations and with the impact of many different individuals and many different cultures is, like the vast majority of arts, a practice undertaken with exchange in mind, and with the meeting of individuals and groups at its heart. That is, Creative Writing is an intensely human activity, with all that fact entails.

IN THIS BOOK

The *Creative Writing Guidebook* begins with an exploration of the writing of Short Fiction by Catherine Zobal Dent and Silas Dent Zobal, who explore subject and plot and the nature of contemporary short story practice. The authors also relate the contemporary back to the tradition of the short story. Jeri Kroll, workshopping the nature of Poetry writing, looks not only at the journey from start to finish in poetry writing, but at ethics of teaching and learning, and at the public and private space offered to poetry. The chapter on the Novel, then, focuses on the work ethic connected with novel writing and explores the ways in which a longer piece of prose fiction might be organized and structured.

Oliver Mayer, offering a workshop on Playwriting, explores the spirit of playwriting as well as its background and context. He also considers such things as rhythm and intention, character and direction. He makes the point that 'film is a closely related art to our own' and, indeed, the next chapter, by Ken Dancyger, explores exactly that: the nature of Scriptwriting for film. Here is an explanation of structure, of plot and of genre. The importance of visual action is explained and the management of surprise and energy in the script is highlighted. Graham Mort, in his workshop on Radio Writing, reflects on the importance of formats – something equally notable in Ken Dancyger's workshop – and on the technical history that has impacted on creative writers for the media. Here too the impact of voice and of time-transitions is discussed. There's a definite contrast here, however, with Hazel Smith's chapter on New Media Writing because it can be quickly seen that the impact of digital technologies has both harnessed old Creative Writing forms and initiated new ones. Layering, interactivity, the use of the shape, animation, 'morphing': new media writing, while perhaps no more than a new technological aspect of Creative Writing, generates many additional options for the working writer.

Two workshops return us from the world of electronic media to that, most often, of the book. William S. Penn's workshop on Creative Non-Fiction takes the reader/writer through the actual practices of developing work, highlighting some of those creative non-fiction writers who have had a notable impact on the field. The exploration of ideas and the importance of considering language use are explored. The last of the genre-specific workshops, by Gill James, looks at Writing for Children and Young Adults. Gill James defines the ways in which works here are categorized, and in her section on the 'emergent reader', gives a productive picture of the audience the creative writer needs to consider. There's background information and some consideration of the theoretical and critical hinterland to the writing of works for children and young adults. The chapter concludes with a consideration, given the vibrancy of the field, of where new stories might be found.

The final section of the *Creative Writing Guidebook* is devoted to two workshops that extend beyond the boundaries of individual genre. The first, by Adrianne Finlay, focuses on Structure, Style and Theme. There are a lot of examples here, and lots of possible ways of thinking. This workshop brings up questions about communication and metaphor, the evolution of craft and understanding, and about the creative writer's individualism. The second Across the Workshops chapter, and the concluding chapter of the book, is concerned with Voice, Form and Point of View. The link between the modern book market and the way in which these techniques are currently employed is noted. Likewise, the chapter offers exercises that explore the universal nature of these Creative Writing practices and their results. And it asks the writer to think about attitudinal approaches, the dispositions of writers and readers/audience, and the nature of cause and effect.

The *Creative Writing Guidebook* is a book designed primarily for those interested in the learning of Creative Writing in colleges and universities, but many of the things discussed here are of equal importance to creative writers beyond education. This book is about the acts and actions of creative writers, and about how they understand their field, and contribute to their own Creative Writing knowledge and the knowledge of others. Onward!

PART I
WORKSHOPS

Chapter 1

Short Fiction

Catherine Zobal Dent and Silas Dent Zobal

1. WELCOME TO THE SHORT FICTION WORKSHOP

A short story might arise from a mess of ideas. We observe a troubling situation – a brother with a heroin addiction, or schoolchildren confronting the death of a gerbil. Or ask a question – what does a criminal's compassion mean? Do we live based on memory? Or notice a single image: a worm on wet pavement, a falling blue feather, a fish-hook. Sorting through the mess, selecting and adding materials, we begin to make the connections that form plot and character. In the process, if we are lucky and devoted, we create layers of meaning. Short fiction writer Lorrie Moore's 'People Like That Are the Only People Here' opens with: 'A beginning, an end: there seems to be neither. The whole thing is like a cloud that just lands and everywhere inside it is full of rain.'[1] This Short Fiction Workshop is an invitation and introduction to the cloud that has landed in your hands. It will address anyone who writes or wishes to write short fiction.

Writers and Readers, at the chapter's opening, will focus on practical concerns. What might be observed about those who write and read contemporary short fiction? Are you a match? What do you do with the stories you write? The section discusses the potential audience for literary short fiction and provides advice on what to read, current trends and publication opportunities. Workshop participants will consider readers' tastes and what successful writers provide. This section will ask you to familiarize yourself with the short fiction form by reading widely, especially by subscribing to literary journals and thereby preparing yourself to be a contributor to those same journals.

The Background and Context section will consider the formal possibilities and tradition of the short story genre. Stories appear in many varieties of form and voice, and it is useful to point out commonalities and conventions. For example, characters face some sort of struggle or difficulty. Or: plot is the sequencing chosen to best tell a tale, and resolution occurs when the trouble is seen in a new light, either by a character, or more likely, by the reader. Drawing on insight from Edgar Allan Poe, James Joyce and James Baldwin, this section provides a brief overview of the short fiction genre and establishes the framework for the exercises that follow.

The Workshop Exercises will lead participants holistically through writing a short story. The five exercises begin with a look at 'inspiration' and a process by which you might 'collect' a story. Participants are instructed to spend one week taking notes, and given directions on how to work through the fragments to find the story. The second exercise addresses narration and voice as well as participants' ability to create setting through convincing, significant detail. As Gabriel Garcia Marquez once said, 'If you say that there are elephants flying in the sky, people are not going to believe you. But if you say that there are four hundred and twenty-five elephants in the sky, people will probably believe you.'[2] Third, Workshop participants will practice character development, starting from basic status markers and moving to monologues in different voices. The fourth exercise will aid in developing effective, necessary dialogue. The final exercise provides a technique for revision, one that can be applied to any short story. The overarching goal of the five exercises is to give workshop participants a path, from start to finish, which they may follow to produce polished, thoughtful and moving short stories.

The chapter's last section, Follow Up, will challenge you to think of short fiction as connected to a continuum of storytelling. Why and how might you decide to tinker with the form? Several versions of short fiction experiments will be offered in order to suggest new ideas and to encourage participants to think deeply about what it means to be engaged with a narrative form.

On one level, Lorrie Moore's story, 'People Like That Are the Only People Here', shows us a family tragedy, the story of a young child with cancer. It also addresses fundamental issues for writers, of why and how short fiction might operate in the world. The perceived world, as Lorrie Moore tells us, is a provocative, murky cloud. Every beginning and every end is a narrative decision. Where are we? Where do we go from here? As you work through the developmental process that is creative writing, you will begin answering these questions. Moore writes, 'A start: the Mother finds a blood clot in the Baby's diaper. What is the story? Who put this here?'[3]

2. WRITERS AND READERS

It is impossible to generalize about the nature of short fiction writers but easy to observe a link between current writers and readers of the genre. Contemporary writers of literary short fiction are people who (having read something in a class, or by subscribing to literary journals, or buying anthologies, or happening across one of the relatively few contemporary collections of stories published each year by major presses) fall in love with the form. They become devotees, enjoying the expression of ideas and emotions through characters whose concerns must be established immediately and then developed in limited, focused scenes. The intense reading experience is pleasurable in part due to its brevity – a short story can be read in a single sitting – and in part because a good story deserves multiple re-readings. Furthermore, many writers and readers of short stories admire the aesthetic flexibility of the form. A short story might work as a traditional linear narrative, or it might move like a poem, through imagery or associative language, or it might come in the form of a letter, interview or personal ad.

As with any other genre, writers and readers of contemporary short fiction have diverse tastes. Take a look at successful short story collections published in the past ten years. Stories in Lydia Davis's *Samuel Johnson Is Indignant* vary in length from one line to several pages and do not rely on plot but on voice and witty observation. Compare this to Andrea Barrett, whose collection, *Ship Fever*, features stories with historical context and dwells on epistemological questions of science and will. Then look at the sardonic, pop culture appeal of Rick Moody, and at George Saunders's satires and allegories. Consider the surrealism of Aimee Bender; the meandering, sociological eye of Alice Munro; Richard Ford's character-rich tales.

Readers and writers might read anthologies in order to get a look at the newest trends. Annual publications, such as *The Best American Short Stories*, *The Pushcart Prize – Best of the Small Presses* or *Best New American Voices*, draw from a year's worth of fiction and provide a cross-section of strong new work. Some readers look for fiction that fits into a busy lifestyle; they enjoy being able to start and finish a story, as opposed to the delayed gratification of novels. Still other readers prefer anthologies of short stories that reflect a particular interest or cultural grouping, for example, *Peculiar Pilgrims: Stories from the Left Hand of God* (2007); *Separate Journeys: Short Stories by Contemporary Indian Women* (2004); *Short Stories by Latin American Women: The Magic and the Real* (2003); or *Rebel Yell: Stories by Contemporary Southern Gay Authors* (2001). A writer who identifies with a specific cultural voice or special interest group might seek publication in an anthology with this focus.

Despite the popularity suggested by the above, short fiction is not a commercially successful genre in today's global publishing market. The good news is that there are numerous, accessible opportunities for short story writers to see their work in print. Literary journals provide the primary avenue for publication of single stories, and these journals exist in abundance in print form and online. They are funded by private individuals or organizations, linked to university programs, or run as successful businesses. Although the United States houses a majority of these journals, editors generally welcome international submissions, and the number of magazines accepting online submissions grows every year. The relationship between editors, writers and readers is very strong, providing an enthusiastic audience for new short fiction writers. Therefore, if you write a good short story, you may be sure that, eventually, by submitting to literary journals, you will be able to publish it.

The bad news, speaking practically, is that little money is to be made from publishing in literary journals. The more successful the journal, the more likely it can pay writers for stories. Some magazines pay per word, and others per story, enough to buy a fancy dinner, perhaps, or fund a printer cartridge, or occasionally even enough to purchase a nice, old, oak desk! However, unlike during the bygone fiction-in-magazines heyday, which saw writers from Mark Twain to F. Scott Fitzgerald and Ernest Hemingway earning a fair penny with publication in *Harper's*, *The Atlantic Monthly* and *The Saturday Evening Post*, you are not likely to make a living by selling individual works of short fiction. Instead, you will be taking steps in your writing career and, possibly, towards financial success. One of the benefits of publishing in literary journals is that you will build a resume to convince editors and agents of your appeal as a writer. In addition, agents read literary journals and magazines in search of new talent.

The short story writer who has been successfully publishing individual stories may still be hard-pressed to find an agent to champion a whole book of stories. For story collections, you must find the rare agent whose success permits him or her to take on projects out of pure love for the work. Or, publish a successful novel first. Or, enter the annual handful of reputable contests whose prize is a cash award and publication of your book.

Still, readers and writers of short fiction are passionate about the genre; and every year, new stories, anthologies and collections create new devotees. A final word: the accessibility and zeal of literary magazines provide all writers and readers of short stories with good reason to subscribe to at least one or two. Supporting these publications not only provides us all with decent, new short fiction to read but also contributes to the vitality and wellness of the short story genre.

3. BACKGROUND AND CONTEXT

Although the roots of the short story go back to oral storytelling, the short story was not considered a literary genre until the nineteenth century when Edgar Allan Poe wrote that he believed it to be the highest form of prose. The short story, Poe said, 'affords the fairest field for the exercise of the loftiest talent'.[4] He believed that the brevity of the short story allowed for a total unity of effect, that every element – plot, detail, form, atmosphere and characters – could be aligned in a single direction to suit the author's purpose. The short story strives towards this single effect. It is dense, focused and intent. For a reader to glean the writer's full purpose, Poe believed that a short story should be read in a single sitting, requiring from a half hour to one or two hours in its perusal. We, as readers, are then able to see a short story in its entirety. We can hold it in our minds, turn it, and see the way its pieces fall together to become whole. This ability to read the short story in one sitting, coupled with the story's single effect, provides the short story with 'the immense force derivable from totality'.[5]

Today, this understanding of the short story still provides a workable definition of story length. We should be able to read a story in one sitting. Attempts to define length through word count, though sometimes useful, are inevitably faulty. Definitions of acceptable short story length vary widely, but generally speaking, a short story is considered to be composed of somewhere between 1,000 and 20,000 words.

In short stories, as in all fiction, we – the people – are the subject. A given short story generally involves itself with only a few characters: a central character and, perhaps, one or two others. They are the actors. It is the characters' actions that we hold morally accountable. Appropriately or inappropriately, we judge and sympathize with and finally, in the best of fiction, we come to understand that – even though a character's despicability or nobility may far exceed our own – we are reflected within each character and they are reflected within us. So, like us, each central character must face a challenge or difficulty, must struggle, must yearn. Though the best characters achieve a kind of universality, they are created as specific individuals through techniques including voice, significant detail and dialogue. The writer aims to differentiate her main characters as precisely as possible. Each detail of each character has meaning. So, in James Baldwin's 'Sonny's Blues' the central character is a math teacher. He is logical and structured and seeks control. His brother, Sonny, is a jazz musician and a heroin addict. They exist as counterpoints to one another. A central character, a protagonist, must desire something, must want. We must see a main character leaning towards some aim. The aim might be as simple as the desire to leave a family business or as complex as the desire to keep someone, a brother, safe.

The plot in a short story is formed by the events and actions as they are consciously devised and ordered by the writer in pursuit of a single effect. In life, our linear understanding of time dictates that we move forward linearly, along a straight line. In a short story, the writer can reorder events as she sees fit. The scene of a father's funeral can come before the scene of his death, or a scene in which a brother talks about his heroin addiction can come before a scene in which the brother is a child learning to play the piano. Events can be reordered in any fashion, so long as the author feels that the juxtaposition of events best serves her intent.

Conventionally speaking, plot contains five elements: exposition (background information), rising action (the introduction of some struggle or difficulty), climax (a central action or turning point), falling action (a lessening of tension) and resolution. So we might write a story in which a young man is portrayed as unhappy working at his father's florist shop (exposition); then we have a few scenes in which the son expresses his discomfort following in his father's footsteps and the father, while looking pallid and coughing and behaving rather forgetfully, expresses how he's relying on his son to help run the business (rising action); then the father suffers a heart attack and lies in the hospital with the son at his side (climax); then we see, through a depiction of the father's shortness of breath and weakness, that he'll not be returning to work (falling action); and finally a scene in which the son, at work, arranges a bouquet of flowers commissioned by a stranger to be sent to his father (resolution).

Most often a short story does not precisely follow these five elements of plot. Short stories often begin *in medias res*, or in the middle of things. We begin with the rising action or with the conflict. So, in James Baldwin's story, 'Sonny's Blues', we learn immediately that Sonny, the narrator's brother, has been put in jail for charges surrounding his heroin addiction. Background information in a story is usually kept to a minimum and, when necessary, it is delivered in flashbacks. Further, the short story may not have a fully developed resolution. Instead, we often end with the climax, leaving the resolution unstated but implied. So 'Sonny's Blues' ends with the narrator listening to his brother, Sonny, play the piano in a jazz club. James Baldwin implies that there cannot be a resolution except what is palpable in the trembling moment as Sonny plays. There is no safety to be found in a resolution. The reader, along with the narrator, understands 'that this was only a moment, that the world waits outside, as hungry as a tiger, and that trouble stretched above us, longer than the sky'.[6]

The end of a story must do more than simply resolve the struggle or difficulty presented in the exposition and rising action. James Joyce believed in the epiphany, a moment at the end of a story when, all of a sudden, meaning is comprehended, and the events of the story are seen in a new light. In Joyce's own words: 'when the relation of the parts is exquisite . . . we recognize that thing which it is. Its soul, its whatness, leaps to us from the vestments of its appearance.'[7] A longer form, like the novel, supports loose ends, but the short story demands that every word join together to point towards a single destination, towards the sibilant ending song in Joyce's 'The Dead' when Gabriel's 'soul swooned slowly as he heard the snow falling faintly through the universe and faintly falling like the descent of their last end',[8] or towards Baldwin's ending of 'Sonny's Blues' where each reader finds herself contained in those five last words, 'the very cup of trembling'.[9]

4. THE WORKSHOP EXERCISES

The following five exercises are designed to help you to develop, from scratch, a new work of short fiction, and then to work through several revisions. Of course, you may try the exercises with a story already planned or even written. You may skip around or repeat exercises multiple times. Each exercise is given a short introduction concerning its goal and purpose, followed by a description of the process, and what, in the end, you may hope to accomplish.

Exercise 1: A tisket, a tasket, a story in a basket

While you could start a writing session with a story fully formed – a tale of something you experienced, or dreamed, or imagined based on an idea or character – the moment will come when you have written or attempted to write all the stories that once loudly begged for attention. The purpose of this first exercise is simple: to generate material for a new story. Whatever your stage of the creative process, whether a germ of an idea, or an image, or a character has entered your conscious thoughts, or whether you have not a single preconceived idea, this exercise aims to provide you with a method of 'collecting' a story. Part of its power lies in the process of sneaking up on the world and happening upon its oddity and wonder. In addition, this exercise will encourage you to construct a narrative based on your inner, sometimes unconscious, sense of cohesion, structure and form.

The process: For one week, carry a notebook through your daily life. If you have a predetermined writing time, use your writing time (for this week only) to browse the internet, wander through a grocery store, read all the short stories in *Granta* or *Glimmer Train*, or walk the streets of your neighbourhood. When something strikes you, whether a beautiful, stark angle on a building, or a poetic line or passage of text, or comical hound dog whose ears flapped as it ran, write it down in your notebook. Do not be shy about what you write, for *this is not the story*. You are just collecting material. As the week continues, a story idea may present itself to you, but if it does, jot it down in your notes, and continue collecting.

After one week of this, if you have followed instructions, you will have an assortment of fragments. Take them to your computer and type them up in no particular order. As you type, start looking for connections. When something occurs to you, make a note of it. Maybe all those television screens you saw through a store window featured a dog show, and you have written about several other dogs in your week of collecting. Treat this as significant. Take notice.

Now allow yourself to add to the fragments, to develop small scenes. Follow up on whatever interested you in the first place. If you see connections between fragments, elaborate upon these connections as you develop small scenes. Allow your moments to converge. Look for emerging characters. If some fragments do not seem related, let them develop anyway. Trust that your interest in these varied moments is based upon some underlying commonality.

The literary critic I. A. Richards wrote, 'The mind is a connecting organ; it works only by connecting and it can connect any two things in an indefinitely large number of different ways.'[10] Out of the randomness of the initial collecting, your brain will now do the truly creative work. Once you start to consider your material, turning lines and fragments this way and that, you will see patterns, create order and structure narrative. Tell yourself that the story exists in there and that it is up to you to find it. Read through your text. Select for interesting elements that seem in some way related. Identify characters and possible plots, consider and then choose your narrator, and start arranging the pieces. No matter how messy it may seem, find an arrangement for your small scenes.

Now, once again, allow these pieces to expand. Rewrite for consistency. You may have pieces written in mismatched tones. You may have to decide on which of your many settings is the best for your tale. You may have to force three shadowy personages into one central character. Eliminate or rewrite anything that seems boring or inconsistent or just out of place (but paste it into a second document, for second and third looks at a later date).

The product: At this point, you should have a very rough draft of a new story. In the following exercises, we will see where to go from there.

Exercise 2: A fat, rough, loud, smoky house

Short fiction relies on quickly creating a tangible world and beckoning the reader to enter, so it is your narrator's job, whether your story is told in first, second or third person, to do the beckoning. This exercise will focus on setting, leading you to investigate the sensory elements of your fictional world, but it will also look at how you frame setting in the voice of your chosen narrator. The exercise presumes that you have already started to write a story, but if you are just practicing, without a story in progress, it will work as well.

The process: First, imagine the narrator as a person with whom you might have a conversation. If writing in first or second person, this should be easy, as you are already writing from that person's perspective. If you are writing in third person omniscient (the narrator sees all characters' thoughts and actions), or in third person limited (the narration is centred in one character's point of view, or moves among select characters' points of view), it may be harder to conceptualize. Remember that although your story will not characterize, *per se*, this narrator, s/he exists, making choices about how your story will be told.

Now, take the first scene of your story. Where does the opening action occur? In your narrator's voice (and away from the text of your story itself), write down five descriptive details from the setting of that first scene. These may be in either sentence or fragment form. The exercise stipulation is this: in this list, you must invoke each of the five senses without ever using the words 'looked like' or 'tasted like' or 'sounded like' or 'smelled of'.

Make a similar list for every new scene, especially each change of location, in your story.

In order to accomplish the goals of this exercise, consider how setting may appeal to the senses while simultaneously establishing voice, character or tension. For example, let's say that you have written an opening scene where two despondent characters are trying to hang a heavy gate. Your third person narrator might notice *the stained brick wall*, or *grackles in the sycamore*, or *the rough, sour wind*, or *underfoot, wet dirt like coffee grounds*. Work with the narrator's voice, imagining the kinds of observations s/he might make.

The product: Every detail that you generate will not be used in your story. Instead, select for the best, elements that add to the narrative by reinforcing the action and the tone, and perhaps even the plot of your story. Insert them where they do the most work, inviting readers to see, hear, feel, smell and taste the world your story inhabits.

Exercise 3: Quick, get into character

How well do you know your characters, and have you written them so that the reader can enter into their lives? Take a look at how many characters appear in your story. Do you have a protagonist, or main character (think of Franz Kafka's Gregor, Charles Dickens's Scrooge or James Joyce's Gabriel), who plays off others in the story? Alternately, do you have a cast of characters who interact equally, such as the family in Flannery O' Connor's 'A Good Man Is Hard to Find' or in Alice Munro's 'Labor Day Dinner'? In either case, you will need to delineate among all your characters so that each contributes to the story's particular effect, its pacing and its shape. In this exercise, you will check your imaginative work so far, evaluating the role of each character: can Gina be enhanced, cut or combined with her friend Tracy? Does Alex feel real, and necessary? Then you will brainstorm to improve on any weaknesses. If you are not in the middle of writing a story at this point, use this exercise as a way to generate ideas.

The process: Write down the names of all your characters (if you are not working with an existent story, list three to five names with surnames that suggest character to you). Then, consider what you know about each. As a starting point, think of the sociological status markers of age, gender, class, race, education and occupation. These traits should be established early on for the reader, indicated through name choice, diction, description, action, thoughts, or otherwise. The reader may not recover from the betrayal of making a wrong assumption about a narrator, for example, the gender or age of the narrator, if such information is not provided near the beginning of the story.

Then, examine what 'essential work' each character is doing in the story. Ask yourself whether each is performing some unique function; if not, make the hard decision right now to cut that character, or to combine him/her with another of your characters. Sometimes, as suggested in Exercise 1, two or three weak or undefined characters can be merged into one strong character.

Now comes the creative part of the exercise, in which you will do some writing for each character you have deemed essential. Next to each name, write a short monologue *in that character's voice* that describes his or her typical morning.

The product: You will find that these tasks – listing names, considering sociological status markers and an examination of each character's essential work – will suggest that some additional writing needs to be done. Do it. The monologues have required you to enter into the emotional, intellectual and physical perspective of each of your characters; such writing will give you a foundation for understanding the characters, and when you need them to speak, or act, or react, you will be more fully in control.

Exercise 4: When you speak to me, behave!

To bring scenes to life, to develop characters, to highlight dramatic moments – these are all potential goals of dialogue in short fiction. In this exercise, you will practice writing strong dialogue meant to expose characters' inner drives. Like previous exercises, this one is designed to work with material from an existing story, but if you would like to generate a story with this exercise, pick two characters who might appear in a landscape familiar to you.

The process: Pull two important characters outside the plot of your story, and put them in a public place where they might appear, realistically, considering the world in which they exist. The meeting will be unexpected, and for some reason, unpleasant or uncomfortable for one of the characters. The other character will be bursting with the news of some recent experience.

Start by writing a paragraph or two of setting in which you do not mention the characters (but where they are standing, or sitting, or walking, nonetheless). For example, if your characters are to meet in a park, you might establish the duck pond, the windy weather, the overgrown grass, and two kids making a mess of an ice-cream cone.

Now, have your characters start a dialogue. Remember, one of the characters has a story to share, and the other feels extremely uncomfortable. Practice showing this (not uncommon) dynamic strictly through their speech, actions and context. In other words, you want to avoid simply telling the news or the discomfort, and limit the actual narration to observations about setting and action. The first character might express surprise at seeing the other person by bobbing his head twice and half-smiling, and then immediately ask, 'What's new?' thinking, of course, of his own news. The uncomfortable or displeased person might redirect conversation towards the setting, answer in an awkward manner, turn away or have any number of reactions suggesting an unwillingness to engage. The important thing here is to work on character-driven, spontaneous language and the actions that accompany it, and to see how people's inner lives dominate their ability to talk to each other. The plot of the small scene is, simply, that two people meet, exchange words and then leave, each dissatisfied with the interaction.

After you have written the scene, set it aside for a day. Let the characters fade into a corner of your mind, so that you can go back the next day with a fresh ear. When you pick up the work again, reread, trying to listen for realistic-sounding dialogue. Are the characters speaking as you imagined their voices to sound? Do they answer questions that were not asked, fail to pick up on verbal or visual cues, change the subject? Do they fail to 'hear' each other? Revise the dialogue with this in mind: characters behave strangely when they speak to each other. That is, they behave according to their personalities and situations, and not like ideal conversationalists – unless practiced conversation is their particular skill.

The product: This exercise is designed to increase your awareness of dialogue. After writing the scene and revising it, go back to your story and reread moments where characters speak to each other. Are they withholding? Is something accomplished by having them speak to each other (back to the idea of 'essential work')? Do they 'behave'? As a corollary exercise, go and read passages of dialogue from stories that you admire. See how each writer manages the mechanics (dialogue tags, quotation marks, punctuation, moving between interlocutors, context), and imitate different styles in multiple versions of this same exercise. To further develop your skill, read the same stories, asking yourself this question: how did this specific dialogue bring the scene to life, develop characters or further the plot? Then, return to your own writing to see if you have accomplished those same goals.

Exercise 5: The caper, the cut-up

One of the reasons to write, among many, is to have fun. Write? Whether you believe this final exercise will 'work' – that is, produce better writing – or not, try it. The worst outcome is that you'll have a little fun. The best, and the predicted, outcome is that you will gain significant insight into your piece of short fiction, and that you will alter its shape to great effect. The caper will also entice you to pay attention to how your story moves, or is 'paced', a key element of short fiction, and one that is difficult to teach or learn. (This exercise requires a draft of a short story, so if you have not written at least a first draft, return to Exercise 1 and proceed from there.)

The process: First, read your story aloud from start to finish on the computer screen. Then print out a copy. With scissors, cut it into pieces based on paragraph breaks. You may have pieces composed of one sentence or sentence fragment, or paragraphs that last for pages, depending on your style and voice. You may wish to keep lines of dialogue together, or you may cut every single line of dialogue onto its own piece of paper. After trying this exercise with different stories, you will get a sense of what works best for you.

Now, find a good workspace, such as a large table or open floor, and spread the pieces before you in chronological order. Read your story again, and this time, don't worry about reading from beginning to end. Read to be surprised. Read for possibilities, for unplanned connections. Read for a new opening, or a startling conclusion. For example, sometimes you will find, in the middle or end of a piece, a passage with exciting language, dramatic personality or an interesting hook. Pick it up, move it to the front of the line-up, and see what happens. Often, a single move will suggest a whole chain of events, and you will end up rearranging in ways you never could have predicted.

A word about pacing: one way to conceptualize pacing in a short story is to picture a stamping wheel (a 'rollagraph', if you are familiar with stamp terminology) that prints repeated patterns on a span of paper. The larger the wheel, the more intricate and involved the pattern. Short fiction uses patterns that take advantage of the reader's own desire to see narrative and 'put it all together'. While working through your cut-up pieces, imagine a wheel that is imprinted with significant imagery, characters, language or any other unique quality of your piece. It may be helpful to keep a notebook on hand where you write additional pieces that help keep the wheel rolling. For example, if water imagery is important in your story, you might notice its frequency, as well as inconsistencies in the pattern, and add new passages where necessary.

Once you have worked through the story in this way, pick up the pieces carefully in their new-found order, taping section to section, or clipping them together with paperclips. Then go back to your computer to cut and paste. Reassemble everything, save it with a new file name, and then work through it, in linear fashion, again. (A reminder: always save various drafts of a story just in case you need to return to an older version.) You will have to adjust for transitions, setting and other logical demands. You may need to write new scenes. Work with the text until it is in reasonably good shape, and then save. Read it aloud again. If you are not happy, you can always print and cut it up. Have fun.

The product: The intended result is a thoroughly examined, polished short story. By going through your work in linear form, and then opening it to possible dramatic change, you take advantage of different creative talents. Aleatory, or chance-based, forms of the 'cut-up' have appeared in both literary and musical genres, notably in the Surrealist movement of the 1920s and 1930s and Beat-influenced art of the 1970s. However, rather than originating in the desire to let chance take over, this exercise proceeds from a willingness to see the unexpected. The story you produce will express something that is yours, but which you came upon in a process of allowing yourself to see.

5. FOLLOW UP

The tradition of the short story begins with oral story-telling. Epics, like Homer's *Iliad*, were oral narratives composed of rhythmic poetry (Edgar Allan Poe called the *Iliad* a 'series of lyrics'[11]), and sections of these poems would cover individual stories that could, like Poe's stories, be told in a single sitting. Poe wanted his stories to be read aloud. The roots of the short story lie in work that was meant to be heard. The form continues to benefit from being read aloud, slowly, so that the deliberation of the effect can be savoured on the tongue, so that we can catch the plodding of plot, the subtleties of composition and the way that words can turn into song.

The evolution of the short story continues. Many stories – take works by Robert Coover or Donald Barthelme or Jamaica Kincaid or Lydia Davis – deliberately play with standard narrative conventions. Donald Barthelme is the author of a story called 'The School' in which a teacher struggles to explain death to a class of elementary school children. The class's experience of loss is deliberated exaggerated, so that the litany of loss includes orange trees, snakes, herb gardens, gerbils, white mice, a salamander, tropical fish, a puppy, a number of parents, grandparents and two students. In a conversation about death between the teacher and the students, Barthelme reverses the standard speech patterns, so that the teacher speaks as a child, and that the children speak like adults, asking, 'Is death that which gives meaning to life?'[12] Then the children request that the teacher make love to the teaching assistant. Though the teacher and the teaching assistant do not make love, they do hug. In the last moment, a gerbil walks in, almost as though a new child has been produced. We are given broad (and absurd) representations of the beginning, middle and end of our human narrative. The gerbil represents a new beginning, the school itself stands for the middle and death is the end.

'The School' suggests that the narrative tradition of having a beginning, middle and end – or an exposition, a climax and a resolution – is absurd, and yet, by employing the same narrative structure, the story shows the pattern as entirely necessary. Narrative conventions are often based upon conventional ontological convictions. So the conventional form of the short story throughout time reflects the standard conception of the nature of our lives. We believe that our lives – and our short stories – are an evolving series of beginnings, middles and ends.

As we think about the conventions of the short story, we can use this knowledge to write a story that follows conventions, or one that bucks conventions for some deliberate effect. If character and plot are commonly assumed to be essential to fiction, we might begin rebelliously imagining how a story might proceed without plot, or without character. Or we might imagine a story that strives towards a diversity of effect rather than a unity. Play with convention should proceed cautiously. Conventions exist for a reason. The upset of any convention is likely to upset a reader as well. But having set out upon your rebellious course, you might follow a plot-less story as it jumps from point to point in a character's life. These jumps between moments must happen by some logic other than the cause-and-effect of plot. You might write a story that moves between causally unrelated points in a character's life that are filled with violence, or love – and trust the reader to understand the story's progression to be thematic. Perhaps you write a story in which movement is based purely upon image. That is, each moment in a story might be bound together by the image of, say, a person bound hand to foot.

Or perhaps you might write a story in which you attempt to have no central character. First, you summon a common plot. Say, for instance, you block out a series of scenes as follows: (1) a couple at a restaurant yell at one another, drawing looks from other patrons; (2) at home, the young wife, having finished off a bottle of wine, strikes the husband; (3) the husband walks the streets cursing and talking with strangers; (4) at home the wife makes a phone call; and (5) the story ends on juxtaposed images of the husband visiting a prostitute and the wife entertaining her apparent lover. To eliminate the central character, you might write each scene with a different set of characters, as if you were mix-and-matching five scenes from five stories with identical plots. So, in the first scene, the couple might be older rednecks from North American farm country. In the second scene, we might see young, urban hipsters. In the third, a middle-aged manager of an agricultural supply store. In the fourth, an octogenarian making a telephone call from her room in a nursing home. And so on.

What effect does it have upon the story to eliminate the central character? What does this alteration suggest about the human experience? Why might you want to employ this, or a similar technique?

Maybe this sort of story expresses a congruity of human experience that simply doesn't agree with you. Strike that idea. Instead, in order to eliminate a central character, you follow an object. Yes, you'll have a central object. It will be, say, an ivory-handled boning knife. You might follow the knife into the kitchen of a swanky New York chef; on a boy scout's fishing trip; in the hands of a teenager stabbing an intruder; floating at sea; and so on.

What might the idea of supplanting a central character with a central object suggest? Does it insinuate that the physical world rather than human agency dominates our lives? Our history? Does the chosen object have meaning? What will this knife represent?

Many wonderful stories are not planned in advance but evolve organically from an interaction between a writer's understanding of conventional narrative form and the formless everyday occurrences of life. The story rises organically out of this external disorder (the car crash outside the front window, the pile of laundry in the wicker basket, the water leaking from the roof into a bucket) necessarily based upon the forms we've been exposed to (beginning, middle and end; or exposition, climax and resolution). Building upon an always-growing understanding of other fictions, a new story can be shaped in an infinite variety of ways, can support or defy convention, can reflect the meaning that each writer might build from the exigent curiosities (seven doves on a peaked roof, the words inscribed on a father's headstone, a scarf whose ends flap like wings) of this life.

WORKS CITED

Baldwin, James. 'Sonny's Blues'. *Going to Meet the Man*. New York: Dial Press, 1965. 103–141.

Barthelme, Donald. 'The School'. *60 Stories*. New York: Penguin, 1993. 309–312.

Joyce, James. 'The Dead'. *Dubliners*. New York: Signet, 1991. 183–236.

—. *Stephen Hero*. Ed. John J. Slocum and Herbert Cahoon. Norfolk, CT: New Directions Books, 1944.

Marquez, Gabriel Garcia. 'Interview with Peter Stone'. *Writers at Work: The Paris Review Interviews, Sixth Series*. New York: Viking, 1984.

Moore, Lorrie. 'People Like That Are the Only People Here: Canonical Babbling in Peed Onk'. *Birds of America*. New York: Picador, 1998. 212–250.

Poe, Edgar, Allan. 'The Poetic Principle'. *Home Journal* 31 Aug. 1850. 1. Edgar Allan Poe Society of Baltimore. Last accessed on 9 Sep. 2007 from www.eapoe.org/WorkS/essays/poetprnb.htm

—. Rev. of *Twice-Told Tales*, by Nathaniel Hawthorne. *Graham's Magazine* May 1842: 298–300. Edgar Allan Poe Society of Baltimore. Last accessed on 9 Sep. 2007 from www.eapoe.org/works/CRITICSM/gm542hn1.htm

Richards, I. A. *The Philosophy of Rhetoric*. New York: Oxford University Press, 1965.

Chapter 2

Poetry

Jeri Kroll

> *A poem should be equal to:*
> *Not true*
>
> *For all the history of grief*
> *An empty doorway and a maple leaf*
>
>   *For love the leaning grasses and two lights above the sea—*
>
> *A poem should not mean*
> *But be.*
>
> Archibald MacLeish, 'Ars Poetica', 308

> *I imagine this midnight moment's forest:*
> *Something else is alive*
> *Beside the clock's loneliness*
> *And this blank page where my fingers move.*
>
> Ted Hughes, 'The Thought-Fox', 1

1. WELCOME TO THE POETRY WORKSHOP: WILL THE REAL WRITER PLEASE STAND UP?

More than any other traditional literary genre, poetry is hard to define. What is it and what can it do? The extracts from the two poems quoted above seem to be based on different assumptions about the art. The first foregrounds the poem, and the second the poet in the act of creation. Whether MacLeish and Hughes, writing in the first and second halves of the twentieth century respectively, had divergent aesthetic approaches to creation, isn't my primary concern here. I'm more interested in the questions they raise about the nature of poetry.

Can some poems be 'true' and others 'untrue'? Does this mean some poets are liars, or simply bad poets? Can an emergent writer learn how to make poems 'true' in a workshop? What does it mean for a poem 'to be'? Which comes first, the imagination or something in the world outside the imagination that inspires it? (This is a kind of chicken and egg conundrum.) Hughes' poem begins at the writer's desk. Can reading a text about how to set up one's ideal study prepare the novice to receive the muse? Is there such an entity, and if so, what sex is she/he, and does she/he speak in standard English, Hip-Hop or Aussie slang? Do poets need a spacious study (or simply a functional work station)? Does everyone have an optimum time to write (midnight, dawn, lunch break) that will serve them until their brain retires from active duty? All of these questions reveal how complex being a poet is. In fact, most people find that their relationship to their art changes with the circumstances of their lives. There is never just one answer or one way of achieving anything. My approach to teaching poetry has always been somewhat subversive then.

So welcome to my workshop, where the first thing I'm going to ask you is what you don't like about poetry – including the way you were taught it at school and what you were asked to read. A strange way to begin a poetry workshop? Think of this as a kind of Poetry Prejudice 'Time Out' when you can say anything you have wanted to say about poetry but were afraid would condemn you. These assumptions, preferences and pet hates are often hidden from ourselves and can affect not only our enjoyment of other work but what we allow ourselves to create. A writer can borrow a technique or idea from poets they do not like just as they can from those they admire. Learning to take what you need is part of learning how to educate yourself, which is a lifetime process for any serious writer.

Below is a questionnaire that you can fill out now. Revisit it at the end of a set time (a month if you are writing poetry a lot, six if work or study interferes, for example). Have your ideas changed at all? In this way, you can chart your own artistic journey.

1. Why do you want to write poetry?

2. Do you read poetry for pleasure? Why or why not?

3. Which poets whom you studied at school did you like or dislike? Why?

4. What do you want to achieve by the end of . . . (insert time: a month, a semester, a year)? List at least three goals.

5. At the end of the time limit set in 4, ask yourself: what have I achieved? Were my goals reasonable?

Setting goals is useful, but not simply because it is a way of marking progress, slapping that gold star on your forehead. More importantly, it reinforces a truism for committed writers – committed in the sense of doing it for a lifetime: they never stop developing. Goals are not end products. You kick one, but the game isn't over. You need to go back to the centre line and wait for play to begin again. Or to catch that throw-in that comes from the boundary you weren't expecting when you started the game. There's always a new poem to write, a sequence to plan, a verse novel to imagine, a technology to learn so you can finally embody your most experimental vision. And the 'you' who does these things won't be the same you who answered question 1 or question 4.

Then who will that 'you' be? Will the changes be as dramatic as assuming another personality or undergoing a sex change? I am not suggesting that poets train as method actors and become the voices they speak in their poems, although something like this might indeed happen to writers depending on the scope of the project. I am referring in a broader way to how some post-modern discourses conceive of writers and, indeed, readers, by postulating that they can adopt different subject positions from work to work. Let's consider in particular the identity of the author in a post-modern world by asking how we understood authorship before the twenty-first century.

In the classical age, authors were thought to be divinely inspired, conduits drawing on an original creative principle that underpinned everything. In medieval times that principle was clearly identified as God, the first Creator, the Word in fact that was prior to any human language. The Romantics manipulated this idea, still believing in divine inspiration, but giving credit to individual genius, the coherent, unified self who could commune with higher powers and interpret them for ordinary mortals. Here we have the poet as channeller who inspires awe – having 'drunk the milk of Paradise' (Coleridge, 1951, 45). This conception of the poet, carried over into the twentieth century, has allowed many beginning writers to argue against revision, and to excuse sloppiness and self-indulgence. Most authors who have retained a place in literary history, however, have sweated over their work – libraries hold the drafts, notebooks and letters documenting the struggle. It doesn't matter whether they reported that a brilliant idea first appeared crackling across the sky in a summer lightning storm or an irresistible rhythm came from pounding the streets of a ghetto. That inspiration was only the beginning, not the end-product.

If you could go back in time to ask poets before the mid-twentieth century how they understood their vocation, their answers would have probably fallen under the heading of what we call a liberal humanist tradition – where individual selves write freely in order to communicate with other free individuals. In the 1970s, philosophers such as Roland Barthes and Michel Foucault led the assault on previous conceptions of authorship, suggesting that nothing can be created out of time and place; particular cultures underpin each text. What Foucault deemed the 'author-function' (1991) suggests that any writer can try on multiple personalities, experimenting with style and point of view.

This social and cultural dimension to authorship should concern anyone wanting to write. Workshops cannot just be about imagination and craft. If language lives and therefore alters, then so must poets and the way in which they speak. Further, they themselves will mutate as they grow and so will not find only one 'authentic subject' or one 'true voice'. (Helping participants to find a voice is the stated purpose of many conventional workshops.) The more expert they become with the tools of their trade, the more they can consciously choose how they sound. Like all people, in fact, poets do not own one identity. We have work, family, partner, sport personalities, and so on. All of these shift as our relationships do. Wallace Stevens, the acclaimed twentieth-century American poet, was a Vice President of the Hartford Accident and Indemnity Company. Australian poet and novelist Peter Goldsworthy is a doctor. Becoming a parent often leads to new poetic material and stylistic development; poets can segue into writing poetry or picture books for children, too. Finally, whether we have multiple personalities based on actual experience or not, we can travel imaginatively.

Poets never really work in isolation, therefore; they are embedded in a culture, which not only affects what they produce but also raises ethical questions, some of which we'll consider in the section '3. Background and Context'.

2. WRITERS AND READERS: INVITATION TO THE VOYAGE

> [The poet] wants imagination to be a *voyage*. Thus each poet owes us his *invitation to the voyage*.
> Gaston Bachelard, 1987, 21

Do writers 'owe' their audiences anything? Do they have to think about inviting readers into their poems, planting signs along the route, stopping for tea breaks so they don't get exhausted, watching their language so they don't offend? Is there such a thing as a proper relationship between a poet and a reader or listener? I was once told that an audience owes the writer nothing. Readers are just waiting for an excuse to tune out, since there are a lot of other things they could be doing with their time. If this principle was true 30 years ago, it is even more valid now, given the competition among forms of entertainment for the public's few leisure hours.

Among conventional literary genres, poetry has the greatest challenge to face in our advanced technological society. Poet John Barr claims that in America, for instance, there is 'evidence of a people in whose mind poetry is missing and unmissed' (2006, 2). Why might this be so in a more general way in the English-speaking world? Is it purely a matter of not having a high enough profile or can it be, as Barr suggests, that 'reality outgrows the art form: the art form is no longer equal to the reality around it' (2006, 2). Given that you want to write poetry, it is important that you know something about what has been considered worthy in the past (the canon); why this group of texts has lasted as models; and why those choices have begun to be questioned. We'll come back to these issues in the exercise section.

First, let's consider you as reader. If you can't put yourself in that position at some point, you will have difficulty engaging with an audience, let alone revising work. Ask yourself: what poetry do you seek out in the library? Do you go to readings? What it is about readings that engages you? Some poets might be great performers – electric on stage, with rock star charisma, their words crackling over the audience – but when you meet their lines on the page, the battery's flat.

Answering these questions will help you to determine what kind of relationship you want to establish with the public. In the final analysis, if poetry is going to survive outside of schools and universities, it needs to expand its audience. I am not suggesting writing for the lowest common denominator consumer of entertainment. But anyone who writes, whether as an amateur (a 'lover') or a serious artist, forms poetry's audience. Being part of the poetic culture means supporting it – going to readings, engaging in what Ursula Le Guin calls 'participatory silence, a community collaboration in letting . . . the word loose aloud' (2004b, 118). And, of course, buying or borrowing books. UK poet and novelist Philip Gross talks about 'reading-for-feeding' (Gross, 2005, 4); in other words, self-selecting particular poets who 'feed' a writer's work. This means taking responsibility for your education – asking libraries to order new poetry, for instance. Think about who might be buying that magazine with your first poem in it, or your first book. You have to be that person for someone else.

Here's another question, tossed out so often it should be stale but isn't, because the culture and context in which it is asked is always shifting: what is poetry? I have found the most useful working definition is this: poetry is the best words in the best order, paraphrasing Samuel Taylor Coleridge (1951, 109), a nineteenth-century Romantic poet and an astute literary critic. If we nose along behind this idea, tracking it from the lush Romantic past, we stop briefly at the Imagist Movement in the early twentieth century, which attracted, as either devotees or fellow travellers, some of poetry's major figures at the beginning of their careers (Ezra Pound, Marianne Moore, D. H. Lawrence, William Carlos Williams, Wallace Stevens, *et al.* See Pratt, 1963, 11–39). The Preface to one of the Imagist anthologies suggests how important a 'best order' is. After all, that is how a poet creates rhythm and 'in poetry, a new cadence means a new idea' (Pratt, 1963, 22). For the Imagists, the best words made images, for poetry is 'a visual, concrete' (Hulme, 1924, 134) language. So, we have the beat and the word. What about feeling? How is poetry infused with feeling? That is where the individual poet and the specific time and place of creation come in.

Let's finish our voyage by accelerating to warp speed and landing in the twenty-first century with all its complexity, horror and beauty. Listen to its song: you'll hear elevated language as well as slang, each valid for a particular purpose. This is the present. Your personality and background will suggest to you what the best words are and the best order. Ezra Pound urged poets to 'make it new' back in the early modern period and that newness – of form and feeling – still results from how we arrange words and how they sound. Wallace Stevens talks about poets 'learn[ing] the speech of the place' (1965, 239–240), which leads into understanding the cultural context. Certainly in the past 25 years there has been an increasing number of poets from indigenous and minority backgrounds speaking from their origins (Indigenous Australian Poets, Japanese-Hawaiian, Chicano, etc.). But is this idea of place literal, metaphorical or both? Heather McHugh expresses the flux and permanence of poetry, which is at once a product of its time and outside time in its attempt to capture meaning, when she says: 'The place of poetry is nothing less than the place of love, for language; the place of shifting ground, for human song; the place of the made, for the moving' (McHugh, 1993, 1). The way things are said affects what is said; the words determine the theme as well as the other way around.

If 'authentic' has any useful meaning for a contemporary poet, therefore, it has to do with speaking out of a consciousness of one's own time and place. Historical novelists immerse themselves in another culture and absorb some of that authenticity, because novels are about the pulse and grit of the times – plot, character, setting – more than the richness of words themselves. Immersing oneself in the details of Shakespearean England, however, doesn't help a poet to produce anything more than a successful imitation of a Shakespearean sonnet, phrased in the language of the time. It always sounds artificial to some extent, because poetry *is* words, the language with all its nuances first and foremost. Writing a voice out of the past must always involve some negotiation with a contemporary consciousness and its natural way of speaking.

The lyric poem (as opposed to the narrative poem), therefore, appeals to our individual sensibilities as opposed to our wish to live in another world. It imitates one mind or voice communicating with another. Whether this actually happens or is an imaginative construct (because after all, the voice is a construct) isn't the point. The strategy holds.

Let's close this section by talking for a moment about strategy then, and what it means. We have already grounded you with a base: you are an individual living at a particular time in a particular place. You are not bound simply by those terms, however; you have access to global resources. You know what the language you are comfortable with sounds like, but perhaps you want to experiment with other voices. Perhaps you will write solely out of your personal experience (a poem about a new baby, the loss of a parent, etc.), perhaps you will observe others, analyse the significance of what you see. Or you will start by playing not with a specific subject but with language and form themselves to explore what they let you say, what they make you say. These are not right or wrong techniques. They are strategies that you can choose to manipulate depending on your mood or purpose.

To summarize, you will find it useful to conceive of each poem as embodying specific strategies and establishing a particular relationship with readers. This conscious thought process might not happen in the initial stages of composition, but it can certainly help during the revision process. Most importantly it will make you more objective so that you can stand back and see what needs to be fixed. How am I addressing readers? Who is the audience for this poem? What kind of voice or speaker 'says' it? Will I perform it and how will it sound? You will have the chance to experiment with a variety of strategies in the exercises following.

3. BACKGROUND AND CONTEXT: THE CULTURE OF THE WORKSHOP AND WORKSHOP CULTURE

The imagination invents more than things and actions, it invents new life, new spirit; it opens eyes to new types of vision.

Gaston Bachelard, 1987, 16

I ask them to take a poem
and hold it up to the light

> like a color slide
>
> . . .
>
> or walk inside the poem's room
> and feel the walls for a light switch.
>
> Billy Collins, 'Introduction to Poetry', 58

One of the most prevalent metaphors exploited in poetry and in poetic criticism is based on vision – the idea of seeing more than we normally see. Billy Collins, former US Poet Laureate, suggests the sensuous richness of poems as well as their shifting meanings depending on how, where and when we perceive them. He goes on to reinvigorate the cliché about the light bulb over the head (equals enlightenment) by asking the imagined students in his workshop to look for a light switch; to 'feel' for one, since simply finding it and turning it on is too reductive. Illumination is not achieved facilely, if ever. Bachelard, a twentieth-century French philosopher whose work is shot through with figurative language, is upfront about what imagination can do – it creates new visions. Writers embody those visions.

One of the primary purposes of a workshop is to help us to see with other eyes, some expert, some not. The critical point is that they are not the writer's. By contributing their impressions, tinged by everything they are as individuals, with their own strengths, weaknesses, loves and hates, the owners of these eyes are the poet's first audience. In short, they help the poet to be objective by forcing her to look at and listen to what she has created. Whether you are part of a formal workshop group, or simply share your drafts with one or two trusted readers, they probably comprise the most sympathetic audience you are ever likely to have. If they take their task of responding to your poetry seriously, they will focus on providing the objectivity that every writer needs. The last century shared thoughts predominantly on paper; now we 'think' frequently via email, forums or chat rooms as well as in letters or in workshop conversation. The operative word here is 'think' – we work out our thoughts silently or aloud, but our aim is to reach other minds in the process.

A workshop itself, whether it comprises two or twelve, needs ground rules to function effectively. Over the past half-century, workshop etiquette has developed as a variety of people from different occupations, educational backgrounds and locations decided to engage with writing in a systematic way. Whether the workshop is at a school, university, community centre, women's refuge, hospital, prison or online (a popular format with its own medium-specific advantages and pitfalls), everyone needs to be clear about the group's goals as well as how to be a sensitive participant. Common sense is behind most basic guidelines and I won't deal with them here, but some might not be so obvious. Ethics, for example, does need to be canvassed.

We all have a responsibility to ourselves, our material and our culture. First, let's define ethics and ask why should you be concerned about it as a poet.

Ethics: n. pl. 1. a system of moral principles, by which human actions and proposals may be judged good or bad or right or wrong. **2.** the rules of conduct recognised in respect of a particular class of human actions: *medical ethics*. **3.** moral principles, as of an individual. (*Macquarie Dictionary*)

As writers, you might be working with human subjects and, whether conscious of it or not, you do follow 'rules of conduct'. Novelists and poets have to consider some of the same issues that journalists and broadcasters do. Writing about the living or even the deceased can have social, if not legal, ramifications (you cannot, for instance, libel the dead, but you should be aware of your country's libel laws). What if someone in a writing group writes a piece about someone else in the group? Is that inconsiderate and should you care? If you compose a poem about your brother and perform it at a public reading to which you've invited him, how will he react? When does manipulation for effect become lying? If we expand these personal ethical dilemmas to a general level, we might ask if it is acceptable for writers to distort facts in memoirs or biographies. What happens to the compact between reader and writer if those labels do not mean what we think they mean? Another area of concern is cultural ownership, particularly in relation to Indigenous material (Australian Aboriginal, First Nations, Maori, and so on). Who has the right to use stories that have cultural or religious significance? All writers now publish in a diverse global cultural and, thus, should be aware of the ethical challenges that might arise.

4. THE WORKSHOP EXERCISES: FINDING YOUR SEA LEGS ON THE VOYAGE

> Re-vision – the act of looking back, of seeing with fresh eyes, of entering an old text from a new critical direction is for us more than a chapter in cultural history: it is an act of survival.
> Adrienne Rich, 'When We Dead Awaken: Writing as Re-Vision', 1971/1975

Why reading?

Becoming a poet means embarking on a lifetime voyage and, as for any journey, you'll have the best time if you're prepared. First of all, learn as much as you can about the environment through which you'll be travelling. Poetry is that environment and the most useful guides are poets themselves. What Ezra Pound suggests in the *ABC of Reading* relates to that idea of self-education I have already mentioned:

> You would think that anyone wanting to know about poetry would do one of two things or both, i.e., LOOK at it or listen to it. He might even think about it?
>
> And if he wanted advice he would go to someone who KNEW something about it.
>
> If you wanted to know something about an automobile, would you go to a man who had made one and driven it, or to a man who had merely heard about it?
> Pound, 1934, 30–31

The tradition in other art forms, such as painting and music, has been for novices to sit at the feet of the master by apprenticing themselves, or to take a master class, where the expert tutors intensively. You've probably seen art students in museums sketching paintings, learning about style and subject through imitation. That tradition has not carried over to a large extent (except informally) to literature until recently, with some government bodies subsidizing mentorship programs. The closest we have come institutionally is the creative writing course, led by someone with a regional, national or international reputation. In some cases attending a program with a famous name means you will be trained in a particular style – the Iowa Workshop style, for instance.

In the epigraph to this section, Rich proposes a vital self-consciousness as part of a writer's education by exploiting that 'seeing' metaphor I talked about earlier. She asserts that in order to define what we need to do in our art today, we have to employ 're-vision', or to revise our conception of the past. For the feminists of the 1970s, this became a critical, historical and political project as they analysed the old, predominantly male canon and discovered 'lost' women writers to add to it. This kind of deconstruction and reconstruction is still going on, led by a variety of critics with particular biases (post-colonial, Marxist, and so on). Writers, therefore, can still learn from the past even as they do not to have to accept uncritically what that past says about the world or to employ the styles they used to frame their artistic visions – although they certainly might adapt techniques.

This discussion about the canon can be distilled into this point: you need to learn about poetry because you want to acquire skills that will help you to say what you want to say in the most effective manner. Becoming an expert in any art, in any vocation, demands dedication. Conductors and composers play instruments and memorize music before they are ready to step onto the podium or pen that symphony. Simply because they can hum a tune does not qualify them to do their best work. Educating yourself is your responsibility.

Why exercises?

Artists need to train, therefore, just as elite athletes. Exercises are not simply for emerging writers, however. Whenever energy flags or ideas wane, poets often set themselves a particular task. They might explore a new form, for instance, or write something for a themed contest. The goal of exercises is to stimulate their imaginations and offer opportunities for practising craft; in other words, to allow them to discover all over again what poetry makes possible (and what makes poetry possible). Below are exercises to stretch your powers.

Hundreds of writing texts exist that define the major poetic forms, explain metre and scansion (the process by which we analyse metre) and include glossaries of literary terms. If you do not already have one, buy or borrow one so that you have a reference guide.

Observations and transformations: playing with figurative language

> . . . the greatest thing by far is to have a command of metaphor . . .
>
> Aristotle, *Poetics*

Let's begin in your present and see what waves of meaning ripple below the surface of what you pass every day; or perhaps we should think of meaning here as webs of thought, shimmering when the light strikes them, connecting one thing to another. Connection is metaphor's raison d'être and metaphorical thinking is at the heart of poetry; philosophers, aestheticians and poets have argued this since classical times. Human beings love analogies; we make images in our minds before we learn to express them in language. Just as rhythm stems from how we move and speak, so metaphor arises from how the imagination makes sense of the world. 'Etymologically, *metaphor* derives from the Greek verb *to transfer*' (Rehder, 2005, xvii). In surprising and satisfying metaphors, we apprehend both elements – the original source and the thing, quality, experience we want to illuminate – in fresh ways (Kroll and Evans, 2006, 38–43). It permeates our daily thinking because we know it allows us to say things we could not say otherwise. Metaphor begins with a single image. Ideally, poetry

> always endeavours to arrest you, and to make you continuously see a physical thing, to prevent you gliding through an abstract process. It choose fresh epithets and fresh metaphors, not so much because they are new, and we are tired of the old, but because the old cease to convey a physical thing and become abstract counters . . . Visual meanings can only be transferred by the new bowl of metaphor; prose is an old pot that lets them leak out. (Hulme, 1924, 134–135)

The following exercise can be done daily, weekly or monthly. Divide up the time so you finish with seven to ten responses.

Choose a house or a tree that you pass daily, something in a shop window, or an animal, such as a dog. Write a short observation in prose about your chosen object/creature without any figurative language (just description) and note the date. The next entry should introduce a simile. The following (third) entry should include another simile. Pay close attention to any changes in your chosen item's appearance. The fourth entry can introduce a metaphor. Try to choose one that supports the tone of the original entries. Alternatively, you can make the entries clash each time. Before you add another, reread the previous ones to create continuity.

When you have all seven (or more), see whether the figurative language builds up a consistent picture of the object or animal. Which does not fit, or add to the overall effect? Have you learned anything from your observations about the object? Have you learned anything about yourself? For instance, have internal or external changes in your life affected what you observed and how you chose to frame those observations (the type of similes and metaphors you have chosen)? Have you unconsciously already written the draft of a poem? What does this process tell you about the way in which the imagination works to make meaning?

Hearing the voice of the past: conventional form

We have talked about the significance of a canon, or a group of benchmark works from the present as well as the past against which any new writer's creations will be measured, so let's begin by allowing you a chance to experiment with some of those techniques.

a) Browse through a comprehensive anthology of English, American, Australasian or World Literature. Select a few poems written in a traditional form, such as a sonnet, sestina, villanelle, ode, etc. as models.

You might also find poems written either in traditional forms or free verse that respond to or manipulate the favoured subjects of previous poetic traditions. W. H. Auden, a consummate craftsman, tried his hand at a variety of forms and music over his long career. I particularly like 'One Evening', where (within the ballad form) he parodies and extends clichés and mixes elements of folk song, nursery rhyme and music hall song lyrics. 'The Wanderer', where he exploits techniques from Anglo-Saxon (or Old English) poetry utilizes alliteration and kennings – or phrases that take the place of the day-to-day term for something ('Houses for fishes' in place of sea, for instance). This poem manipulates not simply the technical aspects, but the subject matter of Old English poetry.

These are not parodies of a tradition, but amplifications of it. Through what I call countercreating, contemporary poets reassess the past, re-imagine it to distil its wisdom and critique it at the same time: updating is appreciating and reappraising. Margaret Atwood's *Circe/Mud Poems*, where she reconfigures the relationship between Odysseus and Circe in Homer's *Odyssey*, making them like present-day lovers, is a feminist revisionist model (she exploits both free verse and prose poetry in this complex sequence). Other examples are T. S. Eliot's 'Journey of the Magi' and Diane Fahey's 'Andromeda'. Countless twentieth- and twenty-first century poets have attempted all the major forms, so a wealth of models exist.

b) Write a poem in a traditional form of your choice. Do you feel constrained to write about a particular subject? Do you feel as if you are not sounding as you normally do (if you do not usually write in metre or rhyme)?

c) Scan, or analyse the metrics of your poem. This is one way of revising, eliminating awkward lines. It is always useful to swap poems with another person if you are not in a workshop group, each analysing a stanza of the other's poem.

This is not simply busywork. As Ursula Le Guin has said, 'Rhythm is a physical, material, bodily thing: the drumstick hitting the drumhead, the dancer's pounding feet. Rhythm is a spiritual thing: the drummer's ecstasy, the dancer's joy' (Le Guin, 2004b, 71). All poetry is based on rhythm, even free verse. It is the pulse that drives the poem forward, that controls the pace, that makes it memorable. During the revision process being able to understand what rhythm predominates in your poem will help you to make it more consistent, or to vary it where you want. A totally regular poem will put your audience to sleep. One that swaps its metre or rhythmic beat every line becomes irritating noise or descends into chaos. The best Hip-Hop poetry moves in a predictable pattern, varying its rhythm when necessary. Listen to the beats of the past and you might discover new sounds in the present.

One last word on rhythm. I discovered its primacy experientially when I once taught poetry writing to 5- to 7-year-olds. We had written a group poem on the blackboard and wanted to revise it. In order to explain the idea of a regular beat I asked the children to stand up and form a circle. We linked hands and together paced out each line as we said it. Instead of being bored with this exercise, they were energized. Moving allowed them to tap into their natural enthusiasm and as a group they experienced a kind of contact high. They felt what worked and what didn't. That necessary underlying pulse vibrated through the soles of their feet and was imprinted on their brains; their bodies moved truly.

If you ever become stuck on lines and simply looking at them makes you more frustrated, use your fingers to count out the beats. If that does not break the deadlock, pace the room as you recite the poem. Speak it into a recorder. As you play it back walk to the sound of your voice. Let your body correct what your eye cannot.

Finding your many selves: pen name/alter ego

This exercise can be understood as a variation on creating character, a kind of advanced version for those who already understand the concept of voice and appropriate diction. In this instance, however, you are not writing a dramatic monologue *per se*, where an individual (not you) speaks in their own distinctive voice to an implied listener (such as the Duke in Robert Browning's 'My Last Duchess').

Here you begin by creating a pen name for yourself and constructing an identity to speak with an appropriate voice. Earlier I mentioned Michel Foucault's concept of 'author-function'. He postulated that one could analyse different authorial personalities in works by the same author; each new creation, in other words, is not produced by exactly the same 'author'. Expanding and transforming that idea, this exercise makes the process conscious and playful.

Once you have chosen a pen name, tie it to an alter ego. Construct a profile. You can elaborate characteristics (physical appearance, attitude, likes and dislikes, etc.). Be as detailed as you want. How does this person sound – in particular, what kind of diction does he or she favour? (You can change sex without surgery here.) Can you assign a piece of writing that you have already produced to your alter ego?

Now create something specifically from this alter ego, your other voice. Do you have to put yourself into a different mental space to do this? How comfortable do you feel? Write more than one piece. Does the process become easier as you work your way into this other style? Do you start to know more about your alter ego from what they write? Australian Gwen Harwood created six pen names for herself (www.trinity.wa.edu.au/plduffrc). In one famous instance, she published an acrostic sonnet in the *Bulletin* magazine that spelled out 'Fuck all editors', which caused her subsequent trouble when her 'true' identity was revealed (Page, 1995, 113).

Ask yourself what effect composing from more than one identity has on your writing as a whole. Do you feel more liberated? Have you been able to define your primary identity more clearly because of the contrast? Have you at least had some fun?

Re-vision: seeing with other eyes

Here is an exercise you can do with your own drafts. You will need a partner or a class; in other words, you need those other pairs of eyes we spoke about earlier to encourage you to be objective. As a matter of course, you should always date and number your drafts and never destroy them. I handwrite my initial drafts and only when the poem has settled, found what I consider a workable shape, do I type it. Even then, if I encounter difficulties with lines that just won't behave, I rewrite them by hand as a way of enabling me to feel, see and hear the words again.

Choose a poem for which you already have at least three drafts or write a new one and produce at least three. Type the drafts in an arbitrary, not chronological order, so that your partner/class will have the freedom to judge which they think is the most successful version (and the most recent – they might not necessarily coincide). Number them 1, 2 and 3, however, for ease of discussion. On a separate sheet, comment briefly on each draft, noting why you made particular changes.

You are ready to give the drafts to a partner. Which does he think is the most recent and why? Which the most successful? How far do your partner's reasons coincide with your own? What revisions do you now think are required? How good a reader of your own poetry have you been? How good a reader has your partner?

Drafting and revising skills are vital for poets. Inspiration and perseverance – imagination and craft – must hook up. Some exercises succeed – in other words – become workable poems. Others develop skills that you will use elsewhere in the short or long term. Nothing you write, no effort you expend, is ever wasted.

5. FOLLOW UP: THE PUBLIC AND PRIVATE SPACE OF POETRY

The oral dimension: reading yourself and reading the audience

Writers do not create in a vacuum, nor do they flourish in one. Public exposure aids in skills' development, boosts poets' confidence and also introduces them to a sympathetic community with the goal of keeping poetry speaking to the world. Entering contests, submitting to magazines and participating in readings are all worthwhile strategies for combating isolation, constructing a network of contacts and receiving feedback from minds outside of one's small personal orbit. Remember that writing is a form of discourse, a kind of public conversation – even if it is carried on in private, on the page, between poet and reader.

The Poetry Reading is perhaps the most accessible way of having a 'test run' for your work. It is imperative, of course, that you read aloud to yourself at home – the first step – in order to be able to 'hear' how your poems sound; to tidy them up before they're taken on their first outing. Hearing helps to distance us from the silence of composition and the page's static nature. If you can, record yourself and critique the performance. You never project as well, however, in private as you do to a live audience. A variation on my principle that 'the body will correct what the eye cannot' is that 'the voice will correct what the eye cannot'. In the middle of a reading, you might suddenly realize that a line or lines sound wrong, but now you know how to change them. In fact, you might find that you have already read a text differently, your aural muse making the decisions.

This kind of experiential testing is what happens when you enter a place where workshop decorum does not apply. It isn't hard to disregard someone's feedback whose biases you already know, just as we dismiss certain reviewers for always riding a particular hobby-horse. In the hothouse of the reading, however, faced by a diverse audience, you can see, hear, even feel the reactions. An adept performer needs to be alert; making eye contact is critical. Do listeners look confused, rapt, expectant, bored? Instant communication or misunderstanding can occur in this volatile space, where you always have an adrenalin rush. Audiences can talk over you, walk out and, in more disturbing circumstances, heckle. Every reading venue – lecture hall, book store, school, bar, coffee house – has its place in the poetry culture. Recently the Poetry Slam, or competition, with audience judges, has blossomed, highlighting once again poetry as entertainment. Poets can learn about their impact on others from these encounters in a way they never can mumbling to themselves hunched over a desk.

Chewing it all over

Let's conclude by talking about that creative space where everything you do – read, take notes, research, write, revise – happens. When you expose your work to others in a workshop or at a reading, when you open that letter or email that contains the editor's comments about your first book, you must bring those criticisms back to this solitary territory to chew them over. How much do you accept? How much reject? This is a process of give and take, of letting your poems move out and come home in a pattern that will repeat itself during your writing life. Insights gained 1 day might not be put to use for another year, or 10. This is why poets must be hoarders: magpies collecting bits and pieces. They must also be cannibals, dismembering the world and recreating it.

In truth, they feed on themselves and everyone they know. This is the rapacious and single-minded way of artists – to utilize all things that stray across their paths, to go looking for adventure in other cities or countries, on foot, motorbike, train, plane or, more likely without a patron with a raft of credit cards, within the pages of a book or on the net. Cyberspace has opened fresh dimensions to the poet's imagination. But sometimes being bombarded by all these written and spoken voices causes information overload. What do you do with it all? How do you keep your poems from putting on too much weight and where do you shed the excess?

As a serious writer there is something else you will need, therefore, besides a place to work. That other essential is a bottom drawer – a space where you keep those unfinished drafts, that great line you couldn't fit anywhere, those others left over from the skirmishes you have with words. The truth is that having that drawer makes it easier to tear out material that trusted critics tell you doesn't fit and with whom you have finally agreed. But at least those lines still live in the drawer and maybe you can resurrect them some day. Poems are living creatures; they can subdivide, giving birth to two. Revisiting what you've published or foraging in that bottom drawer often sparks off something new. Without quite knowing how you've become a magician, you have, pulling ideas out of yourself like coloured scarves, one corner tied to another in a rainbow stream. But this isn't irrational magic, based on another power that bestows these gifts, although it's your clever subconscious that often knots the scarves. What William Meredith once told me in a writing course I took as an undergraduate still holds true. The poets who have 'happy accidents' are the ones who do the hard work; they live with words.

So even if poets go for months without writing, they are thinking about it, about why they are not writing, about what they might write, about whether they will ever write again. About how to find time to begin. If you ever face that point where nothing comes, or you have simply not had time because all those tasks that generate guilt have steamrollered over your creativity, leaving it lifeless as road kill, start small. This is a minimalist exercise – the last one. Write:

> A line a day.
> Just a simple line
> about anything.
> No punctuation.
> Maybe a comma or two,
> perhaps a full stop;
> a semicolon's too much.
> Don't think of this as a line
> of verse to sing.
> Just one scant line,
> lonely on a page.
> See if you can do it
> – leave it as one line, that is.
> Bet you can't.

WORKS CITED

Aristotle. *Aristotle Selections*. W. D. Ross, Ed. New York: Charles Scribner's Sons, 1955.

Armistead, Claire. 'Can Creative Writing be Taught?' *Guardian*, Saturday 17 February 2007.

Atwood, Margaret. *The Circe/Mud Poems* in *You Are Happy*. Toronto: Oxford University Press, 1974, 45–70.

Auden, W. H. 'One Evening', 'The Wanderer', in *Selected Poems*. Edward Mendelson, Ed. New York: Vintage Books, 1979, 60–62, 18.

Bachelard, Gaston. 'The Choice of Literary Examples' and 'L'invitation au Voyage' in *On Poetic Imagination and Reverie*. Colette Gaudin, Ed. Trans. Intro. Dallas, Texas: Spring Publications, 1987, 15–18, 19–24.

Barr, John. 'American Poetry in the New Century'. *Poetry*. Available at www.poetrymaggazine.org. magazine/0906/comment_178560.html (Sep. 2006), 1–12.

Barthes, Roland. 'The Death of the Author' in *Image Music Text*. S. Heath, Ed. Trans. London: Fontana Paperbacks, 1977, 190–215.

Coleridge, Samuel Taylor. *Biographia Literaria* in *Selected Poetry and Prose of Coleridge*. D. A. Stauffer, Ed. New York: The Modern Library, 1951, 109–428.

Collins, Billy. 'Introduction to Poetry' in *The Apple That Astonished Paris*. Fayetteville: Arkansas University Press, 1988, 58.

Eliot, T. S. 'Journey of the Magi' in *The Complete Poems and Plays: 1909–1950*. New York: Harcourt, Brace & World, Inc., 1962, 68–69.

Fahey, Diane. 'Andromeda' in *Metamorphoses*. Sydney: Dangaroo Press, 1988, 23.

Foucault, Michel. 'What is an Author?' in *The Foucault Reader*. P. Rabinow, Ed. London: Penguin books, 1991, 101–120.

Gross, Philip. 'Taken as Read?: Creative Writers and the Trouble with Reading'. *New Writing: The International Journal for the Practice and Theory of Creative Writing*, Vol. 2, No. 1 (2005), 4–11.

Harwood, Gwen. 'Gwen Harwood: Australian Poet (1920–1995). Available at www.trinity.wa.edu.au/plduffrc/subjects/english/aust/harwood.htm

Hughes, Ted. 'The Thought-Fox' in *Selected Poems 1957–1967*. Harper and Row, New York, 1972, 1.

Hulme, T. E. *Speculations: Essays on Humanism and the Philosophy of Art*. Herbert Read, Ed. New York: Harcourt, Brace & Co., 1924.

Kroll, Jeri and Steve Evans. 'Metaphor Delivers: An Integrated Approach to Teaching and Writing Poetry'. *English in Australia*, Vol 41, No 2 (July/Aug. 2006), 35–50.

Le Guin, Ursula. 'Off the Page: Loud Cows' in *The Wave in the Mind: Talks and Essays on the Writer, the Reader and the Imagination*. Shambala, Boston, 2004a, 117–123.

—'Stress-Rhythm in Poetry and Prose' in *The Wave in the Mind: Talks and Essays on the Writer, the Reader and the Imagination*. Shambala, Boston, 2004b, 70–94.

McHugh, Heather. *Broken English: Poetry and Partiality*. Hanover and London: Wesleyan University Press, 1993.

MacLeish, Archibald. 'Ars Poetica'. *The Pocket Book of Modern Verse*, Oscar Williams, Ed. Washington Square Press Pocket Books, New York, 1973, 307–308.

Macquarie Dictionary. The Macquarie Library, NSW: Macquarie University, 1996.

Page, Geoff. *A Reader's Guide to Contemporary Australian Poetry*. St Lucia, Q: University of Queensland Press, 1995.

Pound, Ezra. *ABC of Reading*. New York: New Directions, 1934, 1960.

Pratt, William. Ed. and Intro. *The Imagist Poem*. New York: E. P. Dutton & Co., Inc., 1963, Intro: 11–39.

Rehder, R. *Stevens, Williams, Crane and the Motive for Metaphor*. Houndmills: Palgrave Macmillan, 2005.

Rich, Adrienne. 'When We Dead Awaken: Writing as Re-Vision' in *Adrienne Rich's Poetry*, Barbara Charlesworth Gelpi and Albert Gelpi, Eds. New York: Norton, 1971/1975, 90–91.

Stevens, Wallace. *The Collected Poems of Wallace Stevens*. New York: Alfred A. Knopf, 1965.

Chapter 3

Novel

Graeme Harper

1. WELCOME TO THE WORKSHOP

> The process of writing is something in which the writer's whole personality plays a part. A writer writes not only with his ideas but also with his instincts, with this intuition. The dark side of a personality also plays a very important role in the process of writing a book.[1]

So Mario Vargas Llosa begins his essay 'Discovering a Method for Writing'. Therefore, entering this novel workshop, welcome to the Dark Side! To quote possibly the most famous contemporary resident of the Dark Side: 'We meet again, at last. The circle is now complete.'[2]

Of course, this is not least the case because it is frequently true that those seeking to write a novel have thought about it before; that they have said, as quite a number of non-novelists do also, 'I could write a novel about that' or even 'I'm writing a novel', but that they have not yet done so, or have not yet finished writing one, even if they have started. Circularity is a common novelistic experience.

Here in the writing of a novel you will, therefore, revisit the darkness of mere possibility while gazing on the brightness of probability. The writing of a novel, in essence, is about conquering both that dark and that light – sometimes quite literally, because the writing of a novel is based on a work ethic that often extends beyond the parameters of day and night, that can be part reality and part fantasy, partly clear and easily defined and partly hidden and rarely understood.

Novels are not all written the same way. This is important. In fact, in the darker moments of trying to write a novel it is a good thing to repeat this sentence. *Novels are not all written the same way.* There are many 'how to' books that will ignore this fact and set out methods of construction, or suggest planning techniques or encourage the reader to deal with the novel as a kind of singular structural puzzle in need of specific actions to bring about a solution. There's safety in this approach, a sense that with the right information a solution will eventually be found to any novel-writing problem. However, the needs here are not informational. Rather, what is needed is a way of thinking, a way of imagining, a way of envisaging. These things are not concerned with finding a generic 'key', but about finding ways of accessing your own creative sensibilities.

That said, much has been written generally on novelistic workloads; and much of this seems designed to provide fundamental, inside information on the labours involved. One of the most well-known descriptions is that of Anthony Trollope, who recalls:

> It had at this time become my custom – and it is still is my custom, though of late I have become a little lenient with myself – to write with my watch before me, and to require from myself 250 words every quarter of an hour.[3]

If Trollope's word counting seems a little extreme, it is merely one example of many in which novelists declare the importance of targets and the methods by which they seek to achieve them. Even when the arithmetic is not noted, a sense of pressing need, or work pressure, is frequently present. Take Carolyn Chute, for example, author of *The Beans of Egypt, Maine* (1985) among other novels, who writes 'Typewriter with page 1,994 of novel screams from another room: I WANT YOU'.[4] Or Vladimir Nabokov, who says:

> I generally start the day at a lovely old-fashioned lectern I have in my study. Later on, when I feel gravity nibbling at my calves, I settle down in a comfortable armchair alongside an ordinary writing desk; and finally, when gravity begins climbing up my spine, I lie down on a couch in a corner of my small study.[5]

Whether Chute or Nabokov, the message is the same: that the labour of novel writing is insistent; it takes its physical toll, and it is unforgiving. Nabokov, with his typical ironic stance, suggests that there is a juxtaposition between the 'lovely' and the 'comfortable' and this constant labour. However, even his experience at lifting the mundane into the realms of the lyrical doesn't disguise the relentless nature of the practice: for Nabokov one physical position follows the next, writing continues obsessively.

If it is true, then, that the length of a novel – not least – initiates a sense of supreme effort, then it is equally true that novelists have developed strategies for dealing with this. What is most important is that these strategies are linked to the individual, that they are rarely exchangeable between individuals, and that they are necessary. Thus, here in the novel workshop, you're encouraged first to think of yourself as a distinctive writer, a participant in writing culture, no doubt, but an individual with individual ways of viewing such significant methodological aspects of novel writing as structure, style, story, character and tone. While a generic description of how you come to understand these things is relatively useless, it is possible to speak in general terms about discoveries that might be made, to look at the ways in which the writing of a novel involves a set of acts or actions, and to consider how a novelist can become more capable of clearing the hurdles that might appear on the journey from starting a novel to finishing a novel.

It would be dismissive of the complexity of the exercise here to suggest that the thing that most often prevents someone from becoming a novelist is the simple act of completing a novel! However, certainly there are many examples of novels begun but never finished. It would, thus, not be overly dismissive to suggest that the reasons for this often include the inability to assess the shape or condition of a work-in-progress and to make decisions that allow the work to continue successfully towards a conclusion. It would not be overly simplifying this issue, either, to suggest that the solution here lies in developing confidence in the acts and actions undertaken, and seeing these as part of a process that will eventually lead to completion. How long it will take, and how difficult it will be, cannot be predicted.

2. WRITERS AND READERS

With the exception of media scripts (film, television or computer related), the novel is the most visible of creative writing forms. And, of course, though we might talk of 'reading' the media, we're more frequently inclined to think in terms of 'watching' it, or sometimes even 'playing' it. So the novel, it might be said, is our most pervasive creative writing *reading* experience: widely read, and widely referenced, it is a familiar and formidably conveyor of writerly ideals and human creativity. It carries with it a history of exploration – of knowledge, of places, of cultures – and it holds within it a condition of engagement with human interaction, emotion and disposition, with events and histories, with individuals and with groups. And it is an experience in which writer and reader bridge a gap between production and consumption – even in the case of the hypertext novel, where attempts to make the reader also, in some sense, a writer, don't entirely combine the making and consuming of the text, because construction of formats and links still proceeds consumption.

The novel, also, holds a prestigious place in world writing cultures. There is a continued sense in which, despite the origins of the novel having specific cultural context, that any nation cannot have a fully developed 'literary' culture unless novels have emerged from within it. Literary prizes have emerged that highlight the importance of the novel in this regard, and within the international context, and they continue to draw media attention in a way that few other writing prizes can achieve. When, for example, was the last time a prize for historiography featured in a major news bulletin? When did some of the World's prizes for science writing impact on the size and extent of bookstore displays? The novel holds its place in writing culture not least because of the work ethic associated with it. That is, the novel is seen as a marathon, the long distance event, the endurance trial for the creative writer. Rightly or wrongly, this both draws readers and inspires writers. It also initiates debate. Because the novel is associated with the evolution and management of a range of ideas and writerly actions – enough to fill such a lengthy piece of creative work – interest in successful interpretations of the form, and in the incorporation of individual responses to it into a recognizable genre, are considerable. And yet, as Michael Korda in his cultural history of the twentieth-century American bestseller, *Making the List*, notes:

> The lesson is, yes, there are rules, but they don't apply to writers of real talent, and they're not absolute for anybody. The only thing you can say for sure is that, yes, the ability to tell a story matters a lot, in fiction and in non-fiction, and having something new and interesting to say about familiar subjects is maybe at the heart of it all.[6]

Korda's interest here is primarily in the selling and consuming of all kinds of books, but it interesting how often the novel features and how his comments on 'the ability to tell a story' relate to it. Of course, what he is not overly concerned with in *Making the List*, is the nature of critical opinion in regard to particular creative writing genre.

It is very easy to fall into habit of thinking of creative writing as if it is primarily the fodder for literary criticism – by which I mean *not* that it is not the primary fodder for literary criticism; but, rather, that it's primary purpose is not to be the fodder for literary criticism. This is not a chicken-n-egg argument; simply, creative writing exists because writers undertake to produce it and, to a smaller or larger extent, because someone decides to consume it. Literary critics are some of the consumers of the novel; but the novel is consumed by many more readers who would not remotely be considered literary critics, and whose attachment to the modes of methods of literary criticism is tenuous at best. In some respects, the question of who has the right to define what is a good novel and what is not a good novel comes into play. Likewise, the question of which genre have found critical favour and which have not becomes interesting and reflects, if not simply, on the nature and history of literary criticism, and on the aspects of control and social control that is contained in the professional act of 'literary criticism'. It is somewhat beyond the scope of the chapter here to debate this issue, but as it reflects on the nature of the writers and readers of novels it is not an entirely avoidable discussion.

The novel comes in many guises; publishers and booksellers have long recognized and promoted that fact and novel design and printing, developing in tandem, are fields as well developed as novel writing. A wonderful book published by The Philosophical Library of New York during World War Two, titled *Dictionary of World Literature: Criticism, Forms, Technique* describes the novel this way:

> The novel, the most protean of literary forms, is the least amenable to formal definition. At various stages of its development, it has assimilated the characteristics of other ways of writing – essays and letters, memoirs and histories, religious tracts and revolutionary manifestoes, sketches of travel and books of etiquette, all the popular varieties of prose. Since it has never had to face the circumstances of public performance, or even of oral recitation, it has managed to evade the stricter conventions of drama and poetry. Since, in contradistinction to those more conventional forms, the novel is based upon a more private relationship between reader and writer, it opens up wider possibilities for the direct communication of experience.[7]

Amazingly, over 60 years later, this outline still holds true. Anyone today undertaking the writing of a novel is faced with an incredible number of choices. Similarly, the reader of historical fiction is not necessarily the reader of the fantasy novel, the thriller reader will not necessarily take to science fiction, the romance reader won't always embrace the crime novel, and so on. In some ways, talking about the novel as a singular form for either the creative writer or the reader seems not useful at all. However, the origins of the novel carry with them some sense of the links between its various genre; equally, it is in the context of the appearance of the novel in English in the eighteenth century that an understanding of its principles and performative attitudes emerges.

That we can still talk about 'the novel' today owes much to ways in which we've come to understand it singularly, protean though the novel form may be, and to see its diversity as core to the form. A writer attempting to complete a novel should not, therefore, fear difference, but perhaps be reminded of Korda's general comment on bestselling books that 'there are rules, but they don't apply to writers of real talent, and they're not absolute for anybody'.

3. BACKGROUND AND CONTEXT

> There are three points of view from which a writer might be considered: he may be considered as a storyteller, as a teacher, and as an enchanter. A major writer combines these three – storyteller, teacher and enchanter – but it is the enchanter in him that predominates and makes him a major writer.[8]

Here Vladimir Nakobov certainly shows his bias; he was, after all, the author of a novella titled *The Enchanter*.[9] For those reading *Lolita*, it'll also be all too familiar territory. It is in Room 342 at 'The Enchanted Hunter's Hotel' that the novel's Humbert and Lolita spend their first night as 'lovers'.[10]

Nabokov's three 'points of view' approach raises enchantment above the other ways of considering the writer: alternatively, as storyteller and as teacher. The link between the novel and enchantment extends beyond Nabokov's adoptions; and, the notion of storytelling and teaching through creative writing – particularly in the case of the novel – are not introduced by Nabokov randomly. Indeed, the eighteenth-century origin of the novel in English recalls directly the three viewpoints Nabokov outlines, and the predominance of enchantment might be considered within that context.

Importantly, the industrial changes in the latter part of the eighteenth century in Europe had increased the ability of the novel to reach its audience as developments in printing technology, before and after the turn of the century, brought about increased manufacturing efficiencies and distribution opportunities. But if this was the case at the end of the period, throughout the century and back into the seventeenth century the exploration of the world undertaken by Europeans increased their appetite for new and wondrous things. If the novel was later supported by industrialism it was supported initially by desire and fascination, intensely human traits that informed an age of European reconnaise and that drove not only a cultural revolution but a set of dispositional changes that encouraged the increasing educated populace to engage with what the novel had to offer. As J. Paul Hunter notes in *Before Novels: the Cultural Contexts of Eighteenth-Century English Fiction*:

> We do the novel – and not only the early novel – a disservice if we fail to notice, once we have defined the different world from romance that novels represent, how fully it engages with the unusual, the uncertain, and the unexplainable.[11]

The novel, therefore, has two key antecedentary considerations: the birth of the modern creative writing marketplace, most certainly, but also the rise of a new way of dealing with human individualism. In that respect, the novel drew out from an evolving Europe a sense of how the expanding World might enchant the decidedly more 'average' or common modern reader. But it also brought to the fore a greater sense of the importance of maintaining traditions of storytelling and teaching. It was, in other words, a knowledge provider. This is often overlooked – though not by novelists as skilled as Nabokov.

The novel is, and was from its origins, a place for the meeting of two individuals, writer and reader, for the sharing of knowledge between them, and for the providing of entertainment that could boldly take the reader beyond the ordinariness of their daily lives. It could, and can, paint on a huge canvas, with events and ideas beyond those immediately observable in the reader's world. Or, just as simply, it could, and can, sketch in minute detail the surrounding streets, the familiar and yet partially hidden, the personalities and dispositions, and make from all this an experience that was entirely identifiable yet wonderfully new. As J. Paul Hunter rightly points out:

> Few things about novels are as simple as they try to seem. Not only do they share, at their best, complexities available to all verbal constructs and forms, but they have almost always – perhaps by definition, certainly by tradition – achieved elaborate contextuality as well: they make and they refer. But more too: even in their making, even beyond their desire to refer, they grow out of historical moments more than do most other referential new creations, for in the nature of the novel – in its very definition – there is a new extension from a temporal world, a flowing out of things as they are.[12]

This is a very fine commentary on the novel, and possibly one of the best descriptions of what a novelist seeks to achieve. The only change, perhaps, to make to Hunter's description being this one: that the novelist may not seek to make things seem simple but, indeed, in the acts and actions that add up to the creation of a novel, might certainly seek to leave behind the complexity of composition in favour of displaying, in the very final draft, the integrity of the thing created.

4. THE WORKSHOP EXERCISES

The following exercises relate to the composition and creative consideration of novels. They are presented from the point of view of a creative writer. This would seem an obvious statement, but the point here is both simple and significant: they are not presented from the point of view of a literary critic, after the construction of the work-at-hand; rather, they are presented in action, in process, relating to the act and actions involved in producing a novel, not only to the act or actions of assessing the final product.

The word 'exercise' is interesting, of course: it comes with connotations of highly charged effort, even effort that is morally enlightened, effort that intends to lead to satisfying results, not just personally but somehow also for the world around us. The obvious analogical link to jogging, 'power-walking' or a few hours lifting weights, is as intriguing as it is disturbing; and the similar sense that someone might pop out of a darkened corner and shout 'Exercise is good for you!' does nothing to calm the sense of dread. Of course, there has been forewarning in the use here of the conceit of the 'workshop'.

Workshop, workhouse, work ethic: if there is a creative writing form other than the novel that better recalls the ethos of hard labour then it is yet to be invented. Interestingly, the evolution of writing and printing technologies has, in many ways, only brought about a greater sense of the work ethic connected with the creation of a novel, rather than reducing it. 'Hardware' solutions to such creation have merely shifted revision and editing from pen and paper to the computer screen. Despite the reduction in actual physical editing effort this involves, the discourse of creation around the novel frequently asks the writer to go the extra distant, make the effort and certainly not be enamoured of computer-packaged solutions. No need to recall here the number of times new fiction writers have been encouraged not to just 'tinker' with onscreen edits but to print out and revise in the old, traditional manner. Odd software attempts to provide structural or editing support for novel creation have also been largely ignored. Whereas with screenplay writing computer packages have reduced the labour of formatting and have even been adopted to create narrative shape and character profiles for films and television drama, the novel has largely resisted attempts to cut corners in its creation.

But, of course, the reader is already aware of this, having read earlier about the labour of novel writing. So perhaps the rhetoric here needs to relate, instead, to the endorphin effects of exercise, the exhilarating rush of adrenalin that a writerly swim, run, surf, climb, jump, paddle, ski, swim brings about.

The exercises that follow are offered on the basis that to write a novel doesn't solely involve being able to critically discuss a completed one. The act of novel writing, and the critical consideration of that act and its results, needs to be undertaken 'in process', in order to approach both method and understanding. That is, it needs to be seen as movement not stasis: the writer gains very little from a discussion of writing that insists on it being solidification, detached from the human acts and actions that produce it. Because the writing of a novel can occupy much real time, this fact can be even more significant for the novelist than it is for other creative writers.

Exercise 1: Shape and form

Length. That question 'What is a novel?' often draws the familiar response beginning with something like 'a work of prose fiction greater than 50,000 words . . .' This is one of the definitional fallbacks for almost anyone who finds themselves discussing the novel.

When struck with length as a key definer, and when faced with the variety of prose strategies that writing a novel might entail, notions of shape and form almost innately come to the fore. Pose this as questions. If writing a long piece of creative prose how might I shape it? If writing a novel, how can I orchestrate the movements within it to meet my vision of its final appearance? If theme and subject help shape a novel, how does this happen? If content is best informed by structure, rather than simply being the filler of structure, how can this be achieved?

Shape and form are natural human considerations. We see this in how we humans have managed our living spaces, as well as our works of creative writing. For example, when talking about writers and cities, in a book titled *The Image of the City in Modern Literature*, Burton Pike notes:

> The city has always been man's single most impressive and visible achievement. It is a human artifact which have become an object in the world of nature . . . On the one hand there is the visible city of streets, and buildings, frozen forms of energy fixed at different times in the past and around the busy kinetic energy of the present swirls. On the other hand there are subconscious currents arising in the minds of the city's living inhabitants from this combination of past and present . . . The city has been used as a rhetorical topos throughout the history of Western culture.[13]

Pike's observation that the city is both a physical structure and the stimulus for 'subconscious currents' is a good way also of thinking about the novel's shape and form. The subconscious element, too, refers to both the responses of the writer and those of its reader.

Thus, when writing a novel, consider its shape and form as part of the visible territory; but also consider it as part of the subconscious building of a 'mind bridge' between writer and reader. Consider, also, that form and shape send out a variety of messages. Lewis Mumford, one of the greatest writers on the nature of the city, once recalled that 'the physical organization of a city, its industries and its markets, its lines of communication and traffic, must be subservient to its social needs.'[14] Mumford is alluding here to the nature of human interaction that occurs in a physical location such as the city. Whether we think of the novel, metaphorically, as a human built 'city' or as a nature built 'landscape' we gain a lot from remembering that shape and form are suggestive of function, attitude and ideal and that these things create relationships. The relationship between novelist and reader is as closely tied to shape and form as it is to content. Certain novelists, and certain readers, react differently to certain shapes and certain forms. If we begin with this idea, and rightly consider it as a human natural reaction, then we are reminded that the nature of creative practice, and critical understanding attained in practice, is fluid, a continuance.

a) You are writing a novel. What is its shape and form, and why? Using either a simple description (say 100 words), a graphic representation (e.g. a sketch, scribble, diagram, doodle) or a collection of different representations (e.g. a photo of something, a few words, a sketch) try to depict its shape in a way that feels comfortable to you. Consider how you like the novel to *look*. How does this look impact on how you manage the information the novel will contain. The word 'information' might, on first reading, appear too sterile to describe what you intend to include in your novel. But consider this: the 'information' has increasingly been 'technologized' by the flourishing of the electronic age, the age of digital technologies. However, the word really only means 'something that is known or perceived or discovered'. Thus, the question here is: what will inform your reader? What choices in relation to the shape will inform you, as the novelist, about the direction your novel should take?

For example, these two – your feelings while writing, and the future impact on the reader – should go hand-in-hand. While it is *impossible* to be completely sure how a choice you make as a writer will impact on any given reader, it is possible to make an educated guess as to how the appearance of a page or paragraph or an entire book will be greeted by readers generally. Of course, in discussing shape and form, ideas do extend beyond simple appearances.

b) Thus: how does your prose (assuming your novel is mostly prose as, indeed, most novels are) seek to manage emotional context? For example, do you have a sense of the ways in which different emotions might inform, and be reflected in, the micro structural elements of your writing? By this is meant: any written work has a macro structure (e.g. an overall structure and shape that is both present in its appearance and in the subconscious currents that move throughout the work) and a micro structure, or collection of micro structures (e.g. word placements, paragraphing, chapter sizes) that has the ability to offer the reader some indication of the ideas, thoughts and emotions of the writer. Some of how a writer deals with this is dispositional; that is, some of this is informed by the writer's own sense of the world, by their aesthetic preferences, and by the level of their competence in using different writing techniques, drawing on the vocabulary they possess, even how they use their cultural and personal background. Other elements of this relate to being informed about the choices available.

So: write out a page or two of a novel, something you feel has potential. Start by writing this simply in terms of the information you feel it should contain. For example, information about the story, the characters, the themes of the work you have in mind.

Now approach the same few pages with the intention of getting the writing to reflect for the reader how you would like them to respond to the information you are providing. Be self-conscious about this: how would you like your reader/s to feel? Use word selection and word placement, paragraphing, the physical appearances of the pages, to assist you. Rewrite the one or two pages, noted above, with this in mind.

Now consider what you have achieved – whether elements of the second part of this exercise seem useful or whether, perhaps, they impact negatively on the movement of the work, or on your engagement with plot or story or character. Are there levels of interest in this kind of moulding activity that might be useful to you in creating your novel? At the micro level, how much of this seems 'generic', and how much seems to relate to ideas about the voice, or tone, or timbre of your novel.

Exercise 2: Sound

That is: a novel has a voice. A novel has a tone. A novel has a 'sound'. Many, many examples might be mentioned, but it is just as productive to suggest finding examples of your own. So start with this. Can you find two novels whose voices – that is, just as with a human voice, the voice of a friend or relative or unknown person in the street – whose voices appear to be vastly different? Succumbing to the desire to mention some examples: perhaps compare, if you have access to them, Saul Bellow's *Henderson the Rain King* with Virginia Woolf's *Mrs Dalloway*, or Salman Rushdie's *Midnight's Children* with Patrick Süskind's *Perfume*. Not one of these novels has the same voice. Not one of them, if thinking metaphorically, would be the same person. Do these novels sound like the ideas they wish to portray? If they do then this is quite an achievement for the novelists; many factors come into play. But it is not an impossible achievement – as indeed these novels *do* prove.

Novels speak. How does yours sound? Much of this relates to earlier discussions about arranging information. But some of this also relates to other things that are the common tools of writers. For example, from whose perspective is your novel written? Whose point of view informs the action, the description, the dialogue? Is the viewpoint consistent throughout the work, or do different viewpoints enter and depart? Try this:

Using the earlier method of writing a few pages, and then rewriting them with an alternate result in mind, write a page or two that sounds like a close friend. Then rewrite these pages to sound like a stranger. What did you do to achieve the tonal change? How did the voices alter, and why? How much does the memory of other sounds, voices, tones, elsewhere in the novel, impact on your writing?

Exercise 3: Memory and real time

Having such distance to travel, and such space to use, the novel frequently brings to the fore ideas about time. That is, even the more linear of novels can work between present and past, forward movement and sideways movement, immediacy and memory. There's little doubt here that a rule of thumb for any exploration of this fact must be: form is best when it doesn't overpower content. Of course, this is a point for debate! But the following exercise is based on a simple bias: that linear movement in the novel, if largely abandoned, lessens the reader's engagement with the final results. To put it another way: the exercise that follows assumes that novel reader is interested in narrative drive, forward trajectory – at least in some part, if not solely.

Thus: begin by setting out a list of acts or events that occur in a section of your novel. These might be large events – substantial and multifaceted – or small acts – minor happenings. Set these out in point form, down the page, one following the next.

Now: consider which of these might trigger a sideways movement. That is, which of these might be expanded upon, juxtaposed, or contrasted with something that is not happening *in the immediate*. This could be something from the past (a memory) or something from the future (a speculation). There are formal, narratological terms to describe these movements (analepsis and prolepsis), forward and back, but it is more productive here to simply imagine these as part of the patterning of novel composition. These movements, alternatively, could be generated by the internalizing of the narrator, by the use of metaphor (a change in plane of reference that assists in adding depth to an idea), or by descriptive or expositional extension. In all cases, the result is to upset forward movement.

Now compare the two lists: the first list that simply moves the story onward, from one action to the next; and the second list, that textures the story through the use and, indeed, manipulation of time. As a matter of debate: which of these seems more likely to produce a truthful picture, an interesting narrative, an appealing novel?

5. FOLLOW UP

My method is one of continuous revision. While writing a long novel, every day I loop back to earlier sections to rewrite, in order to maintain a consistent, fluid voice. When I write the final two or three chapters of a novel, I write them simultaneously with the rewriting of the opening, so that, ideally at least, the novel is like a river uniformly flowing, each passage concurrent with all the others.[15]

Joyce Carol Oates, prolific, experienced, revealing. What Oates deals with here is the notion of continuity, the fluid nature of creative writing and, in this case, the writing of novels. It is bizarre that, despite considerable record of this kind of thinking, and this kind of human action, that we continue to treat creative practice as something that can be fixed still and examined with very little reference to the ongoing flow of activity and thought. In other words, we often falsify the nature of creative process in order to critically examine creative product. This must, logically, move us further away from the act of creating – in this case, Creative Writing – itself. This must, surely, create a situation in which creative process is made subservient to a particular brand of critical examination.

Such static critical examination may be a necessary evil in subjects that rely heavily on post-event analysis (e.g. the study of History, Literature, the critical examination of Film or Theatre or Music), but this is not the case in subjects involved in creative practice and discussions highlighting continuity, such as that offered (above) by Oates, helpfully remind us that the creative writer is involved in an organic, moving relationship with their world.

Oates also reveals directly, in the words 'a river uniformly flowing', her own sense of how a relatively large and often complex piece of creative writing – that is, a novel – is managed in her day-to-day practice. Her notions and, indeed, the methods by which she deals with managing the information (recall the earlier definition of this) contained with her novels are interpreted and influenced uniquely by her. That is not to say that others don't use these methods, nor is it to suggest that methodological discussions like hers can't be of benefit to other novelists – indeed, quite the opposite. Simply, it is important in creative writing to keep in mind the individualism of the writer (i.e. their unique way of interpreting and influencing their actions), the ways in which creative writing, while a cultural activity, and therefore connected with the 'mass', 'society', even the 'nation', is essentially a communication between individuals, and a communication that does not stop at one point, still and fixed. It is also an activity in which choices are made by individuals – even in the case of the co-written film script or the jointly composed television drama. The novel is one of those forms that strongly highlights this one-to-one relationship between practice and completed piece of creative writing.

Oates notes that her 'method is one of continuous revision'. She does not mean, of course, that she never, ever completes a novel. Thus it is important, finally, to consider the decisions made to feel comfortable – in any sense – with a novel being completed. These decisions may be imposed externally (e.g. by the terms of a contract, or by the need to move on to new work, or by personal, family or, for the relatively few novelists who are paid well for their work, financial circumstance). Or these decisions may be internally determined. In the latter case, something tells the novelist that their work is done. Not, it has to be said, that their work is perfect. And, equally, as many a publisher's editor will attest, not either that their opinion on what is 'complete' will be supported by *all* those bringing their novel to the public. Equally, even when published, there are those who might comment that something is inadequately developed or poorly articulated. But the novelist, involved in the continuity of creative life, balances their response between a creative sense of the shape, and sound and attitude of their novel. Their own critical response is informed by these things, continually; their sense of success is most often determined by them.

WORKS CITED

Chute, Caroyln, 'How Can You Create Fiction When Reality Comes to Call' in *Writers on Writing: Collected Essays from the New York Times*, New York: Times, 2001

Hunter, Paul J., *Before Novels, the Cultural Contexts of Eighteenth-Century English Fiction*, New York: Norton, 1990

Korda, Michael, *Making the List: A Cultural History of the American Bestseller 1900–1999*, New York: Barnes & Noble, 2001

Llosa, Mario Vargas, *A Writer's Reality*, London: Faber, 1991

Lucas, George, *Star Wars*, 1977

Mumford, Lewis, 'What Is a City?' in *The City Reader*, ed. Richard T. LeGates and Frederic Stout, London: Routledge, 1996

Nabokov, Vladimir, *The Enchanter*, New York: Vintage, 1991

— *Lectures on Literature*, New York: Harcourt Brace, 1980

— *Lolita,* London: Weidenfeld and Nicolson, 1959

— *Strong Opinions*, London: Weidenfeld and Nicolson, 1974

Oates, Joyce Carol, 'To Invigorate Literary Mind, Start Moving Literary Feet' in *Writers on Writing: Collected Essays from the New York Times*, New York: Times, 2001

Pike, Burton, 'The City as Image' in *The City Reader*, ed. Richard T. LeGates and Frederic Stout, London: Routledge, 1996

Shipley, Joseph T. (ed.) *Dictionary of World Literature: Criticism, Forms, Technique*, New York: Philosophical Library, 1943

Trollope, Anthony, *An Autobiography* (1883), chapter xv, in Miriam Allott, *Novelists on the Novel*, London: Routledge, 1959

Chapter 4

Playwriting

Oliver Mayer

1. WELCOME TO THE WORKSHOP

What is really going on? Who are we? How do we really feel? What do our actions reveal about us that we cannot hide? What unanswerable questions reside within us? Of all the arts, dramatic writing unearths the most and best of who we really are, now, on the skin, in our most naked immediacy, onstage for all the world to see. It is an art created for active group involvement, yet it works in a deeply intimate fashion, connecting privately and differently with one person at a time. More than any brother or sister art, playwriting 'plays' with these connections in space, over time and history, exploring dangerous themes and taboos that anywhere else might never see the light of day. More than novels or movies, plays force us to see ourselves – to laugh, to cry, to burn in anger or in embarrassment – in an eternal immediate present moment.

And yet, I have yet to pick up a text on playwriting and truly feel the beating heart of the beast that drives someone – Euripides, Shakespeare, Williams, Shepard, Fornes, Stoppard, you or I – to write a play. There is an undeniable continuum, a veritable *La Ronde*-like daisy chain passing the spirit of dramatic writing from play to play; from its grey beginnings to the greyer fog of today's theatre scene. But this spirit is not grey. Rather, it is bloody and loud, unformed, bold and full of big feeling.

This continuum is strongest in the questions that it asks – not the answers but the questions – asked and asked again by characters and left to us (the readers, the audience) to struggle with and sort out within our own hearts and minds. As you can see, I am speaking of passion more than structure. Both are needed, but emotional fire comes first and matters more than the finest technique.

Perhaps it is time for a text to emulate the actual experience of birthing a play. This demands a heightened (elevated) commitment to the senses within each character, an ambitious hunger to find universal stories, and a deep exploration of who the writer the really is – revealed by the transgressions and untrammelled big feelings unleashed in the drama.

Here goes. Let this essay travel from my heart to yours – with or without our minds' consent – through the channels of the blood, where feeling lives.

2. THE NATURE OF THE PLAY AND THE PLAYWRIGHT

Plays work best when dealing with big feeling: not just feelings – big ones. My wife – Cuban-born – says *Filin* (accent on the second 'i') when she talks with passion about feeling; this seems a perfect word. *Filin* has the Lorca-like power of summoning the *duende*, the blush of all that is truly alive, within us all. Plays are designed for precisely these blushing revelations.

Feelings are faster than thoughts; you can feel something pass over or through you before you can identify necessarily what it is exactly that you just felt. Since this is essentially true of the human vessel, and since plays are about people, this must be a home base, a taking-off point, for the young writer. Plays are emotional constructs before we even begin to deal with intellectual architecture. They hit the bloodstream and can actually cause the blood to rush in an actor, which enacts a chain of feeling causing this same blood rush – or blush – in an audience, almost as if for a moment we were all one great organism.

This blush is the coming together of big feelings and open-ended questions. It is the moment when we are caught somehow with our pants down, embarrassed and naked, yet truly ourselves without spin or style to hide behind. In this moment, we can feel free and safe to ask the biggest questions in our hearts. Answers come from elsewhere – critics, politicos, and best of all from the dreams and nightmares of each audience member long after the play itself has been read or performed.

As ee. cummings said, 'Always the beautiful answer who asks the more beautiful question.'[1] The beautiful question is inside you. As you continue to live and grow, more beautiful questions present themselves. By 'beautiful' I don't mean that the questions need to be pretty or flowery; they may well have a terrible beauty, dark, deathly, frightening. The only thing they must be is unanswerable. The worst plays are those that ask questions that are easily answered. Then, no matter the technical facilities or intellectual heft of the writer, the play becomes forgettable, a treatise rather than a dramatic text. The drama lives in the question.

Characters exist to struggle with the big questions, the big feelings. Whether the play is comic or tragic, the struggle must be there. And the struggle comes from the writer. If the struggle is raging, the play will rage. If it lives in irony, or if the writer copes with the question through humour, the play will be formed along those lines. The big feelings and questions within us are so powerful and necessary that being true to them will affect a play on all levels. In the wake of such elemental feelings and questions, that most difficult of technical concerns – story – will often take care of itself, forming on its own into a plot that makes emotional sense, unique structure, and home-grown integrity.

The young dramatist needs to ask the beautiful questions with every line written, to take note of each blood rush, and to build from there.

3. BACKGROUND AND CONTEXT

Plays exist in an eternal present. They live on the skin. They happen tonight, whether Medea is about to kill her kids and take to the skies, or Hedda blow her head off, or Stella vacillate between filial and sexual bondage. Novels are often written in the past tense; plays hardly ever. No matter the style, plays have in common that they work themselves out in the immediate, on the skin, in the constant and unforgiving present tense. The stories of plays may well take place in the distant past, or in myth, but they always function in the now. Because of this, they are prisms for each day as it comes into our lives. Whether it is a bad day at work, or war in Iraq, each audience member will enter *Medea* or *Hedda Gabler* or *Streetcar* or your new play with the residue of today's reality, and today's reality may do your play good or ill. This is out of your hands. Yet because it must occur, be aware. Allow the light and darkness of the larger world into your obsessive questioning and emoting on the page.

This may seem alchemical, but like all real magic it stems from something amazingly simple: stay present, take your own temperature as you write, and transmit the breath and heat of your being into your characters. Don't let go.

Plays are meant to be played, not read. Plays are literature, but of a different kind than novels, or poems. The best plays are often difficult, challenging and unfinished when read on their own simply as text. They come to life when read aloud, and don't really assume complete three-dimensionality until actors assume these dimensions in space. Conversely, plays that read gorgeously, poetically and with a finished narrative flair are very often less effective when played aloud, and become impossible, earth-bound, when performed.

You must know that the struggle and the questioning inside you demand a certain jaggedness and lack of polish. Rewrites and dramaturgical influences from others will provide the sheen and finished quality of literature with time. But do not lose your edge, and do not be fooled by 'writing' that lionizes the playwright's voice. Be true to the original full-blooded dramatic writing that flows from the heart of your characters (which is your heart).

Students often confuse story and plot. As David Edgar succinctly states, 'Story is the succession of events, while plot is the way those events are represented in a play.'[2] In other words, plots are the way we choose to tell stories, foregrounding what's most important to us and placing in the background or discarding the rest. Choice is all, as any artist can attest. The choice affects the order, the shape and the meaning of the play you write. How to choose? Ask yourself, as simply and deeply as possible, what's most important to you about a story; what pulsates, what is hot, what feels dangerous, what inspires fear or questioning inside you. What is sexy? Where does the mystery reside? Where are you in relation to the tale you wish to tell? You have to be there, if you wish us as audience to come along.

Breathe into the choices. Give them blood and bile, and the blush that comes with lived experience. Keep the writing firmly in the blood and on the skin, and take courage in the continuum of open-ended immediacy. Drama is a shared communal experience that will never die. Shakespeare did it in his day. Now it's your turn.

4. THE WORKSHOP EXERCISES

Plays have their own music. Elementally this is rhythmic, like a heartbeat or a drumbeat. But it's more than that.

Historically, plays have included songs in their texts. Shakespeare used songs to his advantage again and again. In our present theatre scene, original music can be a wonderful highly effective element to the production of a play; but I also believe that existing songs and music can work wonders towards unearthing the foundational rhythms and music within a play. Writers sometimes demur from using existing material, perhaps for copyright or other business reasons. Although this will often be an eventual concern at a late phase of a play's development to production, I still urge the young playwright not to worry. Use songs that naturally come to the fore, that remind you of feelings and memories and moments, and surf those songs as if they were waves of emotion (which they actually are). Sometimes the songs or music will fall away once the scene or play has been written; sometimes they will become pillars within the play's foundation. Either way, songs and music live in each new play.

Neuroscientists point out that music involves nearly every region of the brain that we know about. Apparently, there is a close proximity of music and speech in the frontal and temporal lobes.

This suggests that music and language may start out undifferentiated in human growth. Daniel J. Levitin has a wonderfully spirited new book called *This Is Your Brain on Music* that tries to explain the power of music and its connections to the human brain. He writes that:

> Babies are thought to be synesthetic, to be unable to differentiate the input from the different senses, and to experience life and the world as a sort of psychedelic union of everything sensory. Babies may see the number five as red, taste cheddar cheeses in D-flat, and smell roses in triangles.[3]

How amazing to be able to reconnect what might be termed a true innocence to stimulus! Better than mescal, mushrooms and a host of mind-bending stimulants, I believe that music mixed with language has the potential to open and 'dimensionalize' our elemental connections of the mind and heart.

I am no neuroscientist; rather I am a professor of the heart as all committed playwrights can be. I know how the blood can rush based on pointed use of language and song in a play. It starts with the writer, flows into the actor and ends up causing an audience – one person at a time – to experience synesthesis – even for a moment, as they approach the core of they (we) really are.

As a tool, music may not be the best way to engage thoughts, ideas, intellectual constructs; but it is undoubtedly the best way to engage, arouse and suggest emotions and feelings – particularly the big juicy ones we dramatists so prize.

Exercise: 1
*List the following: (This is a private list, meant for yourself, so you can be as honest as you like!)
(a) What song/music triggers feelings about the one you love? (b) What song/music triggers feelings about your childhood? (c) What song/music triggers feelings about your mother? (d) What song/music triggers feelings about mortality? (e) What song/music triggers feelings about the Spirit?
Now, sing a bit of one of these songs – for yourself (for us). Blushing is okay – revelations are bound to occur. Now, write a scene including the lyrics and THE FEELING of what was just sung. How does the song/music help the scene move?*

Likewise, plays need air – not just to just to breathe, but to fly, the way a bird needs air beneath its wings. I tell my students that plays are like those balsa wood gliders children play with as toys. The writer throws his/her play into the wind with impetus, velocity and with a certain sense of aim; but when the glider/play leaves the writer's hand, all bets are off. Perhaps it will fly in the intended direction, perhaps not. Perhaps it will break into pieces, or loop wildly in unintended directions. Chances are likely that the glider/play will go anywhere other than its intended trajectory – but it will go somewhere. With experience, and with luck, the writer can find the wind patterns to help the glider/play navigate. As previously stated, the world's changeable nature affects the way a play is played: in other words, the winds are ever changing. This is the air that a play must have to fly.

Plays are like people; they make mistakes – some fatal, most not. Like people, plays can survive mistakes by nature of their character, of their ability to fight back when wounded, to bounce back when knocked down. When audiences pull for a character in a play, 'character' is what they are reacting to. Mistakes are actually what reveal character. It's not what characters say, but they do when challenged, that keep a story going. As the Greeks proved, even Gods err; these errors of judgement set into motion all manner of dramatic confrontations. Characters who don't err have no breath in them and cannot fly; not only do they not seem human, they lose their watchability. Likewise, plays that seem all-knowing have a schoolmarmish hectoring quality that can make the most intriguing story seem boring.

How to avoid these pitfalls? Go back to the source, the open-ended question from within, and the inexplicable feeling in your heart's or stomach's pit; then give this to your character(s) with all the energy, immediacy, humour and seriousness you can muster.

> **Exercise: 2**
> *Write a first date between two characters. Every move and utterance reveals character, particularly when the stakes are high. Using powers of perception, reading and misreading behaviour, and distinguishing between truth and lies, each character must determine how the date is going, and whether they are on track for more.*

Plays are best when they include what you fear. I don't mean spiders or Halloween bogeymen; I mean the adult fears that come from lived experience, that can adversely affect your happiness and home life and upset the balance we all strive so hard to achieve. Murder, rape and dismemberment are universal fears – unfortunately they are also largely the stuff of melodrama, based in sensationalism and exaggerated emotion. Perhaps a more helpful self-investigation of fears asks what it feels like to be caught in a lie, or to be embarrassed in front of those you love or work with. What does it feel like to be forced to make a speech when you're unprepared? What happens when old secrets are revealed at inopportune times? These are adult fears that cause a rushing of the blood. They tend to make us blush, to make our heart rush.

> **Exercise: 3**
> *Write about what makes you blush. Literally, write a scene that makes your blood rush. The scarier and more revealing the better!*

Plays include secrets: The deeper and darker the secret, the better. Perhaps the secret is so deeply buried that it will never be unearthed by an actor or an audience, but it should be there regardless. Bury your true beliefs within the structures and accepted norms of the larger society, as the Jews in Spain did after 1492, and what the Mexican Indians did after 1520: you. This phenomenon is called syncretism. In this way, your true feelings (secret though they may be) can live protected – hidden yet pulsating – from the elements and violence of the world. Spanish Jews hid their *mezuzah* within the foot of the statue of the Virgin Mary; thereby, each time they kissed the Virgin's foot in obeisance of the Christian dictates, they also reinforced their secret faith. In the same way, Aztec artisans created hidden compartments within statues of the Virgin and placed Coatlicue, their own female deity, inside; in so doing, they could pray to both deities simultaneously. Over time, secret and accepted faiths tend to fuse in strange and complex new forms. Secrets reveal themselves partially, in new ways, and belief transforms – even transgresses. Plays built this way will have history, and mystery.

The power of Myth over time and culture is passed down in similar fashion. We don't necessarily always know or remember the finer points of Greco Roman myths (or Judeo Christian myths for that matter), yet we feel a residual power of the spirit – of belief – that gives these stories a larger than life quality. Myths are fantastic for playwrights. Their stories are muscular and often strange, and can be plotted in exciting new ways. Existing or exotic, myths are already borrowed and syncretic – that's how they become new again.

> **Exercise: 4**
> *Make a personal list of myths that are meaningful to you. Pick one – identify its expectations – then reverse off them in a scene. Transform the myth into something new.*

Plays are always about desire. Want is the biggest ache you can give a character. It is a much more dramatic quality than need. When a character wants, he/she should want with all his/her heart, every fibre. Needless to say, the character should go after said want onstage throughout the course of the play; the harder it is to achieve, the better. If it is never achieved, that should not stop the character from trying. Upon the completion of this quest on the page, the young writer will be surprised to see that the play in question has a natural, organic and taut plot-line, achieved without strain – except of course for the desirous character!

Exercise: 5

In a private list, ask yourself what you want, big or small. Give the most dramatic, pulsating, revealing want to your lead character.

Plays are transgressive by nature. *Transgression* is a wonderfully operative word with an open-ended definition. I always ask my students to define it for themselves. Invariably the accepted meaning is that a transgression is a crossing of the line, a violation of limits and quite possibly a sin (for those inclined to believe in sin). Plays are best when they identify a line and cross over it – onstage. The best of the best deal in some manner with taboo, or other kind of moral/ethical transgression and its consequences.

Plays challenge authority; simple as that. Why? Plays re-evaluate what our boundaries really are, here in the now. How we feel about Creon and Antigone will change from generation to generation, based on our political systems and opinions, not to mention specific events that point up the very limits of authority and boundaries that *Antigone* was built to challenge over 2,000 years ago. We will always understand Antigone's dilemma, but depending on our own political and legal affiliations, we may also be highly attuned to Creon's dilemma. The best plays are specific to their time and place, but bring up issues and quandaries that simply do not go away, even over millennia. Antigone must rebel against authority for there to be any kind of play; in other words, characters need to revolt, disrupt and fight against the limitations of the world.

Besides which, transgressions are fun to watch. I always tell my students to live careful lives at home, but to explore the most dangerous paths in their scene writing. Plays use transgressions – encroachments on propriety, crossing over accepted boundaries or foul lines – in order to investigate the limits of the laws we live by. Plays invariably involve infidelities and other taboos, not simply because dramatists are a little depraved but because we need to test beliefs by overstepping or doing 'wrong' – making those very human mistakes that are so watchable. There is zero enjoyment in making such mistakes in our lives, but onstage they delight us. Infidelity is a knockout onstage. But pick just about any taboo and explore it openly and open-eddedly in your writing, and I guarantee that your scene will have that unmistakable watchability that comes with touching and surfing the zeitgeist – who we are, and how we act, as a collective. Of course, like any surfer, you may wipe out – your chosen taboo may be too powerful for cursory scene work, and may lead to more unanswered and unanswerable questions.

But this is good news, because this is proof that you need to write and explore and transgress more, in order to go deeper into how we really feel, and who we really are.

Exercise: 6

List five taboos. Choose the one that most attracts you, and write a scene in which the chosen transgression occurs onstage.

Plays use reversals of expectation to make old conundrums new again, and to awaken us from the slumber of a long-accepted but seldom-challenged 'truth' about the way we are supposed to live. Reversals of expectation often lead to further reversals along the way, because once we have strayed from accepted tracks of belief and law, then anything is possible.

Expectations are highly helpful in cobbling a story together; melodramas in particular depend mightily on the use of already established roles and plot-lines, and never sway from the guaranteed delivery of oohs and aahs in the roller-coaster ride of their tales. But serious plays deviate from the roller-coast tracks, with purpose, by reversing off our biggest and most deeply held expectations; the intent is to leave an audience hanging, suspended, mid-air without assurance that they will ever come down again – at least in one piece. The most questioning plays will have the curiosity, muscularity and downright cussedness to never fully allow equilibrium.

> **Exercise: 7**
> *Review your list of myths and taboos. What do we expect to happen from these stories/constructs? What if the opposite occurs? Investigate in a scene.*

Rhythm is a game of expectation; when we tap our feet, we are predicting what we think the music might do next. The great composers know this, and use our expectations for maximum effect – leading us on only to change up the rhythm, pace, tempo – thereby depositing us someplace new, with the old rhythm reverberating in our heads even as we try to find the new pace of our own heart beating.

If you have ever had the feeling leaving a play that your legs weren't fully under you, or even more if you found you had trouble leaving your seat after the show was over, then chances are excellent that you experienced a special and particularly muscular play, and that it manifested its strength literally on your skin, in your body.

I wish this on every dramatist: May your play make an audience weak in the knees, and may your characters and their dilemmas live in people's minds for as long as memory serves.

Plays often involve outlaws of some kind. This does not mean that playwrights are lawless; it does however mean that we can and must imagine living outside the law, mis-, mal-, and non-feasance of the law, irreligion and disbelief. Plays have the potential – the potential – to be the most revolutionary of the literary arts, because they demand a present and immediate re-accounting of all we hold dear. Young playwrights can become drunk on this potential; by living dangerously, they expect to write with extra edge, explosiveness and knowledge of extreme sensation. I always tell my students Flaubert's very cogent advice: 'In your life be bourgeois, so that in your art you can be revolutionary.' Actively transgress *on the page*, not in life. It is, after all, just a play.

Plays are always – always – about love. This does not mean that they must end in marriage, or involve kisses at twilight and flowers; rather, plays can show what love really feels like from the inside of a character's heart – jagged, torrential, cold, confusing, hungering as well as warm and fuzzy. The love in the play does not have to be for another person (although this is recommended, particularly for the first-time playwright); Albee wrote a play about a man's love for a goat, and many great plays have been written about a character's love for an idea or dream. But love is arguably the biggest feeling, the most difficult to rationalize, and the most dangerous for a person's (or character's) equilibrium; and for these reasons, love is central to the active questionings of just about any play being created.

> **Exercise: 8**
> *What do you love? Who do you love? List actively.*

Fear, love and secrets: these are the tools that uncover, crack, puncture, hammer and knock holes into recesses of a character's deepest feelings.

But how do you find your story? Hopefully, it's happening all the time through natural curiosity. Every time you pick up the newspaper or listen to the radio, or even look out your car window at the world going by, you should be attuned to any story that catches your personal interest, and that might 'have legs' – that is, that might have a broader or even universal interest. The Zeitgeist is always there, the connections somewhere in the ether, and the smart playwright looks for stories that cut through the fog and connect not only to how any one person feels, but how we all react and agree or disagree with a problem. The bigger the problem, the better the play will be.

Exercise: 9

Write a scene based on something reported on television or in a newspaper. Dramatize the moment that caught your eye about it in the first place. How true do you need to be to the original document? Is it possible to make the story new?

There is a private language of plays that lives in stage directions and parenthetical suggestions about tone and colour; it is a shadow language because it retains an aura over the proceedings, suggesting and cajoling and inspiring the kind of actions needed for the particular moment. An audience will never see or hear the stage directions as writing, yet they will feel the active suggestion of this shadow language throughout the experience of watching a play unfold.

This is a good way to think about the 'writing' in playwriting: intentions, themes and the biggest feelings are written in shadow. We feel them without having them expose themselves to us. Exposition is necessary at times, but too much kills the immediacy of the writing. Yet murkiness – vagueness – can also kill a play.

So what are we talking about then? Focused, muscular, immediate writing about what happens – suggested from the shadows rather than expressed or underlined in a narrative. Does this sound difficult? It demands a certain trust that the big themes and the big questions, will be revealed without pushing too hard. If you feel them when you write them, chances are good that I will too. If you announce them, I don't have to work to feel them because I'll just take your word for it.

I always ask my writers, 'What is really going on?' Beneath, behind, and inside our pat answers to personal questions resides a cauldron of unexplained feelings and half-marinated thoughts about how the world works. When a dramatist prepares to attack a new big question on the page, I want him or her to really ask this question *in the writing*, and to be prepared to be surprised by the answer.

Private language works extremely well in the actual writing of dialogue. If you are able to ask them, characters should know foreign languages, speak in Pig Latin, or have personal references about songs and events that they simply do not have to explain; this gives them integrity, three-dimensionality and secrets. Too much of this creates a moat between the characters and the watchers, but the young dramatist will be surprised by audience tolerance to this kind of interior language. As long as these private languages mean something specific to the characters, the audience will find residual meaning, and it can become a kind of puzzle or mind-bender that can grow over the course of the play.

Exercise: 10

Identify and list the private languages your characters are fluent in. Those who come from religious backgrounds have entire sets of custom and language that they can use in their writing. These private languages of the soul have an immediate freshness when presented – as is – onstage. Even more, they have a natural structure that helps in scene construction, so that scenes and entire plays can begin to make sense along these traditional lines. Write a scene in this private, shadow language.

Plays have themes because playwrights have themes that they cannot help but explore through their plays. The best themes are unifying without being dictatorial. Like the sky overhead, they can alter temperature, lighten, darken and change colour, even as life continues below on land. Usually, themes become visible after a body of work is created; themes are the motifs and questions that come up again and again almost without bidding, naturally, as part of the artist's voice and style.

What is yours? Write it down. Better yet, meditate first. Take your time. All will come clear.

5. FOLLOW UP

As you can see, plays are amalgams – containing pieces of memories, dreams, songs, myths, stories and other texts. Through the process of changing the names to protect the guilty parties (in other words, fictionalizing), plays fuse these disparate strands of thought and feeling into something hopefully stronger and more original than a documentary treatment of the same material.

Plays glean from life experience the already existing structures that we instinctively recognize and adhere to, without thinking too much about them. Plays give us the opportunity to see them – often for the first time – focused, on their own, flaws exposed and strengths proven by active challenge.

Gleaning is the key. The dramatist gleans themes, emotions, motifs, ideas and facts from life and places them – artfully, let's hope – into the characters and stories of the drama; the reader/audience then has the pleasure of the gleaning process once again by deducing and inferring these facets of the play. The pleasure lies in the suggestion – not the exposition or spelling out; you should have to dig a bit, as a gleaner might dig for a potato in the soil.

The absolute best thing you can do as you glean is to read, read and read more plays – with an eye towards analyzing how they work. Reading plays from the past will give you a sense of the continuum of the drama – for example, how Ibsen and Strindberg informed O'Neill and Shaw (each differently, of course), who informed the rest of us – and how the big stories and myths recur and transform from generation to generation. Reading contemporary plays gives you a cross-section of our present moment (or at least our very recent past). Writing a new play will give you the true pulse of what it's like to be alive now.

Even better than reading, see plays. The big glossy ones are expensive, but I can assure you there are plays taking place tonight in your town that are both affordable and worth your time. The Shakespeares and Greek tragedies being performed tonight present tropes that you not only will see but feel when in their presence. New plays are always a grab-bag (you just don't know what it is till you investigate for yourself), but good or bad they share the air you're breathing, the ideas flowing and that Zeitgeist that is out there for us all.

More than anything, reading and seeing plays gets you in the mood to imagine and tell your own stories in workable dramatic forms, adopting dramatic techniques in the very best way: by osmosis. If you read enough, you will begin to establish what you like and don't like, what kinds of plays work for you, which writers reach out to or repulse you – and you will do this without really having to think about it too much. It will simply become part of your life, the way you do things – not unlike keeping in shape over an extended period of time. When it's your time to write, you will find you have stamina you wouldn't otherwise have.

For that matter, see lots of movies too (for our generation, it is pretty impossible not to). Film is a closely related art to our own, with one big caveat. Films use cuts to tell their story, creating a rhythm and a meter that affects both style and content. While dramatists may play with filmic storytelling devices, the general truism is that plays don't use cuts; since we engage in real time, it simply doesn't suit our medium in the same way. Contemporary writers everywhere (including me) have examples in their work to prove otherwise, bits of plays that have galvanizing cinematic tricks; but for every single success, there is a mountain of painful evidence of cinematic effects falling flat on stages and on pages everywhere. So many contemporary scenes end just as they start to get interesting, and 'cut to' another scene with other characters. This is the insidious effect of writers watching too many movies and forgetting that what counts is investigation and revelation in the moment; to do that, characters must stay in their moment and keep asking the big questions.

Still, keep reading and writing and gleaning.

Perhaps your early work will feel derivative – in the style of – no matter how you might try to be original in concept and character. In order to find your voice, you often need to throw it in the style of those who came before you. If you keep doing it – writing plays – then your thumbprint will begin to show through.

It sounds like a mix of metaphors, but the voice and the thumbprint are highly related in this case. The voice is something you grow into. The thumbprint is what you're born with.

By thumbprint, I mean who you really are: the things you know and the things you'd rather hide, but which pop up at the most inopportune times. In essence, your thumbprint is the unmistakable *you* that serves as your signature as you build your play.

'A person is a person through other persons,' Desmond Tutu said[4] during the tumultuous times of *apartheid*, reminding everyone – friends and enemies – of our interconnectedness. A person cannot be himself or herself in a void. You see yourself in the reflection of another's eyes.

You see yourself in the plays you write. That self becomes refracted in the prism of your characters. As they move, these characters – like music – become sound paintings that move. They take the writer, the actor and the audience somewhere new. We are not all guaranteed to go to the same emotional/intellectual/spiritual place at the same time; free will is alive and well in the theatre, and the EXITS are clearly marked for those who don't want to make the journey. But if you the dramatist want strongly enough to take us somewhere, go there and we'll probably go along with you – just to see what all the fuss is about.

Where will you take us? What kind of person will you show me in your play, so that I can see myself with new eyes? What beautiful questions wait to be asked tonight? What *filin* will move from your heart – your blood – to mine?

Revelations await; they begin with you.

WORKS CITED

Cummings, ee. *Poems 1923–1954*, New York: Harcourt, Brace and Company, 1954.
Levitin, Daniel J. *This Is Your Brain on Music*, New York: Plume/Penguin, 2007.

Chapter 5

Scriptwriting

Ken Dancyger

1. WELCOME TO THE WORKSHOP

In the coming 6 months I will give scriptwriting workshops in Amsterdam, Los Angeles, Bogotá and Johannesburg. I am one of the many who through their books, their scripts, their academic or industrial affiliations will teach eager acolytes how to reach their goal, a completed screenplay that will enter the market-place and help the career path of its writer.

The proliferation of scriptwriting workshops, manuals and methodologies in the past 20 years reflects the explosion of interest in scriptwriting as an attractive entry point into the Film and Television industries. This chapter does not seek to support or undermine this observation. Rather it will try to explain what such a workshop might look like, the purpose it serves, as well as the unfinished work remaining at its end. The underlying assumption of the chapter is that the workshop can shorten the writer's learning curve in his quest for the technically competent, compelling and possibly commercially viable screenplay.

Although there is no linear path to a career in the film and television industries, the notion of skill acquisition particularly through the collective experience of the workshop leaders, has fuelled the market for script workshops. The success of a few fuels the mythology of the scriptwriting workshop. Rather than promote the myth, this chapter will attempt to describe the reality of such a workshop and to imply its potential benefit for its participants. It's my hope that the magical mix of knowledge and hope together will benefit the reader in their quest.

2. THE PURPOSE OF THE WORKSHOP

On a general level, workshops veer either in the direction of a catalyst to stimulate the participant about the idea of writing a script or in the direction of learning the how of writing the script. For me the more useful workshop spurs thinking about how to deploy narrative tools in ways useful to the writer as she moves from idea to outline to treatment to full draft.

A second issue relates to the audience of the workshop. Is everyone at the same level or does the group vary from beginners to advanced? The greater the spread the more elemental the workshop becomes. The higher the knowledge base of the participants, the more specific the workshop can and should become. For the workshop leader, the key here is to know as much about her audience as possible in order to pitch the workshop at an appropriate level.

A third dimension relates to content. Is the workshop focused on writing short or feature films? The answer is critical because structurally and from the view of character population and character arc, the two forms look very different from one another.

Assuming that the workshop focuses on the feature film, will it emphasize a particular genre, a particular approach to structure or upon voice, that singular unifying prism that guides the point of view of the writer towards their subject? Inevitably the workshop will be permeated with the views; I'll call them, ideology of scriptwriting of the workshop leader, his voice on the subject of scriptwriting.

Now let me put forward my own biases. I believe in a clear goal for the workshop. I also believe that the main purpose of the workshop should be writer empowerment. Consequently whatever workshop I teach I believe that its first order of business is to clarify for the participants, the narrative tools they will need in order to write as effectively as possible. And so I turn to what I will call the 'narrative toolbox'.

3. BACKGROUND AND CONTEXT: THE NARRATIVE TOOLBOX

The narrative toolbox begins with a series of definitions that in the course of the workshop have to come alive as useful narrative devices that will help the writer solve the script problems that inevitably arise as the writer begins to make decisions about the shape and population of his story.

The first tool emanates from the fact that you and I experience the script through the experience of the main character. That character faces two opposing choices in the script. Those opposing choices, the premise, position the character in the middle of the narrative. The premise, sometimes called the central conflict, the central idea or the spine runs through every scene of the narrative. And the two choices are embedded in the secondary characters of the script. More on this in a moment. The premise in *Titanic* is whether Rose, the main character will choose love or money. The premise in *The Verdict* is whether Frank Galvin will remain the humiliated ambulance chaser–lawyer or reclaim his dignity and self-respect as a person and as a lawyer. Key here is that the premise is two opposing choices. Without a premise the narrative flattens and becomes inherently undramatic. Again the premise is the two choices the main character faces. They must be the opposite of one another.

The second tool is the organization of the character population around the main character. This population lets call them secondary characters, break down into two distinct groups, those who help the main character (helpers) and those who harm the main character (harmers). The helpers represent option one of the premise while the harmers represent option two of the premise. There are rarely more than three to five helpers and three to five harmers. The purpose of the secondary characters is to push, pull, prod, the main character. Whether catalyst or contrast, each has to be purposeful. The most important harmer is the antagonist. Interaction between the main characters and the secondary characters varies in degree from very intense in the case of the antagonist and love interest to catalytic in terms of plot or character development in the case of the other secondary characters. If the writer cannot define a specific purpose for the presence of a secondary character in this script, it may be the case that that character has no purpose, and serious consideration should be given to the idea of dropping that character from the screenplay.

Next we turn to structure. Structure is four elements – the plot layer, the character layer, the genre and the overall organization of the screenplay, the three Acts. The three Act structure holds true for

90 per cent of screenplays. If you visualize this structure, we meet a character in crisis and live with them until the crisis is resolved in the resolution. More on this shortly.

Plot happens out in the world. The plot layer refers to an external event, a war, a sporting event, a career, a crime, that has a direct bearing on the main character. If the plot is too distant from the main character, it becomes no more than background coloration. If the plot is everything, the character becomes no more than coloration. To be effective plot works against the main character's goal. For example, in the war film *Saving Private Ryan*, the goal of the main character is to survive. The plot, save Private Ryan, results in the death of the main character. What's critical here is that the main character's goal and the plot have to be working against one another in order to be effective.

If the plot layer is about the external world, the character layer is all about the main character's internal world. Think of that internal world as the centre of an emotional vortex. If plot is about sensation and surprise, the internal world as represented through the character layer is all about the emotional world. It is the character layer that emotionalizes the script-film for the audience.

In the character layer, the main character explores the two options of the premise. In *Titanic*, Rose develops a relationship with an artist (option: love) and is in a relationship with a rich possessive aristocrat (option: money). Again, it is the character layer that emotionalizes the script. Plot may be exciting, sensational, but it does not have the deeper impact of the character layer. Scripts are strongest when they have strong elements of each, a strong plot layer and a strong character layer. *Silence of the Lambs* is a Police story with a strong plot and strong character layer. On the other hand there are films with exclusively a plot layer (*Raiders of the Lost Ark*) or exclusively a character layer (*Once Were Warriors*) and each has done rather well. Nevertheless the ideal script should have both plot and character layers.

Genre is huge in its implications because different genres have different character and dramatic arcs, so knowing the genre you are working with, and knowing what it looks like, is an enormous help to the early writer. First every film is a genre film. Second, genres have particular shapes. A Thriller is about an ordinary person caught in extraordinary circumstances. If they don't figure out what it's about, they will die. Until they do figure it out, they must evade the danger. Consequently the Thriller looks like a chase. A Police story follows a crime–investigation solution structure. A Gangster film follows the rise and fall of the gangster. A Romantic Comedy follows the course of an unlikely pairing getting together, in short the course of the relationship.

In terms of the character arc, we meet the main character in the Melodrama as a powerless person. In the course of the narrative, the character will try to attain power. Generally they acquire empowerment at a high personal cost (loss of innocence) or more positively (coming of age). In the Situation Comedy, whose arc unfolds more positively than the Melodrama, the outcome is experienced by the audience as a progression while in the Melodrama the change is experienced less positively. Otherwise the Situation Comedy and the Melodrama are from the structure and character point of view, quite similar. The key in both genres is an internal transformation. The character arc in Film Noir is more specific darker and internal. At the beginning we meet a disappointed character who makes a poor love choice and in the end he is destroyed spiritually and or physically by that choice.

The Thriller on the other hand, tends to unfold more externally. The Plot and an antagonist pose a threat and at the end the evasion, understanding gained about the threat usually leaves the character in the heroic position of having survived. Internally the main character may not have changed, but our identification with the character leaves us pleased about their survival. The character arc in its transformative arc will differ from genre to genre.

For more on genre see *Alternative Scriptwriting* by this author and Jeff Rush. Genre to be useful to the writer must reflect a shape to the narrative, a clear goal for the main character, an antagonist who opposes that goal, and the degree and nature of change the main character will undergo in the course of the narrative. Buddy films, Road films, which are often referred to as genres are simply too general to be truly helpful to the writer. They describe a situation rather than a full story form.

The fourth layer of structure is the three Act structure. Whether one views that structure as Aristotelian (beginning – middle – end) or Syd Fieldian (the set-up – confrontation – resolution), the three Act structure is a linear structure that leads the viewer from critical moment to resolution. It's complete, potentially satisfying and the prevailing structure in use. Although most of the balance of this chapter will focus on essentially a three Act approach to narrative, alternatives at the least should be mentioned. At the other extreme is the non-linear film which may have a circular structure (*Pulp Fiction*), a multi-character open-ended structure (*Magnolia*), a meditative multi-character structure (*The Thin Red Line*) or even an MTV (a series of short films strung together) structure (*Natural Born Killers*). Other voice-oriented genres also differ from the linear three Act structure. The Docu-drama has the case structure of the documentary (*United 93*). The Fable (*Forrest Gump*) has a four to five Act structure 'suitable' to the journey plot it follows, while the Experimental narrative has a two Act structure (*In the Mood for Love*). Multiple characters, multiple plots, non-resolution each differentiate these genres from the classical three Act structure narratives.

Turning to the classical three Act structure it's best to look at its characteristics act by act, acknowledging that the plot layer and character layers will form part of that structure but that its uber-structure will be organized by the genre the writer has chosen for his narrative. First let's look at Act I. Act I, the act of the set-up, has a number of important features, the most important being where you begin the story. I call this the critical moment. The critical moment should launch the viewer into the narrative. A crime is committed. A young man leaves home. A young woman walks away from her marriage ceremony. These beginnings are critical moments.

The next, notable point in the screenplay I call the catalytic event. Elsewhere it's been called the inciting incident or the point of attack. In most films if kicks off the plot. This happens about 10 minutes into the script (one page per minute is the general expectation). It is strong enough to change viewer expectations. In *East/West* a group of Russian expatriates return to Russia in 1946, having spent years in exile. The catalytic event is as follows: as they leave the ship now landed in Odessa, one of them is shot by the police for not obeying orders. What seemed a Utopian return, with this event, turns into a nightmare.

The next important point is the turning point at the end of Act I. That turning point has to be surprising enough that it opens up for us the story possibilities. In *The Verdict*, a lawyer who we have expected will accept a settlement from the Church-Hospital he has brought suit against, refuses the settlement, knowing that a trial is risky and against the wishes of his clients. His refusal is a risk that changes the story, and introduces the trial of Act II. To repeat the critical moment, the catalytic event, the act turning point, as well as the premise, the plot layer and the character layer, are introduced in Act I.

Act II, double the length of Act I and III, is best viewed as the Act of confrontation where the main character explores the two options of the premise. A midpoint separates the exploration of the two options. As expected, relational development is at the heart of Act II. Act II ends with the second turning point but this time the turning point closes down the options for the main character. A choice has been made. What remains is to see how the story works out. Does it accommodate or deny the main character his choice?

In Act III, the act of resolution the key element is how the character achieves resolution. The plot layer and character layers need to be resolved and once all these layers are closed off, resolution is achieved and the narrative ends.

Before we leave the narrative toolbox idea, two more of the tools, both mentioned in the commentary on genre, need to be addressed more fully – the character arc and the dramatic arc. When we speak of a character arc generally we are principally concerned with the main character, although increasingly producers and agents talk about character arcs for secondary characters as well.

In terms of the character arc, three points are important. What is the state of the character when we meet him (critical moment), what is the state of the character when we leave him (resolution) and what is the degree of transformation that has occurred in the character? In certain genres, the Thriller for as mentioned, transformation tends to be external, the character is alive at the end. But in most genres, the transformation tends to be internal – unhappy to happy, a failure to a success, for example. In *Tootsie*, Michael Dorsey begins as a lying, manipulative, macho male failure who is transformed into an honest, sensitive male actor. Transformation can only occur through the pressure of relationships of plot or both. The greater the pressure, the steeper the transformation. On one level the nature of the character arc tells us a great deal about how the story will unfold. The other directional narrative device is the dramatic arc.

The dramatic arc and its shape are determined by the genre the writer chooses to work with. Each genre has a different dramatic arc. In Film Noir, for example, the dramatic arc follows a crime and punishment shape. The main character falls in love with a poor choice. To continue the relationship he commits a crime, robbery, more often murder and is the fall guy for his accomplice. The Horror film looks like a chase ending in the destruction of the main character while the Action-Adventure film is an epic journey – struggle that make a super-hero of our main character. Once the writer has chosen a genre to work with, the appropriate dramatic arc should be immediately available to the writer.

4. THE WORKSHOP EXERCISES

Hopefully it's apparent by now that there are many potential areas a workshop could focus upon. On an overview level I myself have conducted workshops on Genre scriptwriting, Alternative scriptwriting, Global scriptwriting and Writing the Short script.

I have also conducted more specific, specialized script workshops on the use of plot, character development, how plot and character work together and on specific genres. Although my 'ideology' rests on bending, breaking, amending the script rules to make an old story seem new and fresh, I find that the most learning goes on for the participants when I focus on a middle-ground workshop. And so for the purposes of this chapter I'll focus on the Genre workshop that has proved to be the most useful for the writers I have encountered in my workshops.

Entry into the workshop depends upon prior experience, the quality of the idea proposed for development and an interview. Prior experience varies, from making a documentary or a short film, having written material in other medium, for example, journalistic work, short stories, even a novel. The point here is to have proved oneself as a storyteller in one public forum or another. With regards to the quality of the idea many elements come into play – the interiority versus externalization potential of the idea, the clarity and unusualness of the voice, the dramatic potential of the idea. A story of a suicide pact between two lovers which ends in their suicide is sensational rather than dramatic unless somewhere in the story the potential to embrace life, hope, is an option. Even if it fails hope has to exist somewhere in this story to make it dramatic.

The next step is to devote a particular portion of the workshop to each project and its writer. A half-day can work but a full day works better. The goal of the workshop leader should be to alert the writer to the problem areas in the idea and to highlight how different genres offer pathways for the development of the idea. But before that the writer's day should begin with the pitch of the idea, a group discussion about it. For me the pitch should answer the following questions:

Who is the main character and what is his/her goal?
Who is the antagonist and what is his goal?
What is the state of the main character when we meet him?

How does the main character change in the course of the story?

Who/what causes that change?

What is the balance between plot and character you intend to use?

What is the premise of the film and who are the characters you will use to explore the premise?

What is balance between plot and character you intend to use?

What is the genre you will use for your idea?

What is the tone you will adopt for your idea?

An aside about tone since it hasn't been mentioned so far in the chapter. Tone tends to be genre-specific although writers like Elmore Leonard tend to challenge tonal expectation (*Get Shorty*). In a sense, tone reflects the voice of the writer. Often the answer to this question will tell me if the writer wants to tell an enabling story or a disabling story.

The discussion among the participants tells me several things about the writer. First, the level of conviction they feel towards their idea. Second are they viewing the idea in fixed or fluid terms? To put this another way, does the writer want to use the script to pronounce a particular personal, social or political view or are they interested, curious to explore the situation/character that they are presenting? Finally the conversation tells me if the writer wants to connect their story to the external world around them. Or conversely is this a more interior-narcissistic narrative with little or no connection to the world at large?

Having discovered a good deal about the writing and too often a good deal less about the potential shape of the script to be, I select a series of film clips that will address specific script issues. For example, if the film is lacking an antagonist, I will choose a clip that illustrates the link between the main character and his goal and an antagonist with his opposing goal. If it works, the clip will illustrate that a main character without an antagonist is less inherently dramatic. The consequent lower level of conflict drains the narrative of energy and tension.

What if there is no plot to speak of in the narrative? In this case how is a steep transformation to be achieved? Here I like to use a clip from *Truly, Madly, Deeply*. In the absence of plot there has to be two strong opposing relationships to put pressure on the main character. Here the premise is whether a young woman who has suddenly lost her lover will live a life of mourning, or whether she will move on and embrace life. Anthony Minghella, the writer and director of the film brings back the dead lover at the Act II break and introduces a very different but equally vivid live option at the midpoint of the act. And so the pressure on the main character is powerful enough to promote change and be dramatically vivid in the absence of plot.

What if the writer is not using powerful relational issues and only relying on a modest or no amount of plot? The writer anticipates a significant transformation in the main character but because he is using a modest amount of relational pressure and little plot to achieve the transformation, the experience of the narrative will seem flat, pedantic. Here I will use a clip that embraces a strong relationship and strong plot to affect the transformation. Here my emphasis focuses on the benefits of plot in the writer's script. Without it, the script can too easily devolve into a series of conversations leading to change. Sounds boring. It will be unless the writer adopts the strategy of a film like *Goodbye Lenin* which is strong on character and plot layers to transform its main character.

Another common problem at this stage is to identify a premise and if one doesn't exist to consider specific possibilities. In this case, a clip from a film such as *Bullets over Broadway* and its main character's musings about art versus commerce in the production of his play makes the point. Here the premise for the main character is to choose art or commerce. In *Tootsie* the main character has to choose if he is going to be a man's man or a woman's version of a man. If he chooses the first, lying manipulation and failure will be his fate. If he chooses the latter, honesty and success in love and work will follow. The presence of a premise in the narrative will create dramatic amplitude and tension. Without it the story will be flat and less involving.

Tone also seems problematic for the early writer. By tone I mean the deployment of specific detail that will guide the reader-viewer towards interpretation. Tone is the way writers editorialize about their story. Does the writer want the main character to succeed or fail? Is the narrative about attaining wisdom or cynicism? And what are the events or relationships that will promote that change? Is realism or narrative exaggeration the appropriate narrative wrench? In a sense the answers to these questions bring us to the main event, the choice of genre. Genres can be enabling or disabling and it is to that process of choosing genre that we now turn.

At this point my goal is to illustrate how different genres provide different pathways for the idea. To contextualize these pathways, I propose a grid from wish fulfilment to nightmare. In the wish fulfilment grouping we find the Musical, the Action-Adventure, the Western, the Science Fiction film and the Romantic Comedy. In these genres the main character heroically achieves all his wishes. To do so they may endure the challenge of a substantial plot and a super antagonist. The plot may be ritualized as in the Western, or energetic as in the Musical or as a mythical journey as in the Action-Adventure. Here the tone is enabling, romantic, far from realism.

The mid-clusters of the grid are the realistic genres – the Melodrama, the Situation Comedy, the Police story, the Gangster film and the Thriller. In this group, narrative events and characters tend to present realistically. If the ordinary main character in the Thriller prevails against a far more powerful antagonist, he will be experienced as a hero. But the process of the chase needs to be believable. Narrative exaggeration is replaced by narrative credibility. No superheroes or super villains here. In this group it is tone that will determine whether they are enabling or disabling. Either remains an option for the writer. In *North by Northwest* the main character prevails and the lightness of the tone verges on the comic. In *Arlington Road* the main character is heroic but dies and is blamed for a domestic terrorist act. The darkness of the resolution supports the tonal intention, a caution to the viewer about the serious issue of terrorism in the United States. Both these utterly tonal opposites are Thrillers.

The third group in the cluster is the genres of the nightmare – Film Noir, the Screwball Comedy and the Horror film. In these genres the fate of the main character is to be a victim, at the hands of a love interest or in the case of the Horror film, a human or animal 'monster'. In each case the plot resembles an event or journey, that is the basis for the downfall of the main character. Here exaggeration, passion, violence can take on an intensity beyond realism. These are the genres of our deepest fears, of the unimaginable.

Each of these groupings has different implications for the character arc of the story's main character. In Film Noir, a disappointed main, character makes a poor relational choice that in the end will destroy him. In Screwball Comedy, the main character simply makes a relational choice that robs him of his free will. In spite of the loss, he doesn't seem to mind being controlled by a woman. In the Horror film, the main character ends up the ultimate victim. He or she is destroyed mentally in *Alien*, physically in *Dr. Jekyll and Mr. Hyde*. In the Horror film the destruction of the main character is feared and experienced.

In the genres of wish fulfilment the opposite occurs for the main character. In the genres of realism, the outcome can go either way. So which is it to be for the main character in the participant's story? The decision made determines the genre choice for the writer.

An example of genre pathways applied

The most useful way to illustrate how genre consideration can be used to open up a story is to take an established narrative and to apply different genres to it to highlight different dimensions of the story and by doing so to reinterpret the narrative.

Although this approach can be taken to any idea or treatment, I choose a well-known tale by an unforgotten writer, Shakespeare's *Othello*. For the purposes of what will follow I focus on the following specifics of the play.

That Othello is a King.
That Othello is black while his is a mixed race Kingdom.
That Othello's wife, Desdemona is white.
That Othello is proud and possessive of his wife.
That Othello's chief advisor, Iago is white.
That Iago is angry and envious of his King.
That Iago is political, even Machiavellian, in his behaviour while Othello seems almost an innocent idealist in comparison.
That Iago will play on Othello's insecurity about his wife.
That Othello will kill Desdemona in a fit of jealous rage.
That Othello will kill himself when he discovers Iago's duplicity and Desdemona's innocence.

The narrative then is a tale of personal and political power set against the backdrop of racial mixing and racial divide. The personal and the political merge and conflict. Now let's turn to various genres approaches to this narrative.

Clearly the straightforward treatment is to see the black character, Othello, as a powerless person in the powerful white majority culture. In this version his courting and marriage to Desdemona is his effort to gain power. Here the main story line is not political but rather personal. As his white lieutenant, Iago is the antagonist who will play on Othello's insecurities, who will drive Othello to madness, murder and suicide. Clearly the Melodrama treatment explores and exploits the perception of miscegenation in the narrative and punishes the powerless main character, Othello, for attempting to secure power. Power here is not political power, which Othello already has, but rather personal power. Can Othello exercise personal power over his white lieutenant and his white wife? It would appear from this treatment of the narrative that he cannot.

The narrative can be amended by using a genre that will change the expected character arc. A shift to a voice-oriented genre can yield a critique of power politics rather than a personal tragedy. And the introduction of a more expansive plot layer can both raise the stakes as well as alter the expected outcome in the narrative. Let's explore how some of these possibilities might present.

If we look at the possibility that Othello is a 'disappointed character' who makes a passionate choice (Desdemona) who uses him for her own ends and exploits his propensity for jealousy, we are looking at a Film Noir genre frame for the story. Here Desdemona rather than Iago is the driving force behind the destruction of Othello. In this version Iago and Othello may be friends as well as King and lieutenant. Here the race issue is important because this may be the vehicle for Desdemona to use to stimulate Othello's sense of jealousy of his white friend and lieutenant. In this version Iago is a far more benign presence. In a sense he and Desdemona exchange roles and narrative purpose.

If we wanted to explore Othello with a less tragic, more positive outcome we could look at the narrative as a clash of values. In this version Othello, the King, represents idealistic values while Iago represents power or political values. To make the clash amount to a choice, I would explore the notion of using Desdemona as the main character having to choose one set of values over the other. In this version, we begin with the marriage to Othello but see Desdemona seduced by the powerful appeal of Iago. To avoid the story becoming overweighted towards race, we introduce a plot where the Moorish Kingdom is at risk. Desdemona, wanting to secure the kingdom is attracted to the power that Iago's character represents; but it's the stronger ideals that Othello represents that win the day.

In this version Othello's beliefs will have to have influence on the evolution of the plot. In this version neither Desdemona nor Othello need to die. To make the struggle credible a lighter touch will have to be applied to the deep passionate issues of the original – race, jealousy, violent destructive and self-destructive behaviours. Although the story begins to look like the musical *Camelot*, the interracial dimension introduces a more modern dimension to the narrative. And the altered tone yields an examination of a clash of values rather than the personal tragedy of racism, envy and murder.

Othello also lends itself to a voice-oriented genre treatment. Because of its interracial as well as political dimension, the story could be treated as a satire on race and politics. Here the racial beliefs and prejudices of each of the three principal characters, Othello, Desdemona and Iago, need to be treated in an ironic and critical fashion. The will to power race over race, man over woman, king over lieutenant, needs to be held up to examination. More extreme characterization, the use of narrative exaggeration and less of an invitation to identify with any of the three characters, generates the voice-oriented treatment. What I mean by less of an invitation to identify is achieved by using irony to distance us from the main character. Here the character is the vehicle for voice. We watch the character rather than put ourselves in their shoes. The strong critical feelings of the writer have to generate a creative mix of humour and outrage, in order for the satire to work. Plot, even excessive amounts of plot can help the satire remain energetic. A film such as Warren Beatty's *Bulworth* is a good example for the writer to study, even emulate.

In this case the genre approach has been applied to Othello. In the workshop, the approach is used to expand potential pathways for each writer as they move from idea to outline to treatment to script. Clearly the earlier in the process the genre notion is applied the more open the writer is to seriously examining alternative pathways for their story. Openness to options is the primary goal of the workshop in this phase. The analogy here is to limbering up in exercise. Pliancy of the creative muscles can lead the writer to creative options and hopefully in the longer run, to creative solutions.

If a genre is not chosen, if the decision is delayed, it is more than likely that the lack of an overall shaping device for the writer's narrative with leave the narrative in an overly loose state where the parts will struggle for coherent progression and the general sense of progression in the writing process will remain elusive.

5. FOLLOW UP: OUTSTANDING ISSUES POST-WORKSHOP

When the genre workshop ends the writer faces a number of decisions that will lead them to a first draft of their screenplay. What needs to be mentioned at this point is that whatever those decisions may be and whatever genre the writer chooses to frame their narrative, loose issues and ends may remain. The most obvious is that the script may be technically effective but may not present a compelling idea or characters. No workshop can assure a quality idea for the screenplay: just as not everyone is an effective screenwriter, so too in the world of ideas.

Beyond the quality of the idea lies its commercial partner – not every script, even good ones, are commercially viable. No workshop can effectively address the commercial issue although many allude to being able to. There are strategies the writer can use to increase the commercial viability of his script. Stories with goal-directed main characters, stories that use a charismatic main character, stories that affiliate with a prominent issue of the day, all enhance the commercial viability of a project. What do I mean by an issue of the day? On a political level, issues of today include narratives about terrorism and terrorists, environmental disaster, and stories that focus on traditional modern and post-modern societies. Films such as *Whale Rider, Wall Street* and *Gattaca* exemplify these thematic possibilities.

On a more personal level, issues of the day include alternative family structures (the examples of the Chinese daughter growing up with a lesbian Jewish mother comes to mind), stories of sexual identity (*American Beauty*), abortion (*Vera Drake*) or murder as linked to sexual abuse (*Monster*), stories that embed a social issue in a personal narrative.

Other script issues that I bump into all too often are the triumvirate of using dialogue rather than visual action, the shortage of surprise and/or energy in screenplays. These issues are so important its worthwhile devoting the balance of this chapter to them.

However clever the writer's dialogue, a script is essentially a blueprint for a visual experience for its audience. Consequently, it is important that the writer uses visual action to characterize and to advance plot. Without visual action the experience of the film slows, even stops. Although there are writers best known for dialogue-intense scripts (Joe Mankiewicz, Sam Raphaelson, Jacques Prevert, Preston Sturges) the prevailing style of screenplays emphasizes the visual. Particular directors such as John Ford, Roman Polanksi and Howard Hawks choose literary writers such as Dudley Nichols, Ronald Harwood and Jules Furthman to complement their passionate propensity for the visual. But writers should not expect the arrival of a visual luminary to translate their screenplay to film. It's best that the writer herself attends to visual action in the articulation of their idea as it becomes a screenplay.

Equal attention needs to be paid to the issue of surprise in a script. When I use the term surprise I am not only raising the issue in the context of plot. Characterization, behaviour, reaction, decisions all should present as surprise in a screenplay. Good models for the use of surprise in screenplays include Mamet's *The Verdict* and Talley *Silence of the Lambs*. I often suggest to writers that they review these films strictly for surprise in characterization and plot. The fact that the mass murderer Hannibal Lechter proves to be Clarisse Starling's greatest helper is the major surprise in *Silence of the Lambs*. The love interest as betrayer in *The Verdict* is the major surprise in Mamet's screenplay. Each film deploys numerous other unexpected turn arounds. Surprise is a very important feature of an effective screenplay. In a sense the level of surprise can be deployed all the way down to the scenes themselves. If the hook that ends one scene and links it to the next is a surprise, the script cannot help but to sustain our involvement with it.

Energy is also a central feature of the effective screenplay. Energy can emanate from character, but it's more useful to pictorialize energy resulting from a number of key clashes/conflicts in your screenplay. The clash of opposing forces generates the desired energy. The opposition of the antagonist and his goal to the main character and his goal is the primary source of energy in the screenplay. The greater that opposition, the greater the energy generated. The same principle applies to plot. If plot progression is a principal barrier to the main character's achievement of his goal, plot generates tension and energy. Think of *The Verdict, Saving Private Ryan* and *Four Weddings and a Funeral*. In each film antagonist and/or plot generates enormous energy in each of these narratives. Whether it is the goal-directed main character, the opposing goal-directed antagonist or the vigour of the plot against the goal of the main character, the upshot is energy and our consequent involvement with the script. Just as in life we are attracted to energetic people, so too in the screenplay. Too often I hear the phrase the energy will arrive with good casting. My response is casting is too late. The writer needs to make sure the energy is there before a cast is brought into the picture.

How does the writer attend to all of these post-workshop issues? I am not building up to the suggestion of a post-genre workshop. Rather my suggestion is that the writer is best served at the early stages of her career by engaging a script consultant/advisor/doctor. The writer needs the capacity to bounce their ideas off a dispassionate professional who is sensitive to the need for energy, surprise and visual action in the screenplay. Later in their career the writer will have absorbed these script qualities into their work. Those who have not will continue as journeymen attending one writing workshop after another in search of the key to the kingdom of script. Best of luck in your writing endeavours.

Chapter 6

Radio Writing

Graham Mort

1. WELCOME TO THE WORKSHOP

Welcome to the Radio Writing Workshop. In this section of the book I will introduce some of the fundamental ways in which radio works and its consequences for the creative writer. This will cover recent changes in the nature of the medium, the range of radio writing possibilities and ways of thinking about technical aspects of broadcast sound that can actually enrich and illuminate other forms of writing. Even if your main priority as a writer lies outside the field of radio, there is much in the consideration of the medium that can stimulate your approach to other forms, from poetry to the use of dialogue. The chapter will also present you with some ideas to stimulate new writing, taking you in stages towards orchestrating some key techniques of radio into a short script – our primary aim is to get you to think about your writing 'radiophonically' or from the perspective of radio.

Radio formats

It's impossible, especially in a workbook designed for an international readership, to give a full sense of the range of possibilities of radio writing. Many forms of radio – including documentary programmes – involve similar techniques to those involved in making programmes underpinned by creative writing. Those common elements are sometimes described as 'radiophonic' – aspects of dialogue, commentary, tone, soundscape and the use of sound effects that have a special relationship to radio broadcasting. Some common forms of 'creative writing' for radio are:

- Short stories – presented as 'straight readings' or as readings with some sound-effect enhancement.
- Contemporary radio plays – dramatic production based on scripts that deploy dialogue and sound effects to create a sense of reality.
- Historical radio plays – dramatic productions set at some point in the past.
- Radio montage – scripted or recorded voices that are closely edited and mixed to produce impressionistic effects evoking narrative or place.

- Poetry – this includes 'straight' readings of poems, verse plays and innovative wordscapes with sound effects.
- Adaptations of existing stage plays, novels and stories, which are given a radio 'treatment'.
- Drama series – ('soap operas') episodic production that go on for weeks (or years!) featuring a well-established cast of characters and already established story lines that writers have to follow and develop.
- Sitcom – a variant of the drama series but with a particular emphasis on humour.

The internet now provides the opportunity to sample some of these radio formats; so, as well as listening to actual radio broadcasts, it's a good idea to search for the kind of programmes you have in mind on dedicated websites and listen to samples. The BBC website is extensive and offers a whole range of recorded work plus advice to new writers.

A short history

Radio was invented in the early part of the twentieth century. A number of entrepreneurs conducted early broadcasting experiments, but the first 'commercial' broadcast is claimed for 2 November 1920, when KDKA AM of Pittsburgh broadcast the result of a presidential election. A number of other US, Canadian and Argentinean stations followed, including advertisements in their broadcast formats to attract sponsorship. By the 1930s broadcasts of live sports events, music, national and international news, soap operas, radio drama, current affairs and religious programmes were proliferating and, during the Second World War, radio was seized upon as a powerful means of propaganda by all sides. The technological revolution that paved the way for radio had begun much earlier in the nineteenth century with the advent of sound recording via phonograph rolls, gramophone records and even pneumatic 'player pianos' that anticipated early computers. They, in turn, had been preceded by the telegraph and Morse code. At the same moment that the notion of sending encoded information down a length of copper wire was invented, the presence of the recipient was also envisaged. This idea really replicated the way in which books worked – a text is written and sent out to be 'received' by an unknown reader. Before such forms of textual and electronic encryption were invented all human communication had come about through direct contact.

The information technology revolution has continued with the advent of television, the miniaturization of electrical circuits via transistors and silicon chips, the invention of the personal computer, the mobile telephone and hand-held devices that include radio and television receivers. Radio has developed through the use of more flexible FM wavebands, stereophonic sound, 'cleaner' digitalized signals, satellite relay and compressed sound files that have led to podcasting and internet radio, which means that broadcasts can be stored and retrieved after the broadcast event. Strictly speaking, the advent of internet radio (which doesn't actually need a radio signal) is more about imitating broadcast format than using actual radio waves as a medium.

In the developed world it's easy to take the ubiquitous presence of radio for granted, but in many parts of the world radio's dependency on electricity has led to a much slower pace of development. The advent of transistor, battery-powered radios in the 1960s radically increased the availability of radio; more recently, solar-powered and wind-up radios have provided new technical solutions. Radio is the fastest growing broadcast medium in Africa with commercial FM stations proliferating and being captured by a whole array of high- and low-tech devices from the personal organizer to a communal transistor radio hanging in a tree! In a developed country with dominant languages, it's also difficult to appreciate the difficulties of broadcasting in Asian and African countries that may have dozens of different languages contained with its political frontiers.

Technical considerations

Radio can take one of two basic forms: a *live* broadcast or a *pre-recorded* broadcast. For the purpose of this chapter I want to focus on the notion of sound recording and on material that is *written* and recorded especially for radio in any of its forms.

Recording techniques have themselves developed in extraordinary ways since the 1950s. At that time radio involving more than one voice or performer – principally music and drama – was recorded live in the studio with live special effects. The recording was made on quarter inch tape and edited by ear and hand with scalpels and splicing tape.

By the 1960s multi-tracking techniques allowed more than one sound source to be mixed and by the 1990s the dominant form of recording was straight on to a digital hard-drive where incredibly complex soundscapes can be shaped, precisely edited and mixed by skilled engineers. Such cutting edge techniques actually highlight the remarkable achievements of much innovative earlier radio broadcasts, such as Glenn Gould's legendary and laboriously multi-tracked 'Solitude Trilogy' put out by the Canadian Broadcasting Association in the late 1960s and 1970s.

Hang on!

If you've glazed over at such technical matters, then you might pause to consider how vital it is to understand the nature of the medium in which you're working in order to succeed as a writer. The technical nature of radio provides all very opportunities that writers can take advantage of in developing their work – it also highlights the potential pitfalls that many writers fall into through a lack of its appreciation. It's easy to grow accustomed to radio as a form of ambient presence without really understanding its collaborative nature or the way in which its elements are combined to provide an apparently seamless broadcast.

The primary aim of this chapter is to get you to *think* about the sonic elements of your writing and radio – literally – dramatizes this aspect of your work.

2. WRITERS AND THE RADIO AUDIENCE

The medium

The act of writing itself revolutionized human communication and continues to do so. Once invented, it became possible to communicate across space and time, to learn from history. The printing press introduced the idea of mass communication and, by extension, mass literacy. Radio itself falls clearly into this category of 'mass media' with many radio stations reaching millions of individuals.

As well as sharing the key advantages of writing, radio shares one key disadvantage – the removal of the human body from the act of communication. Body language underpins all direct human communication and is present (often in exaggerated form) in all performed or televised drama. The removal of this visceral, often subtle, accompaniment to words places huge pressure on the written or broadcast word to communicate fully and unequivocally. Facial expression or physical stance can impart meaning to our words, adding inflections of irony, compassion, anger, humour, sincerity or despair, reminding us of the roots of language in gestural systems. Transcripts of actual conversations are famously misleading as records of what has transpired between two or more people. Conversation is a complex verbal/physical interaction between its participants, with body language acting as a stimulant, a means of encouragement, anticipation and interpretation.

Fortunately, radio brings across some key elements of verbal communication that are not actually contained in writing, but that are implied by it – these are in that very subtle area of *tone* or *inflection*. A good actor can repeat the same phrase 20 times and each time imbue it with a slightly different inflection that changes meaning and inference. A simple phrase like, 'You're not coming', readily lends itself to such treatment and can be shaped as an imperative, a question or an entreaty as emphasis and enunciation shift from word to word.

Radio can also *imply* the human body and its actions in time and space through the use of sound effects; body language and a range of environmental conditions can be suggested by a radio broadcast. We will return to this idea later.

Writers and listeners

Writers do not have to meet their readers to communicate successfully. It's clear from what I've said above that all forms of writing are highly selective – writers take a small part of the experience of being alive and use it to represent the whole. Without the *reading* skills that we bring to a text, writing would seem a very flattened or impoverished version of life. But good writers are adept at providing a level of sensory detail and intellectual stimulus that allows the human brain to imagine – even *synthesize* – experience from the text. We are able to read a book on a train journey and remember very little of the journey while retaining vivid memories of the novel we were reading. Writing is so powerful that it can actually replace or supersede reality, inventing a world of *virtual* experience within *actual* experience. Radio shares this capacity to invoke an alternative reality that the listener shares and inhabits in an intense way.

We have already mentioned the sonic quality of radio – its obvious connection to the experience of speech and the experience of sound. But *vision* is the primary human sense (neuroscientists think that up to 25 per cent of the human brain has been devoted to it). Human beings have sophisticated stereoscopic vision that, although not intense in its acuity, can interpret movement, speed, distance, shapes, patterns, symmetries, colours and textures. Human hearing is stereophonic and works closely in tandem with our vision. The human brain is 'hard-wired' to respond to sound and vision, so that the human head instinctively turns towards the source of movement and sound to get a 'fix' on it and to decide whether it is a threat or an opportunity. That survival instinct has been refined into a much more subtle capacity for communication and means that radio can command the attention of our listeners in vital ways.

In theatrical terms the whole of a radio drama can be said to be 'off-stage'. That poses obvious technical problems for the dramatist. How can a writer involve an audience in a drama they can't actually see? The interesting answer is that the radio soundscape is itself spatial and through the use of recording techniques can imply main events that are central to the soundstage and peripheral or 'off-stage' events that seem much further away. So the auditory stage replicates the visual one.

Radio is made up of sounds that may be verbal or non-verbal, but it is also – by inference – a highly visual medium. I will explore these aspects of radio writing and broadcasting later in the workshop. Radio is also, potentially, a spatial medium. Stereophonic sound allows us to represent the position of sounds by dividing them up along a lateral plane. In simple terms, we can make one voice come from the left, another voice come from the right and a gunshot happen in the middle.

This technical potential of radio brings me to a word of warning about the limitations of broadcasting technology. Radio stations have the capacity to broadcast dramatic and intensely accurate soundscapes. But ask yourself: where do you listen to radio and how? True stereophonic sound requires a highly structured listening environment with the listener placed between the speakers. A quadraphonic system (popular as an accompaniment to television) increases the sense of a 'surround' soundscape, making sounds circle the room. But very few people listen to radio in such circumstances – we listen in the car, in the bath, while cooking, waiting for a bus, jogging or being active in the gym. Radio is often an accompaniment to other activities and – unlike its early manifestation as family entertainment – rarely an activity to which we are solely dedicated. In addition, few all-in-one 'stereo' radios are truly stereophonic, and offer a mere semblance of sound separation. Radio broadcasts have their dynamic range compressed, so that satisfactory results can be achieved in a range of listening environments. Accordingly, it's usually a mistake to make your innovative radio programme rely on amazing technical effects – they will almost never make it to the broadcast stage. Rely instead on the effects of your writing and its interpretation through the human voice – that most extraordinary of musical instruments.

Time passing

Time carries another powerful and crucial consequence for the radio writer. Unlike the reader of a page of text who can allow their eye to move backwards and forwards over the page, effectively reading and re-reading the work until they understand it, the radio listener has to absorb the programme as it moves past them in time. In everyday conversation body language is used to express puzzlement or dismay or understanding when we are listening. A vigorous nod conveys agreement and encourages the speaker; a small shake of the head or a frown of puzzlement might prompt them to repeat or re-phrase something so that they are sure we have absorbed it. Such dynamic interaction is impossible on radio and writers have to convey often-complex scenes and situations in a way that the listener can readily absorb. It's worth remembering at this stage that a key soundeffect is silence! In other words, the way we *pace* a piece of radio work can help the listener's interaction with events over time or their visualization of scenes.

Time travel

In many media, it's possible to play with or prefigure the passing of time. A stock-in-trade of novelists and film scriptwriters is the flashback/flashforward where readers and viewers catch a glimpse of past or future action. The use of such devices can set up the plot of a novel or film and lead the viewer or reader into the story. This is a little trickier on radio, where time markers may be more impressionistic. In a film it's easy to *show* a character as younger or older; in a novel or story it's possible to narrate time directly. This risks sounding vague or clunky on radio. It's also worth bearing in mind that the peripatetic nature of radio listening means that audiences often tune in part-way through a show. That's an occupational hazard rather than a structural aspect of radio as a medium, but it does have a bearing on the whole issue of represented time and how we handle it.

One way of denoting the past or future is through a different 'acoustic'. This effect can directly represent a place (exterior/interior) or indirectly suggest a time associated with that place. Or it might be brought about by the actor's use of the microphone, which we'll discuss later. The human voice is a very flexible device and can become a percussion instrument as well as an expression of musicality and meaning.

Though, there are no rules for any form of writing, it's helpful for the listener to keep the time-scale of radio pieces simple and to make switches in time the result of clear narration or auditory signals.

Music

In film, music has long been a staple of production since the days of cinema pianists who played to accompany silent films. In film, music is used to form a dramatic narrative device; even with the pictures turned off, it's possible to *hear* the emotional mood of a film – whether it's a love story, a thriller or a western, for instance.

Music is almost always used to introduce a radio piece. A series will have its 'signature' tune, carefully chosen by the producer. Individual pieces often have introductory or closing music and this can sometimes relate to content. Many plays use music within them to denote certain settings – a jazz bar, a discothèque or party, for instance – but it is rarely used as part of the narrative texture of the play. We might expect music to form a key part of a historical drama about Chopin, but it is less likely to feature in a play about Sigmund Freud unless he visits a ball or social gathering featuring a string quartet.

Music can play a valuable role in radio, but it tends to be specific to the content of the piece in question, rather than merely atmospheric or anticipatory. The reason for this is that music is much more *audible* on the radio and risks splitting the listener's attention or creating a sense of melodrama. When we watch a film, almost all our attention is commanded by the movement of images on the screen, so the music has a subliminal quality, directing our emotions at a deep level.

What's in a voice?

Earlier we emphasized the visual nature of radio, the way that sound is translated into vision in the head. An aspect of this is easily understood through the use of *voice* on radio. When we first hear a human voice, a key 'biological imperative' is triggered. What sex is the person speaking? How old are they – a child, a young adult, an elderly person? Are they weak or strong? Are they sick or healthy? Are they self-confident or fearful? Which region are they from? Are they foreign? Are they sincere of disingenuous? Are they sarcastic, passive, aggressive, ironical, hesitant, condemnatory, self-important, pompous, shy or downright evil?

Here the skilful actor is the writer's chief ally. A simple stage direction can be translated into a highly nuanced performance that gets across a huge amount of information at an almost subliminal level – perhaps the most powerful level of response of all. So a voice can trigger a visual image of a person – something that each listener imagines for themselves – and it can deliver a whole range of information from emotional mood to whether our character is an insider or outsider a positive or a negative force. Having said that, it's sometimes best to get across the nature of a character on your cast list rather than to pepper the script with minute instructions. Remember that actors and producers are also highly creative individuals and that their interpretations will enhance your work.

Simplicity

Simplicity is a difficult effect to achieve and is often hard-won; it is obvious when we hear it, but our instinct to explain or emphasize can easily get the better of us. In drama productions it's generally better to avoid a complex cast of characters and a multiplicity of voices – even if they are differentiated by accent, age or vocabulary. In short stories, don't try to make the reader ventriloquize too much or the story is likely to confuse or become a pastiche.

3. PROFESSIONAL CONTEXT

Setting out a radio script

A radio script is fundamentally different from published forms of literature: it is a provisional document that only achieves final form through broadcast. Some scripts are subsequently published, but a radio script is really a working document, a blueprint for the production team that will be building and engineering your programme. You can expect it to be scribbled on by producers in its formative stages; even during the recording process you can expect actors to write on it, suggest amendments and generally subject it to modification.

Most radio scripts will comprise:

- a title page with the title of the programme, the name of the author and the date clearly marked
- a cast of characters with notes about each
- the main body of the script
- headers and footers on each page with page number, programme title and author's name

A radio script needs to leave space for annotation, so it should be double-spaced. Characters should be identified clearly on the left-hand side and stage directions and sound effects (usually designated by the letters FX) should be clearly differentiated from the main text that you intend to be spoken, which should appear on the right-hand side of the page as in the example below:

	FX Interior acoustic – the clink of breakfast things. Marie is sorting the post, opening envelopes
Marie	Junk mail. More junk. Another forest bites the dust. Mortgage statement. Bank statement, ugh! Ah, the tickets have come!
Martin	*(Chewing mouthful of toast)* Tickets?
Marie	Airline tickets? Car hire? Holiday? Remember, when we go away to . . .?
Martin	Relax. I remember. Manchester to . . .
Marie	. . . Perpignan. We pick up the car at the airport and then drive all the way.
Martin	We *drive*?
Marie	*You* drive actually, and don't say you didn't agree, we must have gone through it a thousand times . . .

Software script templates are now available to save you the labour of indenting and re-indenting your script; some are downloadable from broadcasting corporation websites.

Radio slots, pitching and editing

Radio is a medium dominated entirely by time. Programmes compete for pre-shaped 'slots' and these are inviolable as far as producers are concerned. Your 15-minute short story must come in at 14 minutes or else it will be discarded or edited. It's good to study the actual slot that you are 'pitching' for, so that when you approach a producer or radio station with your work, you can demonstrate how suitable it is for its anticipated audience.

The best way to control your work is to time the production of it yourself and get it as close to the prescribed length as possible. For longer pieces like radio plays, this is often very difficult in practice. If at all possible, you should try to get involved in the production process, whether in an in-house studio or a commercially out-sourced studio. Learning to cut your work and how cuts can actually enhance a programme, leaving room for the audience to imagine events for themselves, is one of the key skills of radio writing and production.

It's good to think of writing, recording and production as key *stages*. Even when your script is 'finished' it is only work in progress waiting to be shaped in order to move the air through the human voice.

Teamwork

Writing for radio may simply involve creating poems or stories that can fit into allotted time slots. These pieces may be 'radiophonic' in content and structure – easily absorbed by a listening audience. Their production may be a relatively straightforward process of recording and editing.

But one of the main rewards of working in radio is to be part of a team that includes actors, a sound engineer and producer. All are creative people who will have passion for radio and – crucially – a strong sense of what is innovative and what has been done before (radiophonic clichés) and an even stronger sense of what will actually 'work' on the air.

In this context – radio drama, more innovative poetry or documentary productions – writing for radio becomes a collaborative enterprise in which you are the initiating member of a team. You must be prepared to surrender your work to this process, to carry out last minute changes, to think on your feet and to experience and edit the work from the perspective of a listener who may be enjoying your programme from any of the situations that were listed above.

Producers have little patience with writers who are possessive about their work. While standing up for what you think is right – for your ideal of the finished work – it is always wise to listen and respond to the experts who will develop your ideas if you let them.

In the studio

If you're successful in getting some radio work accepted for recording and broadcast, then it's a really good idea to ask if you can be present at the recording session. Working with actors can be a disconcerting business, as they pore over your script with practised eyes. The session itself may seem chaotic, with actors gossiping happily about their latest play, then switching immediately into performance mode when the recording light is switched on.

Actors like to *perform* and they're not always the best people to record some types of work. Poetry, in particular, can sometimes seem overblown or rhetorical in the hands of an actor, whereas poetry read by the poet can be more immediate and effective. The more times any actor is asked to do a 'take' the more risk there is of the performance becoming overtheatrical. Even the most practiced actors may stumble or develop a blind spot over a particular word or phrase and it's sometimes necessary to change a script to get round this.

Very few radio pieces are ever recorded in one smooth session, so the final version is made up of a whole series of 'takes' edited together. Unlike session music, where the drummer may never meet the singer during a recording session, it's usual to get actors together in the studio. This itself creates atmosphere through the tiny accumulation of sounds that indicate human presence.

Editing the takes is done with a computer that represents the actors' voices as a visual display showing highs and lows and this can be cut and sliced with split second precision. In the final stages of editing a radio production it is usually necessary to discard some material to bring the programme in just under the prescribed time. This can be a very revealing and refreshing process, acting out the writer's dictum of 'less is more'. It really is – and the material that is cut is never missed by the listener!

4. WORKSHOP ACTIVITIES

Writing studio directions, sound effects and wildtrack

Studio directions

Studio directions are simply stage directions for a *soundstage*. They indicate the ambience (see Wildtrack) of the scene being introduced and can themselves be specific sound effects:

> **FX** *exterior* acoustic, the sound of a single blackbird calling
>
> or
>
> **FX** *interior* acoustic, the faint sound of a television tuned to the news

Studio directions can also indicate 'silence' or 'fade-up' or 'fade-down' as a scene is entered or exited. These are more than mere sound effects since 'silence' indicates a gap in time, 'fade-up' indicates that something has been going on for some time and 'fade-down' indicates that it is continuing, so all those effects contribute to a sense of time passing.

Sound effects

Sound effects are an essential part of the radio writer's toolkit, though they should be used sparingly. Sound effects are usually actual recordings of sounds, or representations of sounds that are synthesized in some way. These days they are usually pre-recorded and most recording software comes with a comprehensive library of sound effects. Nevertheless, they can be difficult to fit to actual situations. Sound effects recorded live may also have an 'added' ambient quality – an echo indicating a large or small room, faint traffic, distant birdsong, etc. Properly used, sound effects can establish of place and a sense of period very effectively.

Sound effects have also been used to create comic effects by exaggerating or confirming events for the listener. Some post-war BBC radio drama like 'The Goon Show' and 'The Navy Lark' relied heavily on such special effects to make comic points. The high point of each 'Navy Lark' episode was the clang of naval vessels crashing, and the entire programme was structured around this moment. So sound effects can heighten the comical effect of the narrative and in these cases they are often heavily illustrative rather than a subtle presence!

Example 1	
	FX The sound of traffic at a busy roundabout.
Narrator	The market place was busy. Miles crossed the road, picking a space in the constantly moving stream of traffic.
Example 2	
	FX The sound of horses and grinding cartwheels at a busy junction.
Narrator	The market place was busy. Miles crossed the road, picking a space in the constantly moving stream of traffic.

The two samples of script are identical in most ways, but it's clear that the first one presents a more contemporary setting than the second, which suggests a much earlier period in history. Such devices can get the listener there in a flash and save clumsy references in the text. Used tastefully, sound effects can instantaneously establish a world.

Wildtrack

'Wildtrack' is the name given to the ambience of a recorded situation. A wide-open space, a padded room, a concrete yard all have a particular acoustic quality and a microphone picks this up as background sound. The difference between total silence and a few seconds of wildtrack can be very striking and sometimes a recording of a particular ambience can be useful when run over edits to smooth out the tiny atmospheric differences between one 'take' and another.

Exercise

Plan a 5-minute sequence of sound effects in writing to create a narrative with no verbal narration or dialogue. In order to do this you'll need to use your aural and visual imagination.

Experimenting with sound

Now that you have a sound sequence in writing, it's a good exercise for any budding radio writer to make a short programme that is completely non-verbal. To do this you'll need a portable recording device – mini disk recorder, digital tape or portable hard-drive – and a decent hand-held microphone. It's good to record your own sound effects anyway and often a refreshing change from the rather stilted effects that might be stored in a radio studio. It's worth reflecting here that some sound effects are better synthesized than recorded. One way to prove that is to try recording your own heartbeat. You'll soon find yourself wrapping the microphone in an old jumper and beating it gently with a tennis ball!

Exercise 1

The aim of this exercise is to make a recording of the sound script planned in the Exercise in the previous section and to demonstrate that a sequence of sounds can make a narrative. This sequence might be structured in some way – beginning and ending with a door opening then closing for instance. If you're technically proficient, you might download the results and edit them on your PC using one of the many available software programs. But you can achieve reasonable effects through carefully planning a live recording. The first thing you might learn is how long a minutes of radio sound is – much longer than a minute of human experience in which all the senses are active to distract us! If you're really proficient, you might even try multi-tracking different sounds – but remember that 'less is more' and that what you're trying to develop here is a narrative line, a *story* in sound.

For an example of this technique see Michael Radford's 1994 film *Il Postino* in which the poet Pablo Neruda is sent a sound poem by the friends he has left behind in Italy when he returns from exile there to Chile.

Exercise 2

When you've mastered the technique you might experiment with a different range of effects, creating more static soundscapes and more dynamic ones, contrasting urban and rural environments, finding out what happens when you try to capture one sound and end up with another. This is a good exercise for beginning to understand how human beings understand the aural environment. We tend to edit out unwelcome sounds in order to focus on the things that interest us – or what it is we think we *ought* to be concentrating on. Like the camera, the microphone can make no such distinctions and gives equal value to each sound. This is often a revelation and can prompt some valuable thinking about how sounds are hierarchical for the listener with dominant ones and quieter, subliminal ones.

Using the microphone

If you do get hold of a microphone, it's a good idea to think about how the actors approach them. Amplified sound is a potential risky medium and it takes great skill to sing or speak into a microphone effectively. A key effect is the distance of the microphone from the sound source, or if the microphone is fixed in a studio, the distance of the actor from the microphone. Distance from the recording device suggests just that: that some sounds are fainter and therefore further way than others. Some microphones will pick up sound in a 360-degree arc, others are unidirectional and will be sensitive to a narrow spectrum. A stereophonic microphone can indicate small movement in sound, the placing of the mouth on one side or another as the speaker shifts their head. The micro effects of approaching a microphone are very dramatic and the difference between a medium distance and a very close-up 'breathy' recording technique can suggest a whole range of effects from the conspiratorial to emotional betrayal.

Exercise

For this exercise, choose a short passage of descriptive writing or a poem and try experimenting with your own microphone, recording the same piece from a metre away and then with your hands cupping the microphone or your lips close to the pickup. Once such techniques are understood, then writers can anticipate them in conceptualizing and scripting their work.

Writing narration

Single voice narration forms an element in many radio productions. It is implicit in short stories and poetry as a narrative 'persona' which exists at various distances from the author. In this sense, voice is a 'given' element and an actor's voice can help to define and enhance material that is primarily narrative in function and form.

In radio drama a narrator is often used to focus the action through the viewpoint of a single character – though multiple narrative viewpoints are also possible. The narrator has a privileged view of the action and can 'take us there' in a very direct way. The narrator may also be a character in the drama at some point in time. A classic version of this technique is for a character who has grown old to present a drama in which they were young, so that we are constantly reminded of the passage of time through the difference in voice.

A narrator – as in much fiction – may also have a more mysterious or ambiguous relationship to the subject matter. They may be an 'implied' character without taking an active part in the action they are describing. A notable instance of this technique is found in Dylan Thomas's radio play 'Under Milk Wood', where the narrator plays an important part in the narration; he/she has a God-like overview of the town and its inhabitants but never assumes an individual identity. In a sense, Dylan Thomas' narrator can be identified with the author.

Narrators are often used in radio drama because they can supply a dependable voice that is easier to follow than a number of voices in dialogue. Using a 'once upon a time' technique, they can establish period and time-scale. Sometimes characters themselves take on the role of narrator, telling stories within the drama to bring out the action, then sink back into the action. So a dominant or leading character can take this role. In the section of voice we looked at how the quality of a voice can supply a large amount of contextual detail, so the decisions that a writer takes in establishing a narrative presence are vital to the work.

The other seductive effect of narration is to imply a relationship with the listener, so when we hear the opening moments of a play structured in this way, we assume that we are being spoken to directly in an intimate way.

Exercise

Write the opening moments of your radio drama drawing upon the qualities of voice and acoustic ambience explored earlier in this chapter. Remember that you are introducing your character as much as the events they will, in turn, introduce, so locating them in time and place is crucial – and whether that is implied through sound and voice effects or released directly as information. This piece should last no more than 2 minutes, but should include a brief description of the character in the cast list, an indication of their age and background, and sense of their emotional mood.

Writing dialogue

Dialogue forms the staple of most radio programmes in the categories that we define at the opening of this chapter. It is also a technique used in many other forms of writing. The difference is that dialogue in the context of radio is actually heard and not read. That might appear to make it an uncomplicated factor in radio production, but it adds some subtle issues to the making of dialogue on the page.

The problems with writing dialogue all stem from the body language issues identified earlier. Written narration is a synthetic form of dialogue and doesn't necessarily have to replicate the form of human speech – it is a *literary* technique. But dialogue has to be both credible on the page and translate into a good approximation of what we hear. Transcripts of actual conversations can be very difficult to follow, even if we do add detail about body language – such as 'blinking furiously', 'scratching her ear', 'curled up on the sofa'. Those clues to mood are ambiguous and the transcript – which is a representation of 'real time' – will be tediously laden with superfluous speech that is there simply to keep us connected to our listener, or allow us thinking time: 'you know what I mean,' 'er', 'um', etc. What transcripts can show us is that real dialogue is rarely logical or directly sequential ('on the nose') and that's a valuable lesson about its representation.

Good dialogue also has to move the action forward as well as tell us what characters are actually saying. This is a real danger in radio where what characters are saying may be our main source of information. Radio writers have to steer a very fine line between dialogue that feels 'real' and dialogue that is stiffened by allusion. So speeches that are laden with information should be avoided.

Example 1

John	Henry, I've hurt my arm. Come and stand by me on the quarterdeck and throw this rope over to Alison, there on the quayside.

Example 2

John	Henry! Over here!
Zach	Hang on, I'm coming . . . damn! Where are you?
John	Here. On the quarterdeck . . . I've wrenched my arm. Alison's there on the quay. *FX footsteps scrabbling, panting breath*
John	Now, throw this rope to her.

In the first example, the action is told through the speech, in the second, the action is acted out between speakers. Note how the sound effects contribute to a richer interpretation and how the speech doesn't have to follow a strictly alternate pattern. In the second example Zach is too busy crossing the deck to reply to John, so John can speak twice in sequence. It's interesting to reflect upon the implied social class of this cast of characters and how they got into difficulties!

Another great advantage of writing for radio is that contextual information can help actors to *interpret* voice and dialogue, so indicating a Lancashire accent or a very old speaker can free us from slavish representation of speech. If we get the rhythm, and pattern of speech right, the actor can do the rest.

Exercise

Try writing character notes for the short extract above. Now write your own short, two-hander lasting about 5 minutes in which two characters are engaged in conversation. This could follow on from the passage in which you experimented with narration.

Adaptation

It's possible to begin thinking about radio from a blank sheet of paper, if you have a strong sense of the work you wish to create. But before attempting that, a good way to begin to explore the medium as a writer is to take an existing piece of work – your own or someone else's – and to 'adapt' it for radio.

Exercise

The source of your adaptation could be a section of novel, a short story or a poem that lends itself to radiophonic effect. Your task is to create a short production for a single reader and to add in some sound effects. Remember that sound effects are least effective when they are merely illustrative. Sound effects can anticipate something that happens in the text so that it has added force, or they may introduce a new element to expand on an aspect of text and supply *context*.

Choose a time format for your work – 5 or 15 minutes. Read and annotate the original from an actor's point of view:

- Does the dialogue seem realistic?
- Is there too much dialogue or too many voices to confuse the listener?
- How do we know who is doing what?
- How can the text be cut to create a simple production?

Re-work the piece into short script with minimal directions for producer, engineer and a reader. Try recording it yourself for effect.

Putting it all together

Exercise

For the final exercise we suggest that you should create a short (15 minute) radio piece that brings together a central narrator, a temporal structure involving past and present, a small cast of characters, the use of sound and voice effects and some dialogue. The temptation, of course, it to ladle all these elements in with a heavy hand. Decide on the dominant atmosphere of your piece and follow it accordingly. Use studio directions sparingly, leaving space for the interaction of others. When you've created this piece, write a short 'pitch' or 'treatment' for it, identifying its subject matter, atmosphere, main dramatic tensions and who you anticipate the listening audience might be.

Now you're ready to scale that up into a full-length production!

5. FOLLOW UP

Reading the preceding sections of this chapter and attempting some of the exercises should have given you some insights into the nature of radio as a broadcast medium, the technical considerations that govern new radio writing, an alertness to sound and speech in the everyday environment, some professional considerations and requirements, and also how the rest or your work relates to the idea of a soundstage that (a) *deploys* acoustic dynamics and that (b) has to *imply* a huge amount about what is happening through the structure of dialogue, narration and sound effects. In order to write for radio you need to become a *listener* to radio, so take every opportunity to follow programmes in your chosen genre and to explore the resources that are proliferating on the -Internet and in print.

Radio can be a great stimulus to new work or to adapting existing work, whether you find yourself interested in making innovative programmes that challenge listeners or whether you're mainly interested in supplying some of the staples of radio output – plays, drama series, even documentaries. For the writer who has previously only worked in printed media, radio offers one great reassurance – all voice-radio needs to be fed with good quality content and that content is going to be paid for. So from the purely professional point of view, payment follows upon endeavour once the work is commissioned and doesn't depend upon royalties – though additional royalties for repeated programmes may sometime accrue. Even better, your work will reach a mass market rather than disappear into the uncertainty of bookshops and libraries. Through radio, you can literally reach an audience of millions!

WORKS CITED

Il Postino, (film) Michael Radford, 1994

Books and CDs

Radio Scriptwriting, edited by Sam Boardman-Jacobs, Wales: Seren, 2004
Writing Radio Drama by Keith Richards, Australia: Currency Press, 1991
Writing for Radio by Rosemary Horstmann, London: A&C Black, 1997
The Way to Write Radio Drama by William Ash, London: Elm Tree Books, 1985
Making Waves: Three Radio Plays: Mourning Dove, Denial is a River, Past Imperfect, by Emil Sher, Toronto: Simon and Pierre, 1998
There are many recordings of radio programmes available on CD. 'Under Milk Wood' by Dylan Thomas and 'The Solitude Trilogy' by Glenn Gould are still innovative classics.

Websites

BBC Writers Room. www.bbc.co.uk/writersroom/
Packed with information about submitting your work and provides an archive of downloadable scripts.
The Principles of Writing Radio Drama by Tim Crook. www.irdp.co.uk/scripts.ht
A practical guide.
Writernet. www.writernet.co.uk/php/map.php?id=294&ID=
Guide to techniques and practicalities.
British Council Radiophonics. www.crossingborders-africanwriting.org/
Features eight recordings of contemporary short stories commissioned for radio from Ugandan writers and a library of books relating to African radio and mass media.

Chapter 7

New Media Writing

Hazel Smith

1. WELCOME TO THE WORKSHOP

This workshop focuses on new media writing, an exciting and contemporary area of creative endeavour, in which writing interfaces with new technologies. In new media writing – known variously as cyberwriting, digital poetry, e-poetry or networked and programmable writing – you work with language in the context of a computer program. You also create work for the screen rather than page, and this can radically change the way you think about writing. Writing for the screen makes it possible to animate words, link texts together in a non-linear way, increase the interactivity of the reader, and bring together words, sounds and images within the space of the computer. Cyberspace is therefore more fluid and dynamic than the page, but less hospitable to lengthy texts which need to be read in a linear fashion.

This workshop will address the task of creating a simple animation based firstly on words, and then words in conjunction with images. In a more expository context, animating words can simply take the form of the words appearing successively on the screen to progressively reveal a particular meaning. But in the context of creative writing, animation can be much more adventurous. To animate words or letters is to move them around on the screen, rotate them, turn them upside down, break words into letters or build letters into words, and so on. Words may appear or disappear in unexpected ways that subvert the making of meaning or create ambiguities; sentences and phrases may break up and cross-fertilize with each other. The speed of the animation can also dramatically slow down or speed up the process of reading. All these animation techniques have enormous creative possibilities because they stimulate a dynamic interplay between loss and retrieval of meaning.

Similarly, an animation that combines words and images might simply use the images to illustrate the words or the words to explain the images. However, in a more creative context, the relationship between words and images can be more complex. For example, the images may be largely disconnected from – or antithetical to – the words, but suggest new meanings that are, in turn, developed by the words.

The objective of this workshop is therefore threefold. First, it aims to make you more aware of how words can form stimulating and sensuous patterns, by the use of fonts, colours, movement and visual arrangement on the screen: this aspect of language – its potential to function as what W. J. T. Mitchell calls 'textimage' (Mitchell, 1994) – is often lost on the page. Second, it encourages you to explore the ways in which animating words can enrich and subvert meaning – making it fluid and multiple – and extend normal reading practices. Third, it will help you to create synergies between words and images, and think about the way in which visual images can work both with and against verbal meanings.

In order to engage with the exercises maximally, it is useful first to reflect on how we read on the page. Although print is static, reading for the page is temporal, and the process involves flux and movement. As we begin a sentence we may unconsciously expect certain words to appear, or anticipate a number of possible alternatives; as we reach the end of the sentence our expectations are either fulfilled or thwarted. Then the sentence disappears as we focus on the next one, even though we retain traces of its meaning. We also never read in an entirely linear way; as we progress though a novel, for example, we remember (at least partially) what we have already read and continuously reinterpret it in the light of what we are reading now. In the exercises in this chapter we will play with, and intensify, this non-linear aspect of reading by displacing readerly expectations.

Learning to write in new media is a long process that involves familiarizing yourself with computer programs and exploring their impact on your writing. Here we are looking at only one step in the process, but with the objective of opening up a new area to you which you can then explore in more detail. The exercises were devised using the program Flash MX but you can use any animation program to do them. In order to avoid the confusion that arises from the differences between programs, I have avoided referring to Flash specifics too much. The workshop presupposes some basic familiarity with Flash, or a similar program, though the skills needed to engage with the exercises are minimal and can be acquired quite quickly. However, the main purpose of the exercises is conceptual rather than technical.

I believe that the most exciting new media works arise when their creators surrender themselves most fully to a new way of thinking about writing. Our goal in this chapter is not to write texts and then 'set' them digitally. Rather you are encouraged to try out the possibilities of the program and allow them to suggest the direction that the text might take. In this way the exercises in this chapter will help you to take a generative approach to new media writing, and to think both systematically and freely about how you might exploit the opportunities that animation offers.

2. WRITERS AND READERS

As a new media writer you will operate very differently from a writer for the page. A new media writer is a cyborg, half-machine and half-person; Katherine Hayles calls this conjunction of machine and person 'posthuman' (Hayles, 1999). This type of writing is very demanding because you have to think about the technical requirements of the computer as well as the operations of language. But it is also enormous fun because the program is intrinsically playful, and the possibilities of computer programs may lead you to write in ways you never dreamed of previously. Even errors in running a computer program can sometimes lead to exciting developments in your writing.

New media projects can be mobilized by one person, but are also often undertaken collaboratively because of the wide range of expertise they require. Large-scale new media projects are often brought to fruition by an assemblage of workers in different fields, such as a writer, a graphic artist, a programmer and a sound artist; this is part of what it means to be a posthuman writer. Working collaboratively can extend your range considerably as you can benefit from the experience of your programmer and also adapt to his or her ideas. It can allow you to operate in the field without spending an enormous amount of time learning the technology. However nothing can fully substitute for working with the technology yourself; as you play with a program, ideas will arise that will not occur to you if you remain more distant from it. Since the exercises here do not require a high level of technical expertise, hopefully you will be able to manage them yourself.

As a new media writer you also have the possibility to make your work a combination of image, text and sound. Again it is difficult to have all the expertise necessary to do this, and you may want to collaborate with others. However collaboration does not necessarily have to be the answer: you can use pre-existing images or sound files, or search the web for relevant material to use. Don't be put off by the fact that you do not consider yourself to be a sound or visual artist. There is a good deal of capacity within the computer to manipulate sounds and images in ways which make them your own, and you may be surprised, once you start working in this way, how much you can achieve. The idea of 'the expert', and the distinction between professional and amateur, has been shaken up considerably by modern technology; for example, it is increasingly suggested that on the internet some of the best commentators on world news are writers of blogs, not professional journalists.

New media writers work in the context of the internet and other new technologies such as the mobile phone. As a new media writer you are likely to draw on aspects of these technologies; some new media writers include computer code in their work, while others collage material extensively from internet sites. At the same time you can draw on your experience of writing and reading print literature, and you can create unusual hybrids between cyberwriting and the literary tradition.

Publishing can also take a vast array of different forms for the new media writer. Although journals dedicated to such publication exist, even highly reputable writers simply put their work up on their own websites and publicize it by sending their URL – and information about their latest work – to other related sites. Some new media writers have a section on their websites which features works in progress [see the websites of John Cayley and Jason Nelson (Cayley; Nelson)]. New media works sometimes take a long time to develop and this can be a way of obtaining feedback during the process, but it is a radical departure from the writing-for-the-page poet who only publishes finished poems and keeps the stages of the process leading up to them hidden. There are also numerous new media discussion lists, such as *webartery*, which circulate information about new work in the field and act as a forum for discussing it.

The audience for new media writing is potentially vast as new media work circulates most widely on the internet. There are specialist sites – magazines and journals – but such work can also be found on more popular websites such as YouTube. The audience for new media writing therefore has the ability to include, but also go way beyond, the audience for print literature. It is diverse in its readership, heavily internationalized and culturally broad. New media readers also have different expectations from print readers. They are used to modes of reading which are highly interruptive, they may scan texts rather than reading them all the way through, and will expect words to be supported, or even replaced, by sounds and images. Readers who spend a lot of time surfing the internet would be used to virtual environments such as blogs and chat rooms – and the kinds of behaviour and language (including a more casual attitude towards grammar and spelling) which are common on such sites.

In the broader field of new media writing, beyond the scope of the exercises in this chapter, considerable changes are taking place in the relationship between writer and reader. In fact, it has been suggested that in the future we will only need one word, 'screener', because the roles of the writer and reader will no longer be clearly defined. Interactivity is central here. In new media environments the reader can interact with the text at a relatively low level by clicking on links and reading through the text in his or her own way, but at a higher level the reader can become a co-producer of the text, changing or adding to it. At the same time the role of the writer is radically transformed in certain forms of new media writing. In working with some interactive computer programs, the writer activates an algorithmic process which can have variable results, rather than authoring a finished text.

New media writing does not necessarily mean abandoning the page, and some writers produce work that appears in both print and new media formats. Stephanie Strickland, for example, has published two poetry books, elements of which have been transcoded digitally, usually in conjunction with a programmer (Strickland). Moving between different forms of writing can be very productive, if you transmute and adapt the characteristics of one medium of writing into others either directly or indirectly. You may find that the code-based environment of new media feeds back into dramatic changes in your writing for the page.

3. BACKGROUND AND CONTEXT

All writing is about exploring possibilities and limits. Whenever you write, you are setting yourself specific tasks and choosing between alternative ways of responding to the task; consequently there is a productive tension between writing freely and systematic exploration of a defined terrain. In new media writing this interaction between freedom and circumscription is particularly acute because you work with the possibilities and limits of computer code as well as those of language. Different computer platforms offer distinct, if not mutually exclusive, possibilities: Flash is ideal for animation, layering and action scripting, while Jitter is adapted for real-time image processing and allows for the production of variable texts.[1] Poems written in a particular program will share certain features however different they may be, so Flash poems will tend to contain elements of animation and action-scripting.

New media writing is code-based and its technical characteristics include hyperlinking, animation, action scripting and multimedia. Each of these characteristics is multifaceted: for example, hyperlinking allows readers to move from one text to another, or one part of the screen to another, in a non-linear way. Hyperlinks can be obvious or hidden (they may become apparent only when the mouse pointer becomes a hand icon, or not all).

A computer program is, therefore, the basis for a writing process, and provides particular technical opportunities: it is not a genre. However, new media writing does not totally jettison genre: rather it produces an interaction between literary genres and the kinds of writing which are possible by means of the new technologies. The result in some cases has been the emergence of cybergenres. Examples of cybergenres are: hypertext fiction in which readers chose pathways through fictions by means of alternative hyperlinks; the Flash poem which exploits animation and action scripting; and codework, a term for works in which computer code becomes part of the content of the piece rather than a means to its end. In each case some aspects of a particular literary genre are retained. For example, hypertext fiction is a close relation of the novel, the Flash poem has some of the linguistic density of poetry, while codework displays the playfulness of language characteristic of experimental poetry. However, cybergenres tend to push the boundaries of literary genres. For example, the Flash poem turns the unit of the line in the poem into a kinetic unit that can be a letter, word or phrase. In addition, much cyberwriting pulls different genres together into hybrid forms in which prose, poetry and theoretical/critical reflection are juxtaposed.

Like experimental writing for the page, then, new media writing tends to subvert literary genres and is also multiplicitous and discontinuous. It is always potentially multimedia and brings literary genres together with genres from the visual arts and music. My own collaborative multimedia work has involved music by Roger Dean that abuts on, but also extends, the genres of noise, drum and bass, computer music, minimalism, jazz and atonal music: see our website (austraLYSIS).

Writing digitally often overlaps with popular and everyday genres such as computer games, and with developments in technology in a wide range of different spheres. *Arteroids,* conceived by Jim Andrews (Andrews, 2007), is based on the arcade game Asteroids. In *Arteroids* words and phrases take the place of asteroids, which a pilot fighter has to ward off in deep space. Andrews subtitles it 'a literary shoot-em-up computer game – the battle of poetry against itself and the forces of dullness'. Some new media writing projects are also partly blogs, and may include a range of different kinds of approach from journalism to creative writing.

Animation, which is one type of new media writing, is very diverse and there are many different ways of approaching it. A classic of text animation is Brian Kim Stefans's *The Dreamlife of Letters* (Stefans, 2000). Based on an alphabetical sequence of words, it creates an intricate interplay between visual virtuosity and shifting semantics. In Deena Larsen's *I'm simply saying* (Larsen, 2005) animated text is triggered by the reader's mouse movements. In John Cayley's *windsound* and *riversIsland* (Cayley) animation is part of a process he calls transliteral morphing: here one text morphs into another, or a series of texts successively morph into each other through substitution of letters. Komninos Zervos is a past master of morphing words often accompanied by punchy music or manipulated voice sounds; see his works *beer* and *komninos* (Zervos). My own *The Egg, The Cart, The Horse, The Chicken,* created with musician Roger Dean, combines a split screen with different verbal animations in each half, and a minimalist soundtrack (Smith and Dean, 2003). The animation in the upper half of the screen can be interrupted by clicking on hyperlinks which take you to different parts of the movie, so that the top movie is always in a variable relationship to the bottom movie. On the other hand, my collaboration with Roger Dean and Anne Brewster, *soundAFFECTs* (see Figure 7.1) consists of animated chunks of text which are stretched, multiplied and overlaid in real time, and is accompanied by an intense soundtrack (Dean, Brewster and Smith, 2004; Smith, 2007; Smith, 2008).[2] For a more narrative, slower moving piece where static texts are combined with animated text and pictures, see M. D. Coverley's very effective *Afterimage* (Coverley, 2001).

4. THE WORKSHOP EXERCISES

In this section I will engage with a number of exercises based on animation techniques. The main purpose of the exercises is to help you explore animation with respect to (a) the visual display of text, (b) the creation and disruption of meaning and (c) the relationship of words to images. Throughout these exercises we will be playing with notions of predictability and unpredictability. One of the purposes of the exercises is to create texts that force the reader into slightly different reading strategies from those they adopt for the page.

The exercises encourage you to develop your writing as you play with the animation program, rather than to animate pre-existent texts. They are based on generative writing techniques where ideas develop as you work with language. Such a generative process prompts you to think in terms of short fragments initially, rather than whole texts. The exercises will result in small-scale animations, but you can build these up into longer pieces if you wish.

It will not be possible to complete all these exercises in a single workshop, and in fact you may not have the time to finesse even one. You can start a number of exercises and finish them afterwards, concentrate only on one, or spread the work out over several workshops.

Exercise 1

The first exercise is designed to show how you can play with words in an animation and break them up into letters as a means of forming other words. This poises you between deconstruction and reconstruction of meaning.

Using the text writing facility, insert a word in frame 1 and then insert a keyframe[3] at a later frame (say frame 20). In frame 20 use the 'break apart' facility to pull the word apart into letters, so that each letter can be treated as a separate entity. Then rearrange the letters slightly, delete some of the letters or add some others, and pull the letters out of their linear arrangement into a pattern. While you do this be aware of the new words you can create or hint at by deleting and rearranging letters, and the way in which this can shift the meaning. If you start with the word 'reconciliation', you might break apart and rearrange the words in such a way that the words 'con' or 'late' or 'alienation' arise through the processes of separation, rearrangement and addition respectively. You may want to use fonts and colours to pick out the different letter and word formations that arise, so they are highlighted. Also, create a tween motion between frame 1 and frame 20.

Insert a new keyframe at frame 30 and take this process of arrangement, deletion, addition and tweening further, then repeat the process two or three more times along the timeline until you are left with only a very small number of letters or have radically changed the word. The animation will look striking but can you make this change salient in terms of its semantic impact? Do the remaining letters, or the new word you have formed, resonate in a powerful way with the word you started with? For example, maybe you started with 'silent' and it becomes 'silo'.

There are numerous variations on this exercise: you can keep reasserting the word at various points in the animation and then deconstructing it differently each time. Or you can also build the animation on several layers, each time starting with a new word that is nevertheless connected in meaning to the original word. Or you can add extra 'scenes'[4] in which you apply this process with variation to several words.

Exercise 2

This second exercise is designed to encourage you to use animation to produce unexpected and kinetic meanings. You will do this by gradually revealing the content of sentences and by crossing over the meanings of different sentences on the screen.

Think of a sentence, if possible with a little twist to it, or an element of contradiction or illogicality in it. My sentence is 'You can only write dialogue by refusing to hear other people speak.' Then decide how you will divide this sentence up. Any sentence will do (and if you cannot think of a sentence take one from a book or newspaper), but if possible try and maximize the element of surprise in the sentence, so that it raises and then deflates certain expectations. I have divided my sentence up into four segments: 'You can only write dialogue/by refusing to hear/how other people/speak.'

Arrange the segments of your sentence at different points on the timeline, for example, place the first segment at the keyframe in frame 1, and then the second in frame 20, and so on. The sentence will gradually build up, but on the other hand the beginning of it will disappear so there will be a sense of both accumulation and disappearance. This forces the reader to project and recuperate the meaning at the same time. Use fonts and colour to highlight or segment the sentence in any way that seems appropriate, but do not go overboard as this may negate the effect. With respect to my sentence – 'you can only write dialogue/by refusing to hear/how other people/speak' – we do not know what the last word is going to be until it actually appears, but there is an element of thwarting expectation because the word 'speak' seems to contradict the import of the rest of the sentence.

Now add a second layer (layer 2). Think of a different sentence or short phrase. Can you generate a phrase by association from the first one? My phrase is 'the acoustics of deafness', which is related obliquely to the previous sentence through the concept of hearing. Divide your phrase or sentence up in any way that seems effective to you. Place the segments at different points on the timeline from the sentence in layer 1, for example in frames 5, 15, 25. Do not place the segments of the phrase or sentence in a straight line, but instead create some visual movement on the stage (the working area on the screen).

Add a third layer (layer 3). See if you can generate a phrase that has a tangential relationship to the other phrases. Mine is 'the inexplicable enabled'. Again, divide up your phrase or sentence and try to arrange the sections at well-spaced points on the timeline, that is, not at points that coincide with words on the other layers.

If you test your movie you will find that the layers interact and fuse with each other, creating unexpected verbal formations. Different meanings will emerge from those you had predicted. For example, at one point in my movie I can read the combination 'enable by refusing to hear', at another point 'speak of deafness'. The words pop up all over the screen encouraging the reader to scan them in a number of directions. At any one time the reader can make several alternative meanings depending on the direction his or her reading takes. In this way the semantics of the layers cross-fertilize.

You might want to improve this animation by making it look more attractive, or by slightly moving the segments, or by adding extra layers. You should also try this exercise repeatedly, in order to become adept at forging the word combinations that can arise out of the interweaving of the different threads of words. The effect of this interweaving may be less engaging if it disintegrates into a word salad: try to forge some new meanings (or at least hints of new meanings), even if they quickly disintegrate. Unless you are technically very adept, accidents may occur and take you in new directions: this can be annoying when you want to create a particular effect that misfires, but it can also open up new possibilities. Try not to have too many preconceived ideas about outcomes; instead allow unpredicted events to suggest new directions.

Exercise 3

The next exercise focuses on morphing words into each other. The words are chosen on the basis of their association through sound. In this exercise visual patterns, sound connections and semantics work together to create striking transformations.

Use the pencil icon to draw a word (any word you want) at frame 1 (do not use the text function). Let us say that the word is 'political'. Then insert a keyframe at frame 20, and draw another word that is related in sound to the first word, for example, 'polemical' or 'litigious'. Place the second word over or close to the first word, and then use the shape tweening facility to morph between them.

Elaborate on this process by producing a series of words that are related in sound and then shape tweening between them. You might want to conceive of the morph as circular, so that you move through a succession of words and in-between-words and then return to the first word, or you might want to end with a word that is distant from the initial one. The basic principle is to create changes in meaning which parallel changes in the sound of the word.

There are many different ways in which you can build on this exercise. Try creating morphs on three separate layers but choose an interconnecting principle. Maybe all the initial words signify colours (red, blue, purple) or moods (anger, happiness) but in each case you then associate away from the initial word on the basis of sound. You can also develop your technique from morphing words into morphing phrases: this will give you more linguistic and semantic opportunities. Again, use fonts and colours to taste, but at all times think of the connection between meaning, sound and visual appearance.

You might also want to add a soundtrack. This could have only an abstract connection with the morphing shapes or alternatively be a soundtrack of someone speaking the morphing word(s). If you have the technical know-how you could introduce some elements of interactivity into this. For example, you could create two soundtracks of the morphing words, each with a button to start and stop it. The reader or 'screener' could begin and end each soundtrack at will or play both together.

Exercise 4

In this exercise we will build up an animation of several layers with a mixture of images and words. Again we will use a generative approach as you learn to evolve words from images and images from words. The purpose of this exercise is to help you develop facility in combining words and images, particularly in unpredictable ways.

In the first layer (layer 1), insert/import an image at frame 1 and then insert it at two or three other positions on the stage (your working space on the screen). Using the properties panel (if you are working in Flash), transform the image at a number of points on the timeline. For example, elongate, rotate or tint the photo so it becomes light and transparent. Make sure that three versions of the image are arranged at different positions on the stage and make a striking arrangement; don't just line them up in a row. If you are stuck for an idea, use a photograph of yourself or photos of a particular location that interests you. Don't overcrowd the stage, however, as you will be inserting more words and images.

When you have done this, insert another layer (layer 2) but keeping the first layer visible. Insert several phrases along the timeline that respond to the image, but make each phrase quite different. The response may be specific or much more abstract. As far as positioning is concerned, the phrases can overlap physically with the photos, or with each other, or be juxtaposed with them.

Now look at the phrases you generated and see if they suggest ideas beyond the original photos. Suppose your image is of a person and you have generated the phrase 'his mood was fragile'. Can you then find an image, such as one of a delicate fabric or vase, which suggests fragility (even if obliquely)? Insert another layer (layer 3) and then import some images which respond to these phrases but not to the original image. Now insert another (layer 4) and create some phrases that respond to the new set of images in layer 3 and place them wherever you wish along the timeline.

You could obviously go on indefinitely adding extra layers to this animation, generating words from the images and images from the words, but each time adding extra ideas and directions to the piece. However, if you want to do that you may have to extend the animation into a number of different scenes, as one scene will soon become very cluttered.

Exercise 5

This exercise is similar to the previous one but has narrative as its focus. In this exercise we are going to create a narrative through words and images. However, you will not be using images simply to illustrate the story, but also to extend it, and even call aspects of it into question.

First of all think out the beginning of a story. To maximize the creative possibilities, do not plan the story from start to finish as we want it to develop through the interaction of words and images. Animate the beginning of the narrative by making the storyline progressively appear along the time-line. It will be easiest if this only takes up one scene.

Then insert another layer (layer 2) and place images along the timeline. These images should respond directly to the narrative, so you might include an image of a landscape or a house if one is mentioned in the storyline. Then insert another layer (layer 3) and add images that either have no direct connection with the storyline, work against it, or call aspects of it into question. Construct the next part of the narrative by picking up some of the ideas in this layer of images (layer 3) and developing the story through them. This way the story will take you into directions you might never have conceived of initially, through a combination of verbal and visual stimuli.

As the narrative develops don't necessarily spell it all out in words, let the images tell part of the story. Ambiguities and gaps in the storyline will develop but this will make it all the more interesting.

5. FOLLOW UP

As a follow-up to these exercises you should try to extend some of the technical approaches that they initiate. Build each exercise into several scenes so you produce longer movies and, if you can do so without unnecessary clutter, add more layers in any particular animation. Also combine the exercises: for example, introduce word morphing into some of the other exercises to lend more variety and complexity to your work. Try to focus not only on building up your technical expertise but on producing work which employs language in visually striking and meaningful ways. Extend your animation skills, for example, by adding interactivity. You may want to give your reader the chance to stop and start the animation at will, or to move between different parts of it. Or you may want to give the reader the opportunity to generate animated text from a static text through mouse movements, so that the text intermittently 'grows' in surprising ways.

Once you have mastered a degree of interactivity, many possibilities become open to you. Try dividing up the screen into frames, so that clicking on one part of the screen activates text in another; inserting roll over buttons to activate text on the screen in response to mouse movements; or allowing your readers to drag texts round the screen. Also try splitting the screen in two, and run one text-based animation in the upper half of the screen and a second text-based animation in the lower half. Each animation should be independent, but you will find that many interesting and unintended meanings arise when the two halves of the screen are read in conjunction with each other. If you make at least one of the movies interactive (by allowing the reader to stop and start at will or to jump to other parts of the movie through hyperlinks) then the two movies will never coincide in exactly the same way twice.

You will also want to develop the multimedia aspect of your writing more fully. We have seen some of the ways in which images can work with and against words, but you can also use sound to counterpoint words. You can use illustrative sounds, environmental sounds or musical sounds. You can also construct sounds in a non-linear manner, so that the reader can stop and start and control the dynamic level. Spoken text also has limitless possibilities, and the narrative you constructed could be counterpointed by snippets of conversation or short monologues. Another exciting possibility is to use computer programs to sample and manipulate the voice and change its pitch and timbre.

In order to explore new media writing further you need to familiarize yourself with other innovative work in the field. I have already mentioned a number of writers in this area, in particular John Cayley (Cayley) – whose website also contains a number of articles by him as well as his creative works – and Jason Nelson (Nelson). But you should also look at the work of austraLYSIS, Marc Amerika, mez, Talan Memmott and Loss Pequeño Glazier (Amerika; austraLYSIS; Breeze; Glazier; Memmott). There are a number of online magazines where you can view new media work such as *Born Magazine, Beehive, infLect* or *Drunken Boat* (Beehive; Born Magazine; Drunken Boat; infLect). There are also websites which catalogue and give information about such work, for example, The Electronic Literature Organization site (Electronic Literature Organization). Some of the magazines I have just mentioned are no longer adding new work but they still constitute a good archive. Relevant books on the subject include *New Media Poetics* (Morris and Swiss, 2006), *The New Media Reader* (Wardrip-Fruin and Montfort, 2003) and *First Person: New Media as Story, Performance, and Game* (Wardrip-Fruin and Harrigan, 2004). Two books by Katherine Hayles, *Writing Machines* and *My Mother Was a Computer*, will also be very useful (Hayles, 2002; Hayles, 2005). My book *The Writing Experiment* has a chapter on new media writing (Smith, 2005) and an accompanying website where you can view new media works (Smith).

The workshop exercises also have implications for your writing beyond and outside new media work because they encourage you to think about writing in a generative way, rather than by starting from preconceived ideas about content. This may enable you to think of ideas that would not have occurred to you any other way and can take you beyond the limits of your own intentions into unchartered territory. In addition, the exercises motivate you to create texts that are non-linear, fragmented and discontinuous. This way of writing opens up language to multiple meanings and gives an active role to the reader, who then must draw the ideas together rather than simply digest a seamless text. Try to develop your capacity to work in this way; it can be productive both for your new media writing but also for your on-the-page-writing. Such strategies are the focus of my book *The Writing Experiment* (Smith, 2005).

New media writing is a fast-developing field because as the technology develops new ways of manipulating language emerge and new cybergenres appear. This does not mean that works written with older technologies are no longer compelling, that you must continually bow to the latest technological fashion, or that expertise with technology can totally replace expertise with language. But it does mean that this is an area in which you can continually take your writing in unexpected directions and advance it through fresh challenges. The best way to develop your new media writing is to keep abreast of developments in the field and bend them to meet your own creative needs.

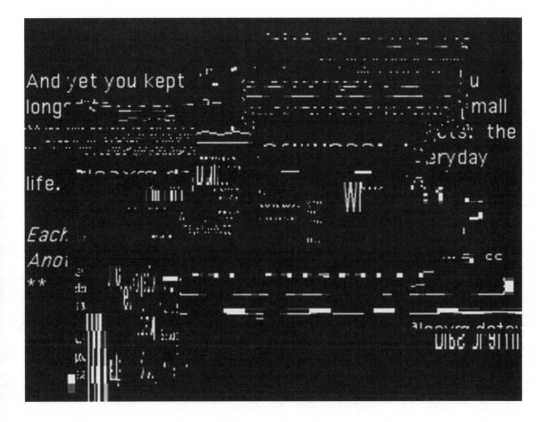

Figure 7.1 Screenshot from *soundAFFECTs* by Roger Dean, Anne Brewster and Hazel Smith
  Source: Dean, Brewster and Smith (2004).

WORKS CITED

Amerika, M. www.markamerika.com/ (Last accessed on 18 July 2007).

Andrews, J. Arteroids. Version 3.11. 2007. vispo.com/arteroids/indexenglish.htm (Last accessed on 23 July 2007).

austraLYSIS. www.australysis.com (Last accessed on 18 July 2007).

Beehive. http://beehive.temporalimage.com/ (Last accessed on 18 July 2007).

Born Magazine. www.bornmagazine.org/ (Last accessed on 18 July 2007).

Breeze, M.-A. (Known as mez) Website. www.hotkey.net.au/~netwurker/ (Last Accessed on 22 July 2007).

Cayley, J. http://homepage.mac.com/shadoof/net/in/ (Last accessed on 22 July 2007).

Coverley, M. Afterimage. *The Salt River Review* 4.3 (2001). http://califia.us/Afterimage/ (Last accessed on 18 July 2007).

Dean, R., A. Brewster and H. Smith. *SoundAFFECTs. Text* 8.2 (2004): www.griffith.edu.au/school/art/text/oct04/content.htm (Last accessed on 18 July 2007).

Drunken Boat. www.drunkenboat.com/ (Last accessed on 18 July 2007).

Electronic Literature Organization. http://eliterature.org/ (Last accessed on 18 July 2007).

Glazier, L. P. http://epc.buffalo.edu/authors/glazier/ (Last accessed on 18 July 2007).

Hayles, K. *Writing Machines*. (Cambridge, MA: MIT Press), 2002.

Hayles, N. K. *How We Became Posthuman: Virtual Bodies in Cybernetics, Literature, and Informatics*. (Chicago: University of Chicago Press), 1999.

—. *My Mother Was a Computer: Digital Subjects and Literary Texts*. (Chicago: University of Chicago Press), 2005.

infLect. http://www.canberra.edu.au/centres/inflect/ (Last accessed on 18 July 2007).

Larsen, D. I'm simply saying. *inflect: a journal of multimedia writing* (2005): www.ce.canberra.edu.au/inflect/02/larsen/simply7.html (Last accessed on 17 June 2007).

Memmott, T. www.memmott.org/talan/index.html (Last accessed on 18 July 2007).

Mitchell, W. *Picture Theory: Essays on Verbal and Visual Presentation*. (Chicago: Univerity of Chicago Press), 1994.

Morris, A. and T. Swiss. *New Media Poetics: Contexts, Technotexts, and Theories*. (Cambridge, MA: MIT Press), 2006.

Nelson, J. www.secrettechnology.com/ (Last accessed on 18 July 2007).

Smith, H. *The Erotics of Geography*. Book and CD-Rom. (Hawaii: Tinfish Press), 2008.

Smith, H. SoundAFFECTs: Transcoding, Writing, New Media, Affect. *Scan: a Journal of Media Arts Culture* 4.1 (2007): http://scan.net.au/scan/journal/display.php?journal_id=89 (Last accessed on 19 July 2007).

—. Website for the Writing Experiment: Strategies for Innovative Writing. www.allenandunwin.com/writingexp/ (Last accessed on 23 July 2007).

—. The Writing Experiment: Strategies for Innovative Creative Writing. (Sydney: Allen and Unwin), 2005.

Smith, H. and R. T. Dean. The Egg, the Cart, the Horse, the Chicken. *inflect: a journal of multimedia writing* (2003): http://www.canberra.edu.au/centres/inflect/01/eggsite.3/eggindex.html (Last accessed on 17 June 2007).

Stefans, B. K. The Dreamlife of Letters. 2000. www.arras.net/RNG/flash/dreamlife/dreamlife_index.html (Last accessed on 23 July 2007).

Strickland, S. www.stephaniestrickland.com/ (Last accessed on 18 July 2007).

Wardrip-Fruin, N. and N. Montfort. (eds) *The New Media Reader*. (Cambridge, MA: MIT Press), 2003.

Wardrip-Fruin, N. and P. Harrigan. (eds) *First Person: New Media as Story, Performance, and Game*. (Cambridge, MA: MIT Press), 2004.

Zervos, K. www.griffith.edu.au/ppages/k_zervos (Last accessed on 18 July 2007).

Chapter 8

Creative Non-Fiction

William S. Penn

1. WELCOME TO THE WORKSHOP

You may ask what Joseph Heller has to do with a chapter on Creative Non-Fiction writing. Glad you asked. It allows me to tell you my favourite recent anecdote (note the way 'recent' limits a lifetime of sins and errors, along with the forgetfulness that not only comes with age but is demanded by it in order properly to be age at all).

Joseph Heller attended a cocktail party and a friend introduced him to the manager of an investment hedge fund on Wall Street and, as the man walked away, said, 'What do you think, Joe? That man earned more last month than you've made from all of your books.' Heller smiled and without envy replied, 'Maybe. But I have one thing he'll never have.'

'What's that?' his interlocutor asked.

'Enough', Heller replied.

That is what a writer has, if he is lucky enough to realize it, and the only words I might add, given the good fortune of my writing life, would make it read 'more than enough'. Unable to help myself, to restrain the desire to educate as well as entertain which is one of the sins of writers that is more allowed in the commission of non-fiction than fiction, I might go on to say that we – you're in it now with me, sort of like jumping out of a plane at 13,000 feet holding hands – are not in it for the money, or the renown (I can't use 'fame' when referring to myself; heck, even 'renown' is a bit like the pot calling the kettle . . . well, a kettle), or even publication. Though I do think that we write to be read and read by others (writing for oneself seems to me, at least, a bit self-absorbed). But first and foremost, we write. And write. Maybe revise. And then write more. 'Writer's block', to me, is an excuse a bit like the same dead grandmother, used several times in one semester by a student to explain his absence.

There is another lesson in my Hellerish anecdote, and that is while we write, we cannot hedge our investment. Instead, we enter into it fully, and we have to train ourselves not to worry about anything more than sound, clarity and basic meaning as we manipulate our reader. For it is our reader's thinking and feeling that we are trying to manipulate, to control, perhaps to change. We are less like mutual fund managers than investment brokers who are in my view all corrupt, selling clients/friends investments in which they themselves have a particular interest (such as what may be crudely called a kickback). You may agree, but mainly because you, as a budding non-fiction writer, do not have enough money to bother with investing beyond the safety of guaranteed bank deposits. You may never. But you will have enough because you will have the things that do matter – imagination, language, a joy in serious or playful manipulation, and an ability to understand point of view, context and most of all, the importance of process.

Recently, I received an email from a student thanking me for my 'system overrides' to let her take my courses, adding her thanks for taking away her ability to read for entertainment. Now, she can't read without asking why this structure, this point of view, or why these words and implications or explications. She has yet to find out that though I know she's trying to be amusing, and is, I also have a response: writing is not about entertainment, it is about pleasure. America's problem, certainly, is to confuse the meaning of the two while denigrating the full volume of pleasure by including in it things as shallow as driving cars the size of mastodons, houses where you never see your children and the general wastefulness of too much money.

Writing is hard work, and hard work is rarely entertaining. Every morning or every evening you sit alone, nowadays probably at a computer keyboard and with hope for luck put words to paper (metaphorically). Words don't always come with ease and even if they do never come shaped and formed, the sentences and paragraphs rhythmical or structured. We spend our time learning about those things, and adding in point of view, context, balance (if appropriate), rhetoric – the use of language with attention to its effect upon the very audience we have to imagine as being there in order to have it at all. In addition, we think about the questions that 'non-fiction' raises in relation to 'fiction'. Ugly, nagging questions about truth or beauty, meaning, intention. Questions to which some teachers will teach you there are no answers, but questions you and I know must be answered or else. It is with these questions that workshops may be useful, giving us a perhaps instant and therefore slightly artificial community, inviting like-minded people with relatively large (possibly uninformed) egos to read or listen to our words and then respond with acerbity, compassion, and not a little brutality – or at least it can feel like brutality.

But gentle or overly kind and therefore vague criticism is not helpful at all. Think of when you were young – or when I was young, which is ancient history, now – and a friend tried to set you up with his girlfriend's best mate and you asked, 'What's she like?'

'She's nice', came the reply.

Oh, right. 'She's nice' means that she has no other characteristics that your friend can call to mind quickly because she's 10 feet tall and weighs 40 stones. True or false, the imagined 'date' stretches before you like a darkling plain.

The same is true if you switch the genders and make 'he' into 'she' and 'her' into 'him'.

And you see? I chose to put in the previous sentence after 51 per cent of you said, 'Yeah, well, what about guys your girlfriends set you up with, etc.?' Maybe I ought to have opened with that disclaimer. But I am perverse in my writing and love to try to make you think and feel, even if it is really not-thinking and the feelings are stereotypically visceral or trained, so I may go on like this:

The truth is that almost any reply from your friend is insufficient. 'She's cute?' Yeah, if she's so cute then why . . .? Perhaps 'cute' means she's all bubbly and full of silly thoughtless life, or she's immature, or she can't hold her liquor and doesn't have the grace to control her consumption of it while you are trying to discuss Kierkegaard because you're a freaking bore on a date and Kierkegaard is the best you can come up with . . .

All questions after the fact: we assume from the outset that something must be wrong with her or with him if she/he needs a friend to do the work. (As far as I'm concerned, something is also wrong with my friend's idea of me, if he needs to set me up with someone who dots her 'I's with Valentine hearts or who struts about the locker room in underclothes cut for a 15-year-old.)

Don't we?

Maybe I'm wrong. But that's what we're about in this chapter. Taking our topic and writing about it in a way that will keep our reader interested, make him or her think, feel, react, respond, agree and disagree, but most of all, make him want to keep reading.

Our topic? Everything. For to writers, everything is not merely fair game. Everything is our topic and everything is what interests us. Especially to writers of non-fiction of the creative kind.

2. WRITERS AND READERS

Non-fiction writers come in all shapes and sizes, and their interests may resemble the shelves of a discount warehouse with a little of this and a lot of that placed side by side in bins. That is as it should be: there is no subject that is unavailable to the non-fiction writer. Making the phrase 'creative non-fiction writer' does not limit the number of available bins, but it does modify the way in which those bins are searched or displayed.

The other confusion – as easy as it is to make – is to see creative non-fiction as being essentially undifferentiated from fiction. They both do the same things, people tell us.

Yes, they both use inventive language – metaphor, simile, verbs that jiggle the sensibilities with humour or slanted meaning, and even made-up words that seem onomatopoetic. They both use economy and structure to open at a place in the midst of interest and ideational or physical action. And they both try to set up numbered dots like a child's painting that, when connected by the active participation of the reader, make a picture of the truth. Though many of my colleagues insist there is no 'truth', I disagree: it is bad to kill and wars are not good, but it is flat out wrong and evil to murder; a little humility goes a long way and charity makes you feel good while it helps people who have less; there is a difference between entertainment and pleasure; and process is everything – whether you are writing or golfing, it is less about 'winning' than about doing it as well as you are able and enjoying the effort of trying.

Like the fiction writer, the non-fiction writer should consider subject, tone, structure, appropriateness and use of language, and at all times must be interesting to his audience. That audience may be limited – other anthropologists, for example, or it may broaden out to include all thinking human beings. James Merrill, the finely tuned poet, said he wrote for his 'one perfect reader'. Others say they write for a larger group of intelligent but slightly imperfect human readers. Some may even try to define their audience as all human beings, but those lackwits who don't think or read at all (well) are difficult to reach and then what do we do with that basket of used proto-human goods called 'people'? Regardless of how you define your audience, you must define it – it will govern the kind of language you use, as well as the indirectness of your metaphors and the complexity of your structure and tone – in order to be interesting to your particular audience, and if you are not interesting, then you've begun and will finish behind the proverbial eight ball and live the bitter life of blame of the unread writer.

All these are the stuff of fiction, too. So where do the two differ?

Point of view, the place from which the writer sits, inventing a narrator who then invents or uses interior narrators to create his meaning. The fiction writer consciously or unconsciously invents an implied author who then invents a narrator (omniscient, limited third person or first person) who then tells the story using, among other things, interior narrators to modify, alter, move along the scenes. The non-fiction writer is more closely associated with the implied author, indeed, is the author without much implication – it is his point of view we are encountering, not his filtered, hidden point of view. It's like gauze on the camera of feckless beauty: the fiction writer can hide his blemishes more easily than the non-fiction, and perhaps even learn something himself in the process of hiding. The non-fiction writer has to be more careful to manage all the other aspects of writing without the hiding gauze. The fiction writer has to invent an author who is better than himself; the non-fiction writer has to be that author who is better than himself.

Involved with point of view are the attitudes and beliefs of the behind-the-scenes non-fiction writer, which may extend into the realm of agenda. We have to be careful. Our readers will not like us much if our hidden agendas are too heavy-handed or too blatantly obvious, and no thinking person will excuse a writer for having an agenda that is interesting without the feeling that the writer knows he is imperfect and still learning and he is offering these words to his reader in order for them to go on a journey of discovery that leads to a conclusion – what conclusion, however, is not known though perhaps suspected. This seems a possible description of what became of writing in the 1960s – cerebral play turned heavy-handed prescription – and of what is happening to it now – mindless cliché attempting to cross-dress in thoughtful clothes, or simple pandering mindlessness, mostly represented by Hollywood, but also by the frightened marketing men and women of the larger publishing houses. If what you say is truly uninteresting, you may sell well to uninterested minds and hearts.

Why you write remains the essential piece that only you may supply. In this workshop the first two commandments are be interesting and do not know the whole of the conclusion you will come to.

Third, feel free to treat ideas like characters (but never, in fiction treat characters like ideas or you'll end up with flat types) and place them in a context and give them some freedom to find their ways to wherever.

Try to create the truth and stop worrying over the literary theorists who have nothing better to do than fret and worry, parsing out their inventive parsimony like old men discussing their meds (and making about as much difference).

As all truth has a context – religious truth is just that, religious, which means besides the laws one believes in and follows, there is such a thing as faith and you cannot argue – nor should you want to – with faith (unless it is with the complete absence of faith, the colourless all-colour of total evil like Nazism, Neo or Not, and even then you are wasting your time with pinheads). One does not have reasons to believe, one either believes or does not. Though not a Catholic, I have long admired the Catholic Church because you either believe and follow or you disagree and disobey and therefore are not a Catholic, though the Church welcomes you back at any time without making you do too much in the way of penance outside of re-establishing the context in which you live and believe. My favourite anecdote about Catholics comes from when they met my people, the Nez Perce, who used to kneel and rock when they connected themselves to the generations. A Catholic priest wrote Rome and told them this – 'They look like us, a lot', he said with not a little panic in his tone. Imperturbable Rome wrote back, 'Make them stand.' Problem solved. And in the anecdote is a context, one that allows the truth to emerge without too much in the way of tight-lipped, morally superior agenda. So our fifth commandment is to make sure the reader knows the context. Will the reader understand the context? The intelligent one will or will at least try, but then the intelligent one enjoys variety and not the homogenized samenesses that Americans make into laws of 'diversity'.

The sixth is to use language that is appropriate and beware over-stating things or using modern sillinesses such as 'awesome' because in fact, what little we come up with rarely inspires awe at all. Avoid cliché like a plague of locusts unless you are attempting humour or satire and then be certain that your intelligent reader knows it is satire (one of the many failings of workshop teachers is the repetitive stress disorder that comes from reading the same clichéd essay over and over, year in and year out, until we do not expect and therefore fail to recognize a bright young writer trying to be funny; for our sake, one doesn't need to label the piece 'satire', but one does need to work towards the subtleties of humour slowly, beginning more broadly and then working down to specifics if one doesn't want to risk what my daughter says: 'But papa, poopy jokes aren't funny.' (Just wait until you get old, I think. They will be.)

Seven is to remember that all things are connected, and to keep that in mind while you write. You make dislike the Romantics and American Transcendentalists (though I like beans of all sorts, I get tired, too, of Henry David Thoreau's brand). That's okay (sort of) but be careful not to see things as isolated, unrelated or overly individualized. For all our 'isms' and movements, we've accomplished two or at most three things. We (Americans, at least) now accept with a milky mildness the idea that it is best for our children if someone else rears them in the unhappy competition of Day Care and we neither understand why our children hydroponically plant us in old folks' homes when we're old nor why familial cultures find us odd. We were outraged when Communism suggested putting our children in State pre-schools that brainwashed them. But not any longer. Second, we let someone trick us into the apparent need for two people to earn the same money one used to. And third, we let those same people take away retirement pensions (relatively secure) and replace them with our savings and investments (from defined benefit to defined contribution) while bankrupting our children, grandchildren and great grandchildren with national debt.

While avoiding harsh agendas, never, never forget your audience, your reader, and if it becomes a choice between clarity for his or her sake and cleverness for your own, sacrifice your own. Remember that this person is the one you want to pleasurably manipulate and make sure he or she enjoys the journey with you as a firm but attentive guide and do not be content with pre-packaged perceptions, the tenets of the faith in commerce and advertising. Be like the stand-up comical satirist who recognizes the inherent similarity of all feeling, thinking selves and then makes fun not of us-the-audience but of *him and us*, of us-as-community. He joins with us in laughing at us all together. The contexts are broad – men and women, blacks and whites, politics or the absurdities of Modern Life (Lewis Black) or perhaps the creation of the world and a temporal running together of ancient and modern (Eddie Izzard).

3. THE WORKSHOP

The workshop is the most usefully dangerous of all ways to enter the practice of writing. Whether you think your workshop colleagues are smart and well-read, or stupid and unread and very competitive, or your workshop leader is high-handed and very often wrong, you are put in a group whose task it is to comment on your writing and that may be dangerous. On the other hand, the members of your group may be compassionate or not want to piss you off too much because sooner or later you'll be talking about their work. The tendency is towards homogenization and eventually degeneration. Anyone from the Iowa Writer's Workshops can write a competent imitation of a Raymond Carver story. In fact, just about any decent writer can write a Ray Carver story. No one can write an imitation of an Alice Munro or a Flannery O'Connor story, and would have great difficulty writing a Tobias Wolff story.

Hmmm.

The same applies to creative non-fiction. Many think that because they have a good idea or something to write about, that they may be able to write an interesting essay. A recent reading I attended was flat, uninteresting, degeneratively derivative – and strangely, only the person who invited the reader and one – count her – one student thought otherwise. And they thought it because the agenda of the writer was the same as their own personal agendas. The writer read a piece in which she was slightly superior to everyone else except for the one or two 'real' characters she allowed to be her friends in the unbelievable exercise of her old-hat essay. We were supposed to feel slightly superior along with her. Yet it made the audience uncomfortable, made me dislike the writer and discount almost all she said. Her second piece was all about her – look at me, I went to the seashore but I am smarter than other seashore wanderers and I took along my friend the educative biologist who told me things I found very interesting, metaphorically, and so now I am going to display the metaphorical blah of my mind. It was so about her that I cannot recall what the metaphor was, only that her self-love and self-regard, dashed gently with self-pity was tasteless. If non-fiction begins with an idea of the truth and invents a way to talk about it, and ends with a truthful understanding that may be different from the beginning idea, this particular writer – and so many like her – did not make it. She wanted to tell us what she thought – though she had thought little – and mix in an infection of her.

In this tendency lay the reasons I keep marks on students essays simple plusses or minuses, or abbreviated, most often 'int?' for 'interest?' I make students read their work aloud, and I elaborate on my comments along with the rest of the workshop. But it is in the reading aloud that the writers themselves hear their work, forcing them into a relationship with an assumed audience who are assuming that the narrator and author of the essay are very, very close to the same person.

It's a worthy exercise. Did you know that beginning as well as experienced writers hear their work lose energy, can hear it bore their audience, or can hear it succeed, or where it succeeds? Being gay, being a woman, being an Indian, being a man, being a being is not interesting in and of itself if the writing does not sustain the reader or allow the energetic reading aloud of it to real people. How many times have I endured readings where the reader's voice drops and he begins to struggle himself against the incipient narcosis of his prose? The audience reaction, the body language, the looking around, the surreptitious checking of mobile phones always proves my belief that dying is harder on the people around you, even though no one in his right mind wants to die. Hearing a piece read – our own or another's – we get to hear the minor imperfections that allow us to trust that the writer in all his revised perfection expresses and by expressing proves his humanity.

The non-fiction writer, more than any other kind of writer, must remember his own limited humanity and yet reach for a broader, more generalized truth about Humanity, and always remember that he is accompanying the reader on a journey, through a process that leads to understanding – regardless of subject or theme.

4. SOME EXERCISES

The exercises for any workshop should be designed to help the non-fiction writer be creative and interesting, and I hope the following do just that.

Exercise 1

Go home and write a one-page description of the classroom.

The purpose of this one is to begin focusing the writer's attention on detail and its selection. When the workshop reconvenes, the students hear each other read aloud and then comment on which details were visual or aural, meaningful or meaningless. It also begins to give each of the participants an idea of who they are in a workshop with. The leader may also discuss economy: whether in England or America, and I imagine other countries as well, words like cinder block are probably sufficient to represent the classroom. If a student chooses details within the room – the plugless overhead projector, the bemetalled girls (and boys?) around them, that tells one kind of story. If he chooses to focus on the teacher, or the labourers outside the window working hard not to, that tells another story. In both cases, the story begins with him, with our evaluating what he has selected to write about. Further, two main goals are beginning the building of a responsive community of writers, while taking a mundane object and trying to make it interesting. (One might list the interesting elements of description on the blackboard or by plugging in the overhead and spending 30 minutes finding a grease pencil to use on its rolling cellophane and then combine them as an end exercise to create a group description).

Exercise 2

Write three paragraphs. In the first, describe a person using two apparently disparate human senses (hearing, sight, smell, touch and taste) so that you combine them, for example, the sound of colour (or a colour of sound, avoiding clichés like 'blue' for, well, being 'blue', or the bright yellow of silence or the soft acridity of burnt almonds). In the second, describe an idea, and in the third, a place. Explore combinations that help the reader engage the primary senses with altered perceptions. Read what you come up with aloud and encourage others to talk about what they got as listeners (readers) from the juxtaposition.

This exercise begins the process of criticism being about the writing, while it also introduces the concept of looking for metaphor and simile, for things that express something more about what might be a well-described event or moment. Plus, it's fun, and introducing fun into a workshop and the workshopper's perceptual life – the enjoyment of being continuously aware and alive to slight alterations – seems to me essential.

Exercise 3

Write a three-page dialogue between no more than three people to embody and express both a situation and the attitudes contained by their words, each time using one of the other characters' points of view. Avoid all adverbs and adjectives, and in no way add in narrative descriptions of what the speaker is feeling or thinking (e.g. you may not have a man reply to his friend who has asked 'What's she like?' 'She's cute', he said as seriously as possible). As a secondary exercise, have students add in gestures – for example, 'She's cute', he said, squinting at the Thames).

This exercise – perhaps the most difficult – focuses on using dialogue to convey a situation – a good exercise for either fiction or non-fiction – and aims to remove the overuse of adverbs to underpin dialogue that does not contain the feeling, emotion or point of view. The secondary exercise invites the writer to use gesture to convey what otherwise might have been conveyed with an adjective.

Exercise 4

Write a one-page essay on any topic or idea avoiding all punctuation.

This exercise has been fun for students of all levels, forcing them to use conjunctions and coordinating conjunctions to control rhythm and pace, as well as making them think about emphasis – which words comes where and indeed, which word is that which gets used in order to fit into the rhythm of what is being said. Donald Barthelme, the American short story writer, published a story titled 'Sentence' that might be used as a reasonable example even for non-fiction writers.

A secondary exercise may be to write a one-page essay avoiding periods until the very end (and perhaps even then if one wanted to make the essay circle back on its opening, for example). Punctuation, along with the sound of words and the way they create their own emphases may be fruitful or perhaps simply interesting – and the writer, regardless of genre, is always interested in the fact that British pronounce 'corollary' 'co-RAWL-ary', while Americans pronounce the word 'COR-row-larry'. Certainly, the British pronunciation is closer to the original Latinate syllabification; but then do we want to be close to Latin any more? (On the other hand, if we are not close to Latin or Greek or other originating languages, then what are we close to, the wayward mispronunciations of popular music?)

Exercise 5

Describe your parents in one page or less. Once you have done that and read it aloud, then go home and describe your parents as though you are they, and follow that with a second description of them as your grandparents (though now you are describing them as though they are your original parents, though hundreds of years older).

Context. Point of view within context. These are the justifications of such an exercise that forces students to shift their vantage points as well as justify their language within the expressed contexts.

Exercise 6

Write one page about anything of your choice using any and all of the exercises above and arriving at the workshop ready to explain why you did or did not alter the punctuation or why you chose that particular point of view or context. Most important, be interesting.

5. WRAP UP

A final anecdote.

Weeks ago, I helped run workshops for Native American people on a Saturday in a linoleum room that seemed to once have been a Chemistry lab with the fixtures removed with the quickness of theft. People of all ages listened to the main guest – who made surprisingly good sense about this writing business – and when it became my turn to enter the fray the fray was gone. Only good feeling, the desire to write – whether it be stories for a woman's grandchildren or songs that echoed the singing a man had heard as a child. There were questions – the questions of beginners. Regardless of age, none of them were silly, or shallow. Not a single one was about making money or acquiring fame. By the time the day was over, I felt good in a way I hadn't felt for ages. Involuntarily grinning as I left the institutionally ugly and practically impractical building built, it seemed, to house the manufacture of aircraft parts and not the liberal education of uninterested students, it dawned on me why: everyone in the rooms we inhabited understood *process*. Everyone was humbly concerned with telling essays and stories and poems that could transmit something of their philosophies, of their lives and contexts, to their children and grandchildren, and the transmission was everything. We all had shared a morality, and that morality was that we were not individually important but existed in this world as bridges from the previous generations to the next and the next after that and the next again, pushing our transitional powers back towards the seventh generation before us and forwards towards the seventh to follow. Everyone there, in one way or another, felt in his bones and being that the proof was not in the pudding, but actually in the process of intentions and ingredients. Both their sources and their audiences were particular, known – their grandparents or grandchildren, their families, their people and all people who wanted to be like them – and thus their language was chosen for them. Their intentions were not to change or alter, maybe to guide by suggestion, not to express the self but rather to pass along, to give, to transmit what was important, and only if the listener/reader wanted to discover what was important. It was, in other words, up to the reader/listener. You can nudge a grandchild towards the truth but you cannot make him believe it and, more essentially, there is such a thing as truth and whether it is housed in a log hut or on Downing Street or in a linear accelerator or poem it will emit its own kind of beauty.

Beauty.

And it is there that we reach our ultimate definition: everything worthwhile in life, is, has, expresses some kind of beauty in a beautiful way. Sure, you may balk at such a statement, but even your hesitation is, in its humanness, beautiful. By beauty, I mean that which allowed Galileo to see beyond the beautiful music of the spheres (and Brian Green might well argue that string theory contains and expresses its own beauties). Without these beauties, the fitting the as-yet-undiscovered inconsistencies that might modify particle physics, we would not have physical theories that work. It is like the very beauty that allowed Jane Austen to give life to Knightly's restrained, intelligent love, the beautiful addition that life takes on with realizing that Ivan Illych is not (as some of my students said) 'encountering death' but is already dead and thus we can assume that everything Ivan attached importance to in his meagre, afraid and bureaucratic life is a falsehood, or at least the attachment to it is false. It's the beauty of an Italian father dribbling a football down the cobbles of a Venetian campo, or the love of a man that achieves its largeness in patient, above-and-beyond caring for his wife-my-sister dying from cancer, or the sheer, unutterable beauty of a Chopin Nocturne or a Mozart flute sonata, or Kandinsky's paintings hung retrospectively at the Tate Modern.

These beauties are true in ways we are barely able to recognize, and they gain added truth and power by being well-arranged and well-expressed.

So beauty, and that is what this entire chapter is after: engaging you in the beauties of process and the beauties of truth. We are conveying the imagined truth, not writing school reports. Though some people might call our realistic things, our imagined truths 'lies', as long as we embellish for the sake of interest and perhaps even greater truth, their 'facts' do not matter. Facts are for pedants. My son, with his physicist's and classical musician's soul admires the idea of the universe's crystalline spheres turning at different speeds and in different directions and creating the 'music of the spheres'. It's not that he doesn't know better. But he also knows that the spheres in their apparent orderliness create a beauty that is similar to that music, the soul responds to the beauty similarly in both fact and embellished metaphorical fact and in that beauty we find truth.

We all know, or should, Keats' poem, 'Ode on a Grecian Urn', and most of us remember the ending lines, 'Beauty is truth, truth beauty, – that is all / Ye know on earth, and all ye need to know.' But we forget that it is the permanent unchangingness of the urn that makes it cold; we forget that in its permanent truth it remains – always – a friend to Man and it speaks to Man and those two things are essential to the writing of interesting creative non-fiction. Befriend your reader with some shaped and decorated object (an essay) that speaks to the reader's imagination and vision and understanding. So many things do not. As the generations waste into old age, Keats' poem remains and remains true, and that is what we are after. Is it too much, too high an aspiration, too Dorian Gray for us? Is it too difficult, even for first-rate writers like Raymond Carver? Yes. But either aspire or don't, and do not whine or settle for fifth-rate essays, or poems, or stories, or movies that run to sequels with the ease of an oil spill. If only we could return to the understanding that unheard melodies are, or can be, sweeter, and human beings could again enjoy some restraint in their daily and historical lives (or, to use Wordsworth, if we could realize that grief embodied but unexpressed by words is more powerful than all the wailing in the world because we the reader/listener supply our own wordless feelings over the too early death of a child). I care more about the young woman serving soup to needy people than about the frail and frill of Anna Nicole because food is general all over Ireland and charity is more beautiful than self-interested death.

Am I complaining about our age too much? Probably. Sorry. But this is non-fiction and sometimes the truth is not all that palatable. There is little about creative non-fiction writing that does not lead to the kind of dismay that may only be overcome by the hope enacted in the process of writing well. The first place to begin is in understanding process, how it produces its own pleasures and its own beauties regardless of the kind of writing one is doing.

To learn this process is not an easy task because you have to give up so much that you thought mattered and then discover – for yourself – the things that do. Advertising may convince you that mobile phones connect while creating an acceptable image of a young man or woman tied to an electronic leash. You may believe that having someone else rear your children is okay – and I suppose in some circumstances such as poverty it is – but don't believe that a loving bad parent is worse for a child than a kind homogenizing care-giver. Harder than those, you have to give up some of your self, and that is not easy.

Live with silence and slow time and tell the things you need to tell to the spirit that is affected by Mozart and quantum physics. Try to make sure, in the language you select and use, the structures you impose, the voices you move in and out of, you remain interesting which means 'For ever piping songs for ever new' – because even the repeat reader of Flannery O'Connor's *Mystery and Manners* will take renewed and added delight from the truth of what she writes. Tease your reader out of thought, or wheedle or cajole, or make him react in such a way that your words are like burrs beneath his saddle which, as he travels, niggle at him, make him think, respond, even try to disagree. But above all – above ALL – be interesting.

And then kill me off – metaphorically, please. As I tell my students, once you've heard what I have to say, and perhaps acted upon it, you will one day find that I am sitting on your shoulder like a trident-wielding cartoon conscience saying, 'You can't do that or you need to do this.' With a quick gesture like the trapping of a moth or fly your hand needs to snap shut on the embodiment of this pesky voice. Then shake your hand violently, making the fly-moth dizzy, and wash it down the sink drain and send it off to join all those voices you no longer need to hear and that you must be rid of in order to do your work.

Chapter 9

Writing for Children and Young Adults

Gill James

1. WELCOME TO THE WORKSHOP

This workshop explores the nature of the child and young adult reader, and looks at who might write for them, and why, and how they might set about that task. When we write for anyone, we need to include a story arc, the characters need to be rounded and believable, the writer should show, not tell, and every word should be relevant, either carrying the plot forward or showing more about the characters. We also need to make our writing suitable for our reader. Children will tend to be less forgiving than adults, and even experienced young adult readers will not wait for the text to become interesting. It must engage them from the very beginning and hold their attention throughout.

We must take notice of the child's stage of development. The child who has a picture-book read to them is different from the one who has just learnt to read who is different again from the one who reads confidently and wants to explore the world completely on their own. Then come the younger teenagers who want some pictures of the world and finally the young adult who wants to order his own society. Each one of these readers has their own specific needs. Identifying what those are is a crucial component of this workshop.

Some may think that because texts produced for children contain simple language and are short, writing for children or young adults is easy. However, the writer has to make more out of less and has to have knowledge about the reader's specific needs. Those who write for children will certainly possess the same skills as many other writers. The writer must also be able to remember what it felt like when all you could see was a forest of legs in the shopping centre, how cruel the school yard is sometimes, how sad the death of a pet can be, how proud a middle-grader is of baking a cake and how awkward and self-conscious a young adult is as they get their newly acquired adult attributes under control. Then the writer has to talk to their readers in the appropriate voice which is not the one of the adult who has had the growth. It should be the voice of a close friend who has just had something momentous happen to them. That friend is going to be a child or a young adult, so the voice must be that of a child or a young adult.

2. READERS AND WRITERS

The picture-book reader (pre-reading)

Generally, the youngest consumer of texts is the child who shares a picture-book with an adult. These books tend to be between 600 and 1,000 words long. This consumer cannot yet read words, and the book is often read to them as they sit with an adult. The language is usually of a higher register than for the next stage: pre-school children can understand spoken language more complex than that printed for new readers.

The pictures in this type of book tend to complement the text rather than illustrate it and often tell an extra story. Occasionally there is a joke which only the adult understands, but not at the child's expense. An artist produces the pictures, but writers create texts that easily evoke images. They will also need to understand how their text might be divided between the spreads within the book. Most picture-books contain 32 or 36 pages, including endpapers and covers, which leaves room for 24 or 28 pages of text, or 12 to 14 double spreads. The writer will also have a very clear idea of the additional narrative in the pictures.

'Readers' of this level love repetition, and this features highly in these books, but often with some sort of hiatus, between two-thirds and four-fifths of the way through. Rhyming texts, however, are discouraged. In order to recoup some of the cost involved in full-colour printing, publishers have to be able sell these books to many different countries and rhyming texts can be difficult to translate. However, there are exceptions. One of the most popular picture-books today is Julia Donaldson's *The Gruffalo,* written in verse. Also popular and also written in verse is Niki Daly's *Ruby Sings the Blues.*

Into this short text, a whole story must go, with its beginning, middle and end, as well as a sub-plot in the pictures, and much repetition. Those writers who write for this reader and for others claim these short texts are more difficult to write. The picture-book writer is more like a poet than a novel writer.

Everyday stories – the arrival of a new sibling, a favoured pet, the loss of a special toy – are often represented anthropomorphically. This is a useful device for tackling issues which might be painful for the child. Distance is gained by making it all happen to an animal. Realistic stories are often about matters that may seem trivial to adults – a lost trainer, a first journey on the London Underground or an empty biscuit tin. Some stories are about real animals – the seal pup that is rescued, the feral kitten which survives against the odds and the terrified mouse which outwits the cat. There are stories too of pure fantasy. The child may encounter for the first time some of the myths, legend and fairy tales on which their culture is built.

The emergent reader

This reader has learnt to read and is now choosing books from a bookshelf. However, concerned adults will have influenced what they read. The class teacher, the school or the town librarian, and other adults close to them may all censor what is available for them.

Typically, these books, often known as Chapter Books, are between 6,000 and 10,000 words long. Often the writer faces restrictions such as: 'no words of more than two syllables, no sentences with dependent clauses, and no paragraphs longer than twelve lines'. Sometimes they are even asked to include specific words. The stories are usually broken down into chapters and are often in the region of 50-pages long. Frequent repetitions are there to aid the new reader, not just for fun any more. The text is usually formatted ragged right, as this helps the reader to keep their place. In books in inflected languages, the inflected word is not separated from the cause of the inflection, so some lines can become extremely short. A story book text can look more like poetry than prose. Illustrations aid understanding rather than tell a new story.

Anthropomorphism is still popular, though a greater percentage of the books contain incidents from real life. There are often four archetypal characters: the hero, the friend, the mentor and the enemy. Sometimes the enemy may be a set of circumstances. The protagonist often has the support of the friend, though he or she is not actually able to help overcome the enemy. The mentor supplies the know-how – but usually disappears before they are really needed. The hero solves the problem on their own in the end.

Middle-graders

The reader is now confident and is usually aged between 7 and 11. Books for this reader differ mainly in content and length from those for teenagers, young adults and adults. They are a little shorter, averaging about 45,000 words. The content will be suitable for the age of the reader and reflect their interests. The friend, mentor and enemy often still exist. As in other novels, however, the plots are multilayered and contain a close viewpoint of the protagonist, setting them firmly in time and space. Most for this age group will stay with one point of view though longer novels may change point of view occasionally. The reader is familiar with story structure and expects it. They are becoming familiar with the characteristics of the novel, largely through reading novels such as these, so the text itself must guide them gently through its own conventions.

By this age, the reader seeks some adventure and some independence. The writer must do away with the parents. However, all texts must be politically correct, and even though Enid Blyton's *Famous Five* stories are still in print, the modern writer must avoid stories where children go on holiday without a responsible adult, where the girls do all the cooking and the boys do all the dirty work. Care has to be taken about who is actually a responsible adult. Tolkien's Gandalf is a trusted wizard and J. K. Rowling's Dumbledore is a revered headteacher. The mentor often comes in a fantasy setting for this age group. Fantasy gives a distance so that what might be questioned in real life is more permissible. Sadly, a special relationship between a male child and a male headteacher would almost certainly be misconstrued in the twenty-first century. In real-life stories the writer has to find a clever way of getting the parents out of the way. Jacqueline Wilson is a master of this and has created children with schizophrenic mothers, some in foster homes and others who give the slip to divorced parents. Judy Blume and Stephenie Meyer, originally writing for a slightly older age group, but now read by middle-graders, create worlds where the young people are in charge and adults seem powerless.

Teen

In the book-selling and publishing industries the terms 'Teen' and 'Young Adult' are often interchangeable, yet there are actually two distinct readers. The 'teen' reader here will be between 10 and 14, though, as with all of these categories, the type of text needed is determined more by the stage of development of the reader than by their actual age. Readers at the beginning of this stage will just be entering puberty. Towards the end of it, they will have at least entered Piaget's formal operations stage; therefore they will be beginning to understand symbols and being able to think in a more abstract way. They will be capable of functioning sexually.

This reader obviously requires a different content from the younger child. They are more experienced at reading, and are even learning to read more critically at school. The novels are becoming longer and the language more complex, with some texts containing multiple viewpoints and voices. Yet there are some young people who read less well. They need texts that are simple in their language and sophisticated in their content. Thus we have the Graphic Novels – novels that are told through pictures and speech bubbles, rather like in a comic, and what the book-selling and publishing trades, and educationalists call 'High-Lows' – sophisticated stories in simple language.

Adults are still well out of the way. It is perhaps a little easier to create that for this age group: they are genuinely more independent, making their way to and from school and other activities on their own, have considerable spending power, and at the end of this stage, are allowed to be left home alone and even to work for limited hours.

Young adults

These readers have completed puberty and may be sexually active. On average, they are aged between 14 and 17. Other physical changes continue. Nicola Morgan in *Blame My Brain* tells us how at this stage the brain grows massively but is also pruned back and as the potential for some skills is lost forever, others assert themselves. Young adults judge with their emotions as the reasoning part of their brain has not developed fully yet. Hormones and the chemicals melatonin and dopamine, in unusual amounts and appearing at the wrong time, play havoc. Young adults also face many pressures – exams, peer relationships and a world which may have become alien to them, where what had once been black and white is now shades of grey. They are nevertheless in many ways fully adult though clumsy in that state.

Books for them must include characters who resemble them. They need to be fast-paced and at the same time offer characters with whom the readers can engage emotionally. Usually, the growth of the protagonist is central to the plot and often happens in terms of the young person establishing their identity. Language, voice and register can be as sophisticated as in an adult novel. The voice is of the utmost importance and should be as one young adult talking to a slightly less experienced friend. As well as some very sophisticated texts, however, the Graphic Novels and High-Lows also still exist.

Often, the stories will push boundaries, reflecting precisely what the young adult does. The writer must be at once an adult with a duty of care and a player in the risk-taking game that is adolescence. Fantasy, Science Fiction and Science Fantasy provide the same objectivity here as the anthropomorphic texts do for the picture-book consumer. Here, though, the symbols are often of the complete workings of a society.

3. BACKGROUND AND CONTEXT

The shape of children's literature in the twenty-first century

Peter Hunt's *An Introduction to Children's Literature* gives a full discussion of the history of children's literature and thus helps us to understand why children's literature is as it is today. The child was first recognized as being different from the adult at the end of the eighteenth century. Children's literature at that time was written mainly for the Sunday Schools, which had two purposes: to teach reading and writing to the working classes and to teach a moral code founded on Christianity. Even today, literature written for children and young adults takes account of where the child is in their emotional and mental development and offers patterns by which they may make some sense of their world.

Hunt's historical survey of children's literature finds 'strong nostalgic/nature images; a sense of place or territory; egocentricity; testing and initiation; outsider/insider relationships; mutual respect between adults and children; closure; warmth/security – and food' (1991, 184). All of these elements are still present in texts written for children. If we look at the latest Harry Potter book, arguably a Young Adult novel, given the age of the main characters, then those elements are also still present in the Young Adult novel.

As we entered the twenty-first century, some changes took place. First of all, the price of print fell dramatically. In 1998, 30,000 words were considered too long for a Middle-Grade Novel. By 2000, 46,000 words were expected. It was suddenly much cheaper to produce a longer book. A few extraordinarily good longer novels were produced, in the 1990s such as Philip Pullman's *Northern Lights* and *The Subtle Knife.* We were all pleasantly surprised to see that young people can consume lengthy novels. All novels for that age group and above then became longer. Also, from 1980 onwards the technology existed to produce full-colour picture-books at a reasonable price. The preschooler was suddenly offered a much richer diet, though sadly that market is again in decline in 2007.

Secondly, we have to acknowledge The Harry Potter Effect. J. K. Rowling's novels contain many genres and they are rich in symbolism that explains the world to their readers. Because of them some reluctant readers have started to read. Writing for children has gained respectability. J. K. Rowling's success has lead many to believe that writing for children is easy. It has actually become even harder. It is no longer enough to write well and have a solid plot. One has to write better than J. K. (perhaps possible) and have a much more extraordinary plot (virtually impossible).

Thirdly, a new reader, the Young Adult, emerged at the turn of the century. In 1999, Ottakers decided to rename the 'Teen' books 'Young Adult', though the books remained mainly the same. American and Canadian bookshops later decided to shelve their Young Adult books away from the Children's section. Writers such as Melvin Burgess, Judy Blume and Holly Black grew wise to the possibilities and started producing ever more daring texts for older teenagers. Others, such as Kate Cann, Annie Jay and Meg Rosoff tried to be accurate in their portrayal of young adult characters. Some argue that previous generations simply read adult books. Publishers use this argument in their favour and market classics as J. D. Salinger's *The Catcher in the Rye* and Harper Lee's *To Kill a Mockingbird* as books for young adults. The whole genre started to expand and change in the late 1990s and still seeks to define itself up until the present day.

Perhaps most significant, though, is that the human need for story remains unchanged. Children in High School may watch as part of Social Education lessons episodes of popular soap operas and comedy series, in which characters of their own age figure, in order to work on solving problems. Most religious books are full of stories. Even those who prefer to read a newspaper and look at supposed facts do so in order to see the bigger picture and trivialize the problems at the shoe factory.

Stories work best for us when they have a shape and a satisfying outcome with some closure. Otherwise, we just have a series of events. Theories of story abound, and they are worth some scrutiny, particularly those of Robert McKee, Christopher Vogler, Joseph Campbell, Vladimir Propp and Andrew Melrose. Even the youngest child expects a story with a shape. Anticipating the form is part of the fun.

Simply put, at picture-book level, a story arc might look something like this:

Setting and inciting incident
Complications:

1. Oh no!
2. Oh dear, oh dear!
3. Now what do we do?

Crisis: Now we've really done it!
Climax: includes

- A high point: We can do this. We can get out of this mess.
- Rug gets pulled: Whoops! We got a bit too sure of ourselves then.
- Can we really do it? (Often a lack of confidence accompanied by determination that might equal bravery.)

Resolution: Ah, that's better. Now we're back to normal – almost.

For older readers, add a few more complications, a few more layers of plot and slightly stronger language. The stories that work best of all, however, are the ones that have skewed the theory slightly and have allowed the writer's intuition in. The writer's job, therefore is to know the theory and when to use it, and also when to do something a little – or even a lot – different.

4. THE WORKSHOP EXERCISES

Exercise 1: Getting the voice right

Writers usually agree that the voice must be consistent and has something to do with the writer's personality and personal writing style. However, even if voice is consistent, and the text is about child-hood, what is written might be for adults. The writer in that case is addressing another adult, using words that an adult would understand, who has had the growth and expects the reader to be at a similar degree of maturity. They speak adult to adult. The children's writer must speak to the child.

Children generally like to read about characters a little older than themselves. The voice is that of a slightly older friend recounting something that happened to someone like them. However, a first-person narrative rarely works for readers up to the age of 13. There is too much discrepancy between the fictionalized age of the writer and their literary skills. With a third-person narrative, the reader can experience the growth with the protagonist.

An exception is Jostein Gaarder's *Hello? Is Anybody There?* which is probably a Middle-Grade Novel.

> I heard the phone start ringing. Mika did too. He suddenly began shaking his head and trying to clear his ears.
> 'There's a horrid sound in my ears,' he exclaimed in panic.
> This made me laugh. 'It's just a telephone,' I told him. (1998, 37)

Gaarder addresses his young niece, Camilla, whose mother is expecting a baby any minute now. Mika is an alien who landed in his garden when he was Camilla's age. Gaarder tells us his own story, but in fact most of the narrative is a third-person account about Mika.

For this exercise, it is best to use one of your own memories from childhood. That saves you the struggle of finding content and reminds you of what it is like to be a child. If such memories are painful, then use a story you know well. Concentrate on that memory or one scene for a few minutes. What do you see? Hear? Can you smell anything? Is it hot or cold? Where are you? Is there anything touching you or that you can touch? Does anyone say anything to you? How are you feeling? What is making you feel that way?

Now write about the scene for 20 minutes. Don't worry too much about structure, though one may come in. Write about the central character – yourself or someone from a scene you have chosen – in the third person, remembering you are speaking to someone a little younger than the person in the scene. You may want to disguise yourself. If you were a blond-haired girl write about a red-headed boy. That helps to make the third person narrative seem more plausible. However, don't struggle with that too much. It is more important to portray accurately the scene you have just studied.

After 20 minutes, read your work. Honestly ask yourself if that is what a 6-, 7-, 8-year-old etc. would have seen. Did you remember that when you didn't have to bend all that much when you played 'house' under the dining table? Did you remember the smell of the furniture polish? What was it like without the adults around? Did you care? Was there a feeling that you had a big secret? Have you inadvertently spoken to an adult or made an adult observation about what you experienced? When any of those discrepancies have been ironed out, does the piece have an acceptable voice? I'm expecting it probably does.

This is a useful exercise to do before you start writing a whole story, though at that point you will probably choose a scene from the story. Nevertheless, references to your own memories will be useful.

Exercise 2: Less is more 1 – writing a picture-book text

This exercise should be conducted over about three weeks. You will need to keep the ideas at the front of your mind throughout the time.

Within the first week, look at as many picture-books as possible. If you can, observe how pre-school children and adults interact with the books. Ask yourself these questions: What are the story arcs like? How do the pictures and the texts work together? Just how complex is the language? Is there anything in the book just for adults? How is tension built? Is there a hiatus two-third to four-fifths of the way through? (Don't just take my word for it!) How does that work? How does the reader react to that? How does the repetition work? Do young children really like it? Why? What else do they like? Carry on with this if you can throughout the second and third week – and in fact throughout your picture-book-writing life.

In the second week, though you can start earlier if you wish, and you can certainly do this forever, look for a story line. It can be a very ordinary event or something extraordinarily fabulous. A good source of ideas can be what the French call 'chiens écrasés' (run over dogs, that is, articles about relatively trivial matters) in the local newspaper.

Many of the following examples might be familiar.

- A caterpillar gets rather hungry.
- A big cat comes to tea.
- A little bear cannot sleep.
- There aren't enough biscuits in the tin.
- A young boy meets a lot of monsters before supper.
- There's something funny going on under the bed.
- Jenny kicks her trainer into an electricity substation.

Week three is writing week. The brief is extremely tight. You are to produce your story in no less than 600 and no more than 1,000 words. There is to be much repetition. The language must be clear to a three-year-old. You must include a full story arc or at least a crescendo and a hiatus, followed by an upbeat, satisfying ending. You need to be aware of how pictures will integrate into the text, possibly telling another story. You may even like to make a dummy of how the text and pictures might work together.

You will find that you need both the precision skills of the poet and the insights of the general children's writer. Somewhere, though, the restraints are actually challenging your creativity. Examine your text. How does it compare with those other picture-books you have studied? You will probably have to edit this more than anything else you have ever written.

Exercise 3: Less is more 2 – a recipe for Chapter Books

Just as tight a brief exists for Chapter Books. Findings in educational research change, as do market trends. Therefore the demands change. What is a constant, however, is that the writer has half a dozen or so constraints to work with and those very constraints challenge their creativity. The lack of freedom forces the writer to make more of less.

Completing this exercise is a little like following a recipe. There is a list of constraints – the ingredients if you like, and then a set of instructions. This exercise should be completed over a week – thinking time plus 4 hours writing and editing. High-Lows face similar issues, and if you would rather write for an older age group, then adapt the ingredients accordingly.

The Ingredients

The book is 6,000 words in total.
It is divided into six equal chapters.
No sentences should have more than two clauses.
No paragraph should be more than ten lines long.
No word should be more that three syllables long.
Words of three syllables must make up less than 5 per cent of the text.
No fantasy.
If an everyday story, characters should be presented anthropomorphically.

The Method

1. Take a week to work out your plot and get to know your characters.
2. Outline a plot.
3. Some time before the writing session, decide which chapter you are going to write.
4. At the session, write the chapter freely to start with, though be aware of the constraints.
5. Edit concentrating on one constraint at a time.
6. Edit so that the piece flows.
7. Finally edit to see that rules have still been obeyed.
8. Add icing. The text still needs to sparkle and really must be of interest to the emergent reader.

Examples of Chapter Books are included within Oxford University Press' Reading Tree Scheme. Though these are carefully graded to suit reading levels, they are not a reading scheme as such and offer much choice to the readers. Egmont's Banana series is simply graded and offers even more free-dom of choice to the reader. At the beginning of this stage we have Bel Mooney's *Promise You Won't Be Cross*. Slightly more complex texts are Duncan Ball's 'Selby' stories, for example, *Selby Shattered*.

The Magic School Bus is a highly illustrated series by Joanna Cole and Bruce Degen. Note, though, that the pictures interact with the text in a different way from in picture-books.

As you compare your work with these and other Chapter Books you find, reflect a little on the process of producing this chapter. You may be surprised to find that having these constraints is actually liberating. You have fewer choices to make because you can't do absolutely just as you please.

Exercise 4: Character magic

Writers must know their characters really well. Children's writers must create characters as children see them. In this exercise, you will create characters and put them to the test.

You need to spend at least a week mulling over the answers to the questions below. Your characters can sit with you in the café and help you people watch. They may be in the back of the car as you drive. Don't worry if they even start talking to you.

The questions are aimed at helping you to create characters in a Middle-Grade Novel. Common sense will tell you how to adapt answers and even some of the questions to suit a different age group. However, if you have a plot and you are not sure which age group it fits, ask age-appropriate questions of the characters to find out who suits the plot best.

Answer these questions for two of the characters in your story. One of the characters should be the protagonist.

1. Name? Age?
2. Appearance? (Hair, eyes, height, weight, birthmarks?)
3. Attitude to appearance?
4. State of health?
5. Any disabilities?
6. Favourite colour, toy, activity at school?
7. What don't they like doing?
8. What do they do after school?
9. Who are their friends?
10. What are their parents' jobs?
11. Do their parents smoke or drink?
12. Which newspapers do the parents read?
13. Do your characters have a favourite weekday? Why?
14. Do they have a day they don't like? Why not?
15. Do they like television? What do they like?
16. What don't they like on television?
17. Do they like books? Which ones?
18. How do they spend the school holidays?
19. What is their home like?
20. Do they live in the town or the country? Or by the sea? In your home country or another one?
21. How do they get on with their parents?
22. Do they have brothers and sisters?
23. How do they get on with them?
24. Do they have a pet?
25. Does anyone in their family go to Church on Sunday?
26. Do they see their grandparents often?

27. What is the strongest part of their character?
28. The weakest?
29. What are they afraid of?
30. What motivates them?

After you have lived with your characters for a week, set aside an hour for writing a short scene that includes some dialogue between them. Have a writing buddy lined up to read what you have written. As you write, don't try to show the reader your answers to the above questions. Just write with that knowledge. Leave some time for editing. Before you reread your text, reread your answers to the questions. Ask yourself if your characters are true throughout the scene.

Next, show your buddy the scene. Don't ask for general comments. Ask them the questions you used to invent your two characters. Magically, it may seem, your buddy will get at least 70 per cent of the answers correct in spirit if not in detail. The truth is, if you have accurately 'shown' your characters, and taken the exercise seriously, it cannot fail.

Lee Weatherly's *Child X,* Judy Waite's *Eclipse,* Hilary McKay's *Indigo Star* and Geraldine McCauchrean's *The Kite Rider* contain finely drawn characters about whom we could easily answer the above questions though these writers do not give us those details explicitly.

Exercise 5: Which tense and person in a young adult narrative?

This is the one age group where it makes sense to use the first person. It brings the reader and the protagonists closer together and the literacy skills of the writer and the reader match convincingly. However, there is still the problem that the narrator has had the growth that the reader may wish to experience. Some writers use the present tense to combat this. However, sometimes the narrator is only in the position to tell their story because the story has had a good outcome, so the resolution is no surprise.

This exercise gives you the opportunity to experiment with person and tense. First, study the four passages below. You might find it beneficial to read more of each book, or if you cannot readily access them, substitute them with similar texts.

> The object was a metal javelin, with a barrel-shaped section at its waist, holes running up its side and fins on the tail. Chamus was bewildered. What was going on? They had been in the hangar. How could they suddenly have ended up in a street he had never seen before? It was as if they were all sharing some vivid, waking dream. Then Chamus realised what the javelin was; his heart leapt to his throat. It was a sireniser. (McGann, 2004, 13)

Possibly McGann has chosen a third person narrative because there is another strong viewpoint character. Also, Chamus would not be able to tell us his story unless his mission is successful.

> Rael, Howard's Chief Watcher, opens the passenger door and Howard gets out. Silver blond. Wire limbed. His amazing eyes deep-set and black as coals. He faces us and everything about him seems to buzz and crackle as if he is lit from the inside. Our mood ignites like a spark on tired ashes. I become elated, just looking at him. (Waite, 1999, 5)

The use of the first person and the present tense brings the reader right into the mind and feelings of Elinor, who has been kept by a religious cult for as long as she can remember. Still, however, as we read we have the sense that she is relating the events after they have happened. Logically, if she had remained with the cult, she would not be telling us her story.

An omnibus crowded with passengers sails past us, drawn by a team of magnificent horses. A cluster of ladies sits perched above the omnibus, their parasols open to shield them from the elements. A long strip of wood advertising Pears' soap ingeniously hides their ankles from view, for modesty's sake. It's an extraordinary sight and I can't help wishing we could just keep riding through London's streets. (Bray, 2003, 26)

Throughout this novel we have no idea what is going to happen next. The protagonist describes the scenes as they unfold. This provides immediacy and emotional engagement for the reader.

And Sam and Patrick looked at me like I said the greatest thing they ever heard. Because the song was that great and because we all really paid attention to it. Five minutes of a lifetime were truly spent and we felt young in a good way. I have since bought the record, and I would tell you what it is, but truthfully, it's not the same unless you're driving to your first real party. (Chbosky, 1999, 33)

Here, the narrator admits he has already had the growth. He is explaining how it occurred to someone just a little younger than himself.

Now rewrite each passage twice more so that you have three versions altogether: first person present tense, first person past and third person past. Ask yourself the following questions about each piece.

Does this help the reader to be engaged emotionally with the characters?
Is it logical? – Is this type of narrative plausible?
Do the person/tense combination help to provide tension and pace?
Why did the writer use their particular combination?
Is it the writer's combination the best for this story?
Do any of the other combinations work as well, better or less well?
Is there anything else you notice?

You could now try writing a scene from a story of your own. Which combination works the best? There is also a possible fourth combination, only rarely used, but it does make the reader feel as if they are watching a film: third person present tense. Try this with one of the pieces.

The first person is actually used quite frequently for readers in this age group. Even in a third-person narrative, the point of view is very close. Works where the person and the tense make an impact include Mark Haddon's *The Curious Incident on the Dog in the Night-Time*, Charlotte Kerner's *Blueprint Blaupause* and Emmanuelle Laborit's *Le Cri de la Mouette*.

5. FOLLOW UP

What next?

As writers we use two different mind-sets; some would argue the right and the left part of the brain. There is the instinctive mind, which seizes an idea that may seem to come from nowhere and then formulates a story that almost seems to write itself. Then there is the more logical voice, the inner critic, that asks constantly whether the story really works whether it has obeyed convention or daringly broken with it, whether what is written might be publishable and if so, where? Both of these exist for the children's writer, but perhaps behave a little differently. For the instinctive part, we must learn to play as children. What we create must fill us, and them, with awe and wonder. As we edit, we must remember what it is like to be a child. Our memories and imagination can help us there, and where they fail us, we may get a little more factual help from such experts as Jean Piaget and Laura Berk who give us practical insights into the psychology and development of children. Know your Piaget, know your Berk and avoid creating monsters that confuse your readers.

Where shall we find our stories? They are actually all around us and are there for the taking. Some say that there are just seven. This is not a problem. Think how many versions you know of Cinderella and think how many more you could create. Tell well-known stories from the point of view of a different character. Make the wolf the good guy and the pigs the criminals. Write it for an older age group. Bring it into the twenty-first century. Maybe Rose has to borrow her mother's hideous red anorak to do an errand in the pouring rain for her bed-ridden grandmother and has encounters with Gary Wolf and Tom Forest on the way home. Write the ordinary as the ordinary but make it wondrous. Yes, Kate's parents do actually divorce in the end, but she surprises herself by coping. Or make the ordinary fantastic. The explosion on the hillside is not caused by the build-ers but by the elves that live inside the mountain who are angry with the humans for destroying nature. There are actually millions of stories, even if they are only versions of the original seven, just waiting to be told. If you can't see them clearly just yet, try the Bible or Shakespeare. No wonder we are invited to take them with us to a desert island. They contain enough stories for a lifetime or two. You can always tell one story several different ways – and if you are writing for children you have the advantage of being able to also write for five separate age groups.

Always use your two great tools of imagination and memory when attempting to make your scene fit an age group. Then write with the senses. Don't try to be clever with words. Just write it as you see it, hear it, feel it, in both senses, smell it and think it . . . bearing in mind that you are only 10 and according to your own memory and imagination, and what Berk and Piaget have told you, at 10, it's like this. Using the senses always leads to good writing. In addition, if you are writing for children, it will help you create characters as they should be and you will speak with an appropriate voice to your reader.

Most writers are usually also readers. They often come to writing from a love of reading. Continuing with reading will enhance your writing. So read as many children's books as you can. A subscription to *Books for Keeps* or a glance at their website or *Carousel* will give you some informa-tion about what is being published. Also useful, *Cool Reads* is a website about books for children reviewed by children. You will probably start reading differently as reading becomes a tool to enhance your writing. A disadvantage is that as you read a voice constantly comments and asks questions: 'This is really good use of the third person.' Or 'This is working really well. How are they doing that?' However, the advantage of the jabbering voice is that you can admire a piece that you might not normally enjoy, and enjoy the process of analysing a piece which you neither admire nor enjoy. As you write, influenced by what you have observed, your own writing almost becomes a conversa-tion with that of other writers. You may want to take that a step further, and actually form a critique group where you share your work with other writers. It is important, though, that you work with those who write for children, and preferably for the same age group. As you edit others' work your editing skills improve and you gradually become your own best editor.

As you become aware of which is your favoured age group, try to find out more about those children. Volunteer to work at a local school, though be prepared to supply public liability insurance and have all sorts of checks made about your character and your criminal record. Simply keeping your eyes open while you are out and about will also help, as will watching children's television and television which children enjoy.

Find out what other writers, publishers and booksellers are doing. A writer's life is usually part solitude, part networking and part ordinary day job – which, incidentally, is a rich source of material. There are several organizations that may be of interest to the children's writer – SCBWI,

CWIG, Wordpool, Nibweb and Write4Kids. All of these will help you to network – often without having to leave your desk.

The essential message is to keep writing, keep reading and keep the conversation going. Above all, though, remember the child.

WORKS CITED

Picture-books

Carl, Eric. *The Very Hungry Caterpillar.* London: Puffin, 1994.
Daly, Niki. *Ruby Sings the Blues.* New York: Bloomsbury, 2007.
Donaldson, Julia. *The Gruffalo.* London: Macmillan Children's, 2000.
Kerr, Judith. *The Tiger Who Came to Tea.* London: Collins, 1992.
Lewis, Paeony. *No More Biscuits.* Frome: The Chicken House, 2006.
Manning, Mick. *What's Under the Bed?* New York: Franklin Watts, 2004.
Sendak, Maurice. *Where the Wild Things Are.* 1967. New York: Harper Collins, 1998.
Waddell, Martin. *Can't You Sleep, Little Bear?* Boston: Candlewick, 2002.

Chapter Books

Ball, Duncan. *Selby Shattered.* Pymble: Harper Collins, 2006.
Cole, Joanne and Bruce Degen. *The Magic School Bus Lost in the Solar System.* New York: Scholastic, 1992.
Mooney, Bel. *Promise You Won't Be Cross.* London: Egmont, 2004.

Middle-grade novels

Gaarder, Jostein. *Hello? Is Anybody There?* 1996. Trans. James Anderson. New York: Farrar, Straus and Giroux, 1998.
McCaughrean, Geraldine. *The Kite Rider.* New York: HarperTeen, 2003.
McKay, Hilary. *Indigo's Star.* New York: Aladin, 2003.
Waite, Judy. *Eclipse.* London: Scholastic, 1999.
Weatherly, Lee. *Child X.* London: Random House, 2003.

Young adult novels

Black, Holly. *Tithe: a Modern Faerie Tale.* New York: Simon Pulse, 2004.
Blume, Judy. *Here's to You, Rachel Robinson.* Basingstoke: Macmillan Children's Books, 1994.
Bray, Libba. *A Great and Terrible Beauty.* New York: Simon and Schuster, 2003.
Burgess, Melvin. *Doing It.* 2003. London: Penguin, 2004.
Cann, Kate. *Breaking Up.* London: Live Wire, 2001.
Chbosky, Stephen. *The Perks of Being a Wallflower.* New York: Simon and Schuster, 1999.
Haddon, Mark. *The Curious Incident of the Dog in the Night-Time.* London: Red Fox Definitions, 2003.
Jay, Annie. *À la Poursuite d'Olympe.* Paris: Hachette, 2003.
Kerner, Charlotte. *Blueprint Blaupause.* Berlin: Beltz & Gelberg, 1999.
Laborit, Emmanuelle. *Le Cri de la Mouette,* 1993. Paris: Robert Laffont, 2003.
Lee, Harper. *To Kill a Mockingbird.* 1960. New York: Penguin, 2002.

McGann, Oisín. *The Gods and Their Machines.* Dublin: O'Brien, 2004.

Pullman, Philip. *Northern Lights.*1995. London: Scholastic, 1996.

—. *The Subtle Knife.* 1997. London: Scholastic, 1998.

Rosoff, Meg. *Just in Case.* New York: Wendy Lamb, 2006.

Salinger, Jerome David. *The Catcher in the Rye.* 1951. New York: Penguin, 1994.

Suzuma, Tabitha. *A Note of Madness.* London: The Bodley Head, 2006.

Secondary texts

Berk, Laura. *Child Development.* 17th edn. Illinois: Allyn and Bacon, 2003.

Campbell, Joseph. *The Hero with a Thousand Faces.* London: Harper, 1993.

Hunt, Peter. *An Introduction to Children's Literature.* Oxford: OUP, 1994.

Inhelder, Bärbel, and Jean Piaget. *The Growth of Logical Thinking.* London: Routledge & Kegan Paul, 1974.

McKee, Robert. *Story.* London: Methuen, 1999.

Melrose, Andrew. *Write for Children.* London: Routledge Falmer, 2002.

Morgan, Nicola. *Blame My Brain.* London: Walker Books, 2005.

Phillips, John L. *Piaget's Theory: A Primer.* San Francisco: W.H. Freeman, 1981.

Propp, Vladimir. *Morphology of the Folk Tale.* Trans. Laurence Scott. 2nd edn. Ed. Louis A. Wagner. Austin: Texas UP, 1968.

Vogler, Christopher. *The Writer's Journey.* London: Pan Macmillan, 1996.

Useful websites

Books for Keeps. www.booksforkeeps.co.uk/

Carousel. www.carouselguide.co.uk

Cool Reads. www.cool-reads.co.uk/

CWIG. www.societyofauthors.net/soa/page_id.php4?pid=122&sid=14&urlsection=Subsidiary+Groups

NibWeb. www.nibweb.co.uk/

SCBWI. www.scbwi.org/, www.britishscbwi.org/

Wordpool. www.wordpool.co.uk/

Write4Children. www.write4kids.com/

PART II
ACROSS THE WORKSHOPS

Chapter 10

Structure, Style and Theme

Adrianne Finlay

1. WELCOME TO THE WORKSHOP

This chapter on working across workshops proceeds from a few guiding principles. First, generic boundaries are more fluid than we might initially suppose. Conventions are only conventions. That is, basing our judgement on certain literary characteristics, we tacitly agree to call a piece of writing 'poetry', another piece 'short fiction', still another 'creative non-fiction'. While useful, these conventions need not keep us from exploring in-between, hybrid genres like prose poetry, flash fiction or concise literary non-fiction. In fact, some wonderful creative writing has being written in these genres in recent years, and as a writer you would be served well to be at least passably acquainted with them.

Second, if creative writing makes the world strange again, allowing us to see and experience it anew, then crossing genres does the same important service for literature, allowing us to see and experience (and write) it anew. Unless we are able to write (and see and imagine and experience) beyond the constraints of genre, we run the risk of remaining slavish to convention, and slaves to literary convention only end up composing tired, formulaic work. Our goal, then, in crossing genres is to compose lively, original work.

Finally, working across workshops and crossing genres will improve your writing *within* specific genres. That is, you need not expect to come away from this chapter with polished pieces of cross-genre writing ready for publication, though that is not entirely out of the question. Rather, this chapter will emphasize once more the importance of writing as a process, which can certainly sometimes be frustrating, but will also always be exciting. What you glean from this chapter depends on the care and passion you invest in crossing genres and the belief that writing as a process in this way can (and will) indeed produce great literature. In other words, while our eyes are on the prize of a potentially publishable literary *product*, it must be taken on principle that the only way to reach that goal is to focus our energies on the *process* of writing.

The focus in this section on working *across* workshops may seem to prevent any fruitful discussion of structure, style and theme. After all, hybrid genres tend to avoid the easy classification of such elements. Nevertheless, looking at the ways published writers have crossed genres successfully will offer some useful generalizations from which to proceed. And while the lessons in this chapter will translate well into any genre you happen to be writing in, we will concentrate on shorter, mostly lyrical forms because they tend to make good use of the space between genres.

Crossing genres can be a daunting literary task. When we write *within* specific genres, not only do we have most of the literary canon to offer us models of good writing – hundreds of years of novels, short stories, lyric poetry, essays – but we feel that what we are doing, because there is a long and esteemed tradition behind us, is worthwhile. There are many techniques for overcoming the fear of exploring new, possibly scary ways of thinking and writing – meditating, keeping a dream journal, free writing – but we are going to approach the endeavour pragmatically and contextually. That is, you will be shown what it takes for a writer to cross genres and then what to do with your writing once you have written it. You will also be offered a necessarily brief introduction to the history of crossing genres in the context of structure, style and theme by looking at excerpts from samples of published hybrid-forms. And finally you will find some useful writing exercises and suggestions for future reading. In the end, you will emerge from this workshop with a fuller understanding of the possibilities inherent in crossing genres and a more concrete way of working across workshops yourself.

2. WRITERS AND READERS

In *The Situation of Poetry*, Robert Pinsky says 'the discursive aspect of poetry may come down to a call for "the prose virtues"', by which he means 'Clarity, Flexibility, Efficiency, Cohesiveness'. He asks, 'What happens to poetry when it gets too far from prose, and the prose virtues?' complaining that 'contemporary poetry is often interior, submerged, free-playing, elusive, more fresh than earnest, more eager to surprise than to tell.' The key words here are 'earnest' and 'to tell' because Pinsky, refuting the 'show don't tell' mantra, is more interested in literature that compels readers and writers to have an honest dialogue than revelling in poetic diction or lingering overlong on poetic images. 'When poetry gets too far from prose,' he concludes, 'it may be in danger of choking itself on a thick, rich handful of words.' The same is true when writers cross genres.[1]

Pinsky's call for poetry that is as clear, flexible, efficient and cohesive as prose is a good place to start as you begin working across workshops yourself. Just because you are trying to write in lively and original ways that blend the techniques of the poet, fiction writer and essayist does not mean that you should avoid guiding your reader towards a clear understanding of what you intend to communicate. In other words, writing in hybrid genres does not give the writer licence to be vague or overly abstract. This belief is a common one among beginning writers who mistake daring for impenetrability, and boldness for confusion. Cross-genre writers are, indeed, daring. They dare to challenge long-held notions of what literature is and can be. This chapter, then, challenges you to be daring in your writing, but it also challenges you to be just as clear as when you are writing within specific genres.

But what are you to *do* with your writing once you have begun composing in these hybrid genres? It may be well and good to be a daring writer, but what of the practical question of publication? Lucky for the literary daring among us, never before in the history of literature has the climate for challenging work been as favourable. While many critics lament the decline in contemporary publishing – citing the supposed paucity of serious literary presses and magazines – the truth of the matter is that there are more venues for challenging writing (cross-genre work included) than ever before. Journals such as *Quick Fiction, Brevity: A Journal for Concise Literary Nonfiction* and *Sentence*, to name only a few, not only embrace such writing, but they make publishing and promoting it a vital part of their missions.

3. BACKGROUND AND CONTEXT

But what exactly do we mean by 'crossing genres' in the first place? Is it simply 'poetic prose' or 'prosaic poetry'? In the context of this workshop, crossing genres refers to the writing of literature that uses to good effect the conventions of multiple genres at once, such that it becomes impossible to classify the writing solely as poetry, short fiction, or creative non-fiction. For the sake of discussion, we will offer prose poetry, flash fiction, and concise literary non-fiction as representative of the possibilities of crossing genres.

Structure and crossing genre

Crossing genres suggests a lack of structure, but nothing could be further from the truth. Prose poetry, flash fiction and other hybrid genres rely heavily on a solid structure. The difference between these genres and others is the lack of a clear definition of what that structure will most likely be in the end. When attempting to explain structure, writers and teachers of writing often resort to architectural metaphors – a not entirely inappropriate tack – but good cross-genre writing rarely reminds you of a well-designed building. Perhaps a better way to think of structure in this context is to evoke something more natural, more organic in its design. To borrow a phrase from the great environmentalist Aldo Leopold, writers should 'think like a mountain'.

Thinking (and writing) like a mountain requires you to heed the subterranean, tap into great tectonic tensions below the surface, and allow the structure of your writing to emerge naturally. Such a process may feel messy and unwieldy at first, but when the energy of a mountain is harnessed and directed towards your writing, powerful literature can emerge.

Consider the prose poem, a hybrid genre whose structure relies on the writer to think like a mountain. The literal, physical structure of the prose poem (as it is most often published) becomes obvious on the page, appearing as a block of justified text. In justified text, all the lines of a paragraph, excepting the final line, are made the same length by the adjustment of spacing between words. Most word-processing software today allows you to compose your writing in justified text. Just as punctuation and proper grammar are conventions of standard English, so justified text is a convention of the genre of prose poetry. Beyond its un-mountainlike appearance on the page, the internal structure of the prose poem, as it has evolved over the past 150 years from the French Symbolists to today, develops organically, rising from a poetic subconscious dream-world in which unlikely, often surreal images and associations tumble out one after the other, mimicking the very process of a mind thinking. This may all sound very abstract and difficult to understand, but take, for instance, Charles Baudelaire's classic 'Be Drunk' from his 1869 collection *Petits poèmes en prose* – in English, *Little Prose Poems* – which ends

> And if sometimes, on the steps of a palace or the green grass of a ditch, in the mournful solitude of your room, you wake again, drunkenness already diminishing or gone, ask the wind, the wave, the star, the bird, the clock, everything that is flying, everything that is groaning, everything that is rolling, everything that is singing, everything that is speaking . . . ask what time it is and wind, wave, star, bird, clock will answer you: 'It is time to be drunk! So as not to be the martyred slaves of time, be drunk, be continually drunk! On wine, on poetry or on virtue as you wish.'[2]

Baudelaire is not actually advocating continual drunkenness – or perhaps he is doing that as well, but that is a story for his biographers. Rather, he is demonstrating a kind of metaphorically drunken poetic wildness that is best captured in the prose poem. Notice the tumbling forth of vivid imagery.

Notice the odd but apt speaking of 'wind, wave, star, bird, clock'. Note, too, that a good prose poem like this bears the traces of its own composition process, as Baudelaire has accomplished here, drunk on his own writing.

Style and crossing genre

Baudelaire is a good example of a writer who dared to cross genres and did so successfully. Writers and critics today point to him as an early visionary in this respect. His loose style is reflected in both the structure and the style of his prose poems. By loose style, I refer here to what the ancient Greeks called a 'running style', which appears to follow the mind in the process of thinking, seeming to go on and on and on. Notice in 'Be Drunk' Baudelaire's syntactic reliance on the comma, his going on and on and on, while he is simultaneous clear, efficient, flexible and cohesive. In his book *Analyzing Prose*, Rhetorician Richard Lanham says

> To imitate thus the mind in real-time interaction with the world is to write in some form of running style. The serial syntax registers the first thing first and then the second thing, simple chronological sequence always calling the tune and beating the tempo. Such syntax models the mind in the act of coping with the world. The coping is all small-scale, minute-to-minute tactics, not seasonal grand strategies. There is no time to reflect on grand strategy; the reader goes on patrol with the writer, sharing immediate dangers and present perplexities. Things happen as they want to, not as we would have them. Circumstances call the tune.[3]

Indeed, the specific circumstances of writers in the world – what they think, feel, see, hear, smell, taste – often determine the style and call the tune when crossing genres. Baudelaire's running style has been mimicked by other writers of prose poems to great effect, but let us look at a contemporary concise literary essay for a useful model of a different (but not entirely unrelated) style.

J. D. Schraffenberger's essay 'Full Gospel', which originally appeared in *Brevity: A Journal of Concise Literary Nonfiction* and was reprinted in *The Best Creative Nonfiction, Vol. 1*, uses both poetic and fictive styles and techniques. In fact, Schraffenberger, though known mostly as a poet, has published in multiple genres. In his introduction to 'Full Gospel', he says, 'A poem is more likely to take a snapshot of the world, but non-fiction keeps the camera rolling, resists the urge to say Cut! . . . No other literary form, for my money, allows you to create a world that comes so close to the one we know.' His desire to create such a world suggests two things: that literature is a world unto itself, and that this created literary world can be more or less faithful to our own reality. Schraffenberger begins 'Full Gospel' in a terse, staccato style, establishing a world much like the one we know by showing us what he sees:

> What I see as a child on my way to church with my grandparents: dead barns, CHEW MAIL POUCH TOBACCO faded into the gray wood. Also: Southern Indiana hills, knobs, knolls, ancient ripples where glaciers halted at the Ohio. What I see at my grandparents' church: an Appalachian diaspora. Millions fled the mountains mid-century during the so-called Great Migration, headed north – to Cincinnati, Pittsburgh, Detroit, and Chicago, big industrial Midwest cities holding out the promise of employment.

Notice the heavy use of colons, as opposed to Baudelaire's heavy use of commas. Each represents a stylistic choice that is meant to guide the reader into the writer's consciousness. 'Full Gospel' shifts from this style to a looser one, ending:

> When my cousin David dies, we try to make each other laugh. It's our way of dealing with the death of someone so young. My aunt takes pills, my uncle starts drinking again, my mother makes food nobody eats.

And there at the funeral home, I say it [a family joke], my father and brothers and me gathered in a small circle in the corner: *Jesus. Thank you, Jesus.* Jonathan, who has been released from the [mental] hospital to attend the funeral, laughs loud and can't stop, a frenzied laughter, worried laughter, his eyes frightened and begging me. He clenches his fists, pounds his thighs.

When the others look at us, huddled in our safe corner, I put my hand on Jonathan's shoulder, think *I'm sorry*, say *Shh*, think, *David, this isn't happiness, I swear*, say *It's okay*, think *These are our tears.*[4]

The essay's style in this final paragraph loosens to reflect the emotional tension in the narrative, marked again by Baudelaire's commas and the tumbling forth of images and thoughts, thus letting the reader in on the mind of the writer as he is thinking and writing. If this essay were composed using a more traditional, perhaps academic essayistic style, such an effect could not have been achieved. In fact, this movement into a lyrical style at the end of a narrative will be familiar to readers of contemporary short literature as something akin to James Joyce's use of literary epiphany in his own fiction.

Theme and crossing genre

Let us turn now to flash fiction, which (it cannot be stressed too much) is more than simply a piece of a larger whole, and more also than simply a short story consisting of fewer words. As Lia Purpura argues in her instructive essay 'On Miniatures':

The miniature is unto itself. It is not a mere part of a whole, like a fetish or an excerpt. Certainly many smaller, component parts can make up an epic – I'm thinking of paintings like Bosch's *Garden of Earthly Delights*; Bruegl's *Childrens' Games*, and of Alexander Calder's *Circus* in which all the individual parts are certainly compelling. But the miniature begins and ends in itself. One rank, Boschian egg-shaped, half-human, half-bird hacking at another with a sword is thrilling, but it is not a whole painting unto itself. It's a snippet.[5]

Our goal, then, as writers of flash fiction is to compose something that is not a snippet but something that stands completely on its own. The Albanian writer Ismail Kadaré's 'Before the Bath', which first appeared translated into English by Peter Constantine in the journal *Fiction* and was later reprinted in *Flash Fiction Forward: 80 Very Short Stories*, is a good example of flash fiction that stands on its own. What's more, it is also a good example of cross-genre writing. Neither its structure nor its style betrays the genre. Its repetitive narrative and lyrical style could well confound our attempts to classify it.

At only 843 words, 'Before the Bath' is certainly extremely short, but because the story recounts only the last 22 seconds of the life of Agamemnon (the mytho-historical Greek commander in the Trojan War), time seems to slow down. In Kadaré's version of the story, when Agamemnon returned from the war, he was murdered in a bath by his wife Clymenestra. In the first paragraph, the entire chronology of the story is told: Agamemnon gets in the tub, his wife throws a fabric over him and she murders him with an axe. The next two paragraphs recount the story four more times, each time beginning 'He found himself outside the tub again.' Kadaré's lyrical style then culminates in a very matter-of-fact ending, the opposite movement of a literary epiphany:

He found himself outside the tub again, moving towards her, as he had a million times before, experiencing with different rhythms this final fragment, these last twenty-two seconds of his life. This was the hell of Agamemnon of the House of Atreus, murdered by his wife on the first day of his return from the Plains of Troy, at thirteen hundred hours and twenty minutes, March 31, in the year eleven hundred and ninety-nine before our era.[6]

Kadaré makes brilliant use of both structure and style in crossing and blending genres and in so doing communicates one of the major themes of 'Before the Bath'. That is, the recursive structure of Agamemnon's being murdered 'a million times before', and the shift from a lyrical to an expository mode combine to make clear Kadaré's point about the subjectivity of time. In many ways, Kadaré is also commenting on literature itself, specifically cross-genre writing like his own, which slows time down, rewinds, and repeats with 'different rhythms'. It may be hard to believe that a short piece of writing like this can do so much, but such is the potential in flash fiction. Such is the potential, too, that you have as you attempt to cross genres yourself.

4. THE WORKSHOP EXERCISES

What follows are a series of exercises, each designed to help you develop ideas about how to use structure, style and theme in your writing. Some may give you the opportunity to generate new work and new ideas for your writing. You may come up with a plot, a character or a conceit that you become interested in and want to pursue further. You might write a line that you fall in love with, or create an image that will fit nicely into a piece on that you are already working. Other exercises are designed to give you a specific, guided objective for the purpose of putting you in the position to think critically and specifically about your writing. These exercises are not meant necessarily to give you a finished piece at the end (although in no way do they preclude the possibility). Instead, you should view the following prompts as an opportunity to focus hard on one aspect of your process and why you write the way you do, as well as to consider the ways you can develop or alter how you write and thus better control the impact of your poetry, prose or art. With various tactics, styles and forms at your fingertips, you will have the freedom to define your own method while also moving fluidly from one mode to the next.

These exercises are divided into three categories that reflect the chapter subjects: structure, style and theme. They do not concentrate on one genre, but instead are designed to allow the writer a means of writing across the genres. In each exercise you will find a brief introduction on the purpose of the exercise, followed by a description of the process and then some questions that will guide your consideration of the goals achieved.

Exercise 1: Structure

When talking about structure, we are inevitably led to more fundamental questions: What is a story? What is a poem? What does creative non-fiction look like? What is a prose poem supposed to be, or flash fiction, or a lyrical essay? There are no universal answers to these questions because the borders that delineate these structures are fluid at best, and each genre tends to incorporate elements from other genres. Often when we think about stories, we think about a series of events, of rising action that builds to a climax of some kind. When we consider poetry, structure might mean a sonnet, a villanelle or blank verse. Essays, as we learn in high school, always seem to require outlines that include a thesis statement, a series of examples and then a conclusion. That said, we may also reverse expected order in stories, organize an essay by images, compose a poem that has no rhyme or meter, and thus create something vivid, fresh and moving. The following exercises are designed not only to help you think critically about structure, but also to rethink what structure means in a given piece of writing.

Exercise 1.1

This exercise uses 'found' stories, which is a way of seeking a subject, a plot, an image or a theme from the world around us. It then asks you to consider how structure informs the content of the narrative or imagery that you have created.

1. Find a story in the world around you. It could be something that happened to you last week, something that happened to a friend of yours or a headline in the news (this last is best if it is about a person, and one who is not famous). This story might be about your friend who had to deal with a co-worker's temper tantrum, or a story in the newspaper about a man who was saved from choking on a french fry by the jolt of a car accident.
2. Write this story in three ways: a prose poem, a concise literary essay and a flash fiction.
3. When you have finished, answer the following questions:

    a. In what ways did the content of the story change given the different genres you have written it in?
    b. Did the theme of your story change across genres?
    c. In which genre did you feel most comfortable? Why?
    d. In which did you feel least comfortable? Why?
    e. How did the style of your writing change when you were writing in the different genres? What do you think is the cause of this change?

Exercise 1.2

For this exercise, you will need to be a little sneaky.

1. Eavesdrop on a conversation. You could sit in a coffee shop, pay attention while waiting for the bus or find a bench in a park.
2. Transcribe as much of this conversation as you can. You will have to write quickly, or use short hand. Try not to think too much about what you are writing, just get it down as rapidly and accurately as possible.
3. Consider your end result and answer the following questions:

    a. What do you think you have created in this exercise? Does it look like a poem to you? In what ways is it a story?
    b. Is there a beginning, middle and end in your piece? Is it linear, or does it jump around sporadically and disjointedly? What is the narrative?
    c. Is the language lyrical? How would you characterize the style of the piece?

The resulting text of this exercise should look both chaotic and structured at the same time. When people interact and have conversations, they are usually telling a story or communicating an idea to someone else. However, when we write, we are writing a translation of events and transcribing our perceptions of how things happen and how we convey information. A transcribed conversation does not look like dialogue in a story, nor does a transcribed spoken story look much like the way we write stories. This exercise is one of the ways we can write without thinking about what we are writing or why. Perhaps this was Baudelaire's method when writing 'Be Drunk'. When we scribble down an overheard conversation, we can determine later what the structure is, and only then what the structure should be.

Exercise 2: Style

You may feel that you have a sense of the style of your writing. Consider, however, when you might want to employ a different style to convey tone and content. Occasionally you may wish to soar away with your reader into complex and lyrical prose. At other times, it is prudent to go easy, write clearly and keep it simple. If at some time you are describing a fast rushing river, you might want your writing style to be just that – fast and rushing. If in a story you have a particularly depressed man putting on his shoes to go to a job that he hates, you might want slow, plodding language to illustrate this action. If, when he gets to work, a file cabinet should fall on him, your language could become an abrupt series of short clipped phrases. The style and language that you choose can indicate shifts in the emotion or action of your piece, and while you may feel tied to your stylistic tendencies, it is important to be aware of the impact style can have on content, and the different tactics at your disposal.

Exercise 2.1

I have a novelist friend who claims that all writers can ultimately be relegated into two categories of stylist – the Hemmingway writer and the Faulkner writer. Hemmingway is known for his sparse, clean, declarative sentences, for his economy and restraint. Faulkner's style could be considered more florid and experimental, a stream-of-consciousness prose with great attention to word choice and language. Whether it is true that we all tend towards one style or another can be debated. For the purpose of this exercise, consider what you know of the style of each author and do the following:

1. Write a description of a person (if you like, this person can be doing something, like baking a cake, or feeling something, like anticipation), approximately two hundred words in length, using sentences no longer than five words each. Consider that a sentence could consist of only two words: 'He died', or 'She stopped.'
2. Write a description of the same person, approximately two hundred words in length, that takes the form of one long sentence. Try not to depend too much on the use of 'and', or 'but', which in their own way can act as endings to a sentence because they can join two independent clauses. Let your mind continuously make connections that keep your sentence going without relying on coordinating conjunctions.

Once you've written your two pieces, consider how the different techniques changed your writing and your language. How did the different styles actually change the reader's impression of who this person is that you are describing? In what ways does the rhythm and the pace of the writing change in each piece? How did your writing process change? In one piece did you feel more free to scribble onto the page whatever came to mind, or did you feel frustrated and stifled? Did one more than the other allow you to create a better sense of character or scene? Did one lead you more readily into a story? More readily into poetic language? Take this opportunity to study a piece of writing you have already written. Think of some word that describes what you see as your own style. It could be sparse, flowing, clipped, flowery, precise, sharp or any other adjective that comes to mind.

Exercise 2.2

This exercise will give you an opportunity to consider how style and language can communicate much more than we initially expect. For instance, the author of a poem or a character in a story can describe a flower using words like bright, velvety, fragrant and delicate. Alternatively, the flower could be described as pungent, festering, garish and drooping. The second example suggests someone who does not like puppies very much. Our feelings on puppies aside, the following steps are designed to reveal how what might appear to be a straightforward description is not at all straightforward.

1. Go outside and select an object in nature. Describe that item (a tree, a bush, fallen leaves, rocks on the ground, flowers, grasses. Preferably not something animate like a bird or a squirrel. It should be something you can sit and contemplate).

2. Write about a paragraph describing your object. Try simply to describe the item in front of you. Use only your five senses: sight, sound, smell, taste, and touch. Do not describe, for instance, how the tree makes you feel or of what event in your life that bush reminds you. Rely instead on perception and metaphor. Describe the tree, and nothing but the tree.

3. Once you have your paragraph written, rewrite it, only this time write the description from the perspective of a man who has just murdered his wife. Do not mention the man, the wife or the murder. As before, describe only the tree, but from the point of view of the wife-murderer. Other point-of-view options might include:

    a. someone who is extremely hungry
    b. a physicist
    c. someone who just finished a marathon
    d. a pregnant woman
    e. someone recently in love
    f. someone who just found out their spouse is divorcing them
    g. someone who is depressed
    h. someone who feels alienated

The hungry person might describe the tree branch as reaching, withered and aching. The physicist might see fallen leaves in terms of an equation, or of relativity. The pregnant woman might see a cloud as something bursting with possibility, or something travelling far over the horizon to a place unknown. Even something as mundane as the description of leaves, when in a piece of writing, is laden with signifiers, themes and stylistic manoeuvrings.

Exercise 3: Theme

It would be, if not impossible, at least a mistake to venture forth on a piece of writing with no other foundation for it than a theme. To start with a theme would be to render your writing heavy-handed and clumsy. It is by far better to start with a subject, a plot, a character, even a beautifully written line. We have to trust, as writers, that a theme will emerge organically. The human mind is wired this way, and amazing in its capacity to make connections, create narratives, marry images to ideas and ideas to fundamental human truths. Life is so often made up of random events to which we affix meaning. We see an angry motorist on the road and think about what made him so angry. We wonder how he can tolerate himself in such a constant state of rage. We consider his fatal flaw, that he will die an early death as the result of his high blood pressure, or maybe of a car accident. Even inanimate objects become the focus of our need to make stories. We see a lamp in an antique store and cannot help but imagine whose home it used to be in, the person who once owned it. Was it a wedding present? Was it saved up for before purchase, or did the buyer have loads of cash and buy it to match his Persian rugs and designer furniture? Was it cherished? How did it come to be shuttled in a back room with countless other storied objects? The stories we create inevitably connect to a deeper fundamental meaning, a universal truth of human existence. A story, poem or essay without this connection is, in the end, only a series of words on a page. William Faulkner called it in his Nobel acceptance speech, 'the old verities and truths of the heart . . . lacking which any story is ephemeral and doomed.' Once you have written a draft of any piece, focus hard on it and think about what the meaning is behind what you have written or what the story is that you are really telling. What universal truth are you seeking to capture through your imagery, plot, character or tension? What is it that makes your writing worth reading? Remember that your writing should evoke an inner core of meaning rather than blurt out what the 'message' is. Once you have found your theme, rework your writing to better reflect that theme. Consider the relationships and analogies that your theme brings to mind, and insert them into your writing.

Exercise 3.1

The following exercise is as much about simile and metaphor as it is about theme, which is not by accident. For how, after all, does the author convey theme if not through devices like style, metaphor and simile? If your writing is exploring the violent chaos of nature and the futility of man's struggle against it, you might linger on a beloved pet cat killing a little songbird, or the image of a car decaying and rusting in the woods; if on the hidden depths of man's consciousness, perhaps you would focus on a dark, murky swamp or the contrast of a shadow cast through the window of a home. For this exercise, follow these steps:

1. Get a piece of fruit. It could be an apple, pear, banana, what have you. It is important for this exercise that the fruit be in front of you as you write. Without the physical presence of the fruit, you will not have the concrete detail that you will need to make this exercise work.

2. Address the following questions about your fruit, while paying particular attention to the actual attributes of your fruit and trying to say only what is so. Though the connections may be disparate, try not to exaggerate or inflate. Use exact language about your fruit to evoke the ideas below. Let the fruit work for you, and allow yourself to make connections that might not otherwise occur to you. Most of all, be honest – your connections need not be brilliant, but all writing should feel like truth. Precision, along with imagination, will make a powerful tool towards writing that resonates with your audience:

   a. How is your fruit like a rainy day?
   b. How is your fruit like someone dying?
   c. How is your fruit like forgetting something?
   d. How is your fruit like a word?
   e. How is your fruit like a poem?
   f. How is your fruit like an empty corner?
   g. Finally, make your own connection. For example: The apple is like a _____.

Exercise 3.2

There are writers who have suggested that there are only three basic themes in the world: love, death and birth. Though this may at first seem limited or reductive, consider the work of some of the great writers that we have continued to read and study for generations: Melville, Wharton, Austen, Shakespeare, Faulkner, Woolf. Also consider the ways in which these themes can be interpreted in a myriad of ways. Death could mean literal death, as well as spiritual death. It may mean loss, change or crisis. Birth could mean redemption, renewal or beginning. There are many possibilities within the framework of these three ideas. The goal of this next exercise is to examine the ways your writing can work towards your theme, and the various ways you can express your theme without being unsubtle or ham-handed.

1. Consider one of the three themes discussed: love, death, birth. Choose one.
2. Write about a page describing the action of a character, a person you know, yourself, or evoking images for use in a poem. While writing, try to express the theme you have chosen through this mundane action. The action might be:

   a. farming or gardening
   b. taking pictures

c. organizing a stamp collection
d. knitting a blanket
e. playing baseball
f. making tea

While writing this page, do not mention in your writing death, birth, or love. You should instead simply have the idea in your head, have its feeling in your mind. Your theme should unfold naturally from this piece of writing, rather than make a glaring appearance that leaves the reader little doubt of the intended meaning.

5. FOLLOW UP

Ideas about creative writing and genre are constantly evolving and unfolding, transforming not simply the stories we tell, but how we tell them. Working across workshops and writing across genres opens countless and exciting possibilities. This is not to say that we should buy into the somewhat lazy position that good writing has no form, or owes no allegiance to structure or boundaries. Rather, the idea of crossing over genre allows us to find a fresh approach to content and form. We are not tossing out the concept of clearly delineated genres, but instead opening a conversation between the genres, creating a collaborative link between what has come before and what we, then, can contribute. By using elements from other genres in our work, we open up the possibilities and the directions our writing can take. Thus, we cease to be constrained by our habitual ways of seeing our writing, and indeed, our world.

Poet William Stafford said:

> Writing itself is one of the great, free human activities. There is scope for individuality, and elation, and discovery in writing. For the person who follows with trust and forgiveness what occurs to him, the world remains always ready and deep, an inexhaustible environment, with the combined vividness of an actuality and the flexibility of a dream.[7]

Trust and forgiveness are important parts of the writing process. We need to trust that we have something to say, something worth saying, and we need to forgive ourselves the writing we do that we know is not beautiful, or fresh, or new. We must let ourselves follow our thoughts, engage the connections we make, and explore those ideas and emotions that make us who we are. Only through writing often and writing a great deal is it possible to find the story you want to tell or the poem you need to write. It is like taking photographs and trying to get that one great shot. It requires attention, a keen eye for the world around us, and most of the time, hundreds of pictures before we get to the one where all the elements come together, where the moment is captured exactly, exquisitely and ethereally. The writing that happens in-between is by no means wasted. It is a part of the process of discovery, and the result of training ourselves to be the most constant of observers. Even then, once we find that part that is good, it takes revision, diligence, patience and attention before what we have written can be called 'finished'. It is important work, however, and worth the effort. Writing is a way for us to synthesize and understand the universal truths of the world, of life, of that which makes us human – what it means to have compassion, sympathy and kindness. As writer and novelist James Baldwin said, 'while the tale of how we suffer and how we are delighted and how we may triumph is never new, it always must be heard.'

Challenge yourself in your future writing to write outside of your comfort zone and experience. Experiment with different forms and structures. Perhaps you have a short story you wrote a long time ago. Revisit that story. What would happen if you turned it into a poem? Or a screenplay? What would it look like as a piece of flash fiction and could only be 500 words? What would happen if you sat down and decided to write the opposite of a sonnet? What would that look like for you? You need not avoid convention, but you should feel free to explore outside of our expected ways of seeing. Jazz musician Miles Davis once said, 'Learn the rules, master them, and then forget them.' We learn the rules by reading other writers. We master them by writing. To forget them, we write more. So keep going.

SUGGESTED FURTHER READING

Ray Gonzalez's *No Boundaries* showcases writers whose work embodies the diversity of styles and techniques representing the art of the contemporary prose poem. Gonzalez's brief introduction gives a history of the prose poem.

Brevity: A Journal of Concise Literary Nonfiction (www.creativenonfiction.org/brevity/) is an online journal devoted exclusively to concise literary non-fiction. Look especially at Lia Purpura's craft essay 'On Miniatures', which considers shortness in prose by defining the value of all things small.

The Best Creative Nonfiction, Vol. I, Lee Gutkind, ed. draws from alternative publications, 'zines, blogs, podcasts, literary journals and other often overlooked publications to find the best representations of a hard to define genre.

Analyzing Prose, Richard Lanham. This is an excellent style guide for revising in every writing context. Lanham provides an eight-step revision method called the Paramedic Method that is designed to help writers break bad habits and improve their writing.

Clear and Simple as the Truth, Francis-Noel Thomas and Mark Turner. This book considers classic prose style, and argues that writing is an 'intellectual activity, not a bundle of skills'.

Style: Toward Clarity and Grace, Joseph M. Williams: a rigorous examination of the elements of fine and elegant writing, and precise directions for improving writing.

Autobiography of Red, Anne Carson. A distinctive and inventive novel in verse that joins the archaic with the modern.

The Writing Life, Annie Dillard. Dillard's collection of essays probes her own relationship with writing, and discusses with great intelligence and wit how she writes and why she writes. Dillard is one of the finest lyrical essayists writing in English today.

Short Takes: Brief Encounters with Contemporary Nonfiction and *In Brief: Short Takes on the Personal*, Judith Kitchen ed. Each of these anthologies demonstrates almost every way brief non-fiction can be written.

Here follows a list of books and authors to read for their highly defined sense of style, and for their willingness to experiment with narrative, structure and poetic form. This list is by no means exhaustive, and you should continue to add to this list yourself. Seek out authors that inspire you, spark your creative ideas, or put you in a position to redefine the work that you have become used to thinking writing can do.

1. Barth, John. *Lost in the Funhouse*. New York: Anchor, 1988.
2. Brooks, Gwendolyn. *Selected Poems*. New York: Harper Perennial, 2006.
3. Carver, Raymond and Tom Jenks (eds). *American Short Story Masterpieces*. New York: Dell, 1989.
4. Nabokov, Vladimir. *The Stories of Vladimir Nabokov*. London: Vintage, 1996.
5. O'Connor, Flannery. *Mystery and Manners*. New York: Farrar, Straus & Giroux, 1969.
6. Stein, Gertrude. *Selected Writings of Gertrude Stein*. London: Vintage, 1990.
7. Vidal, Gore. *Point to Point Navigation, A Memoir*. London: Vintage, 2007.
8. Woolf, Virginia. *The Complete Shorter Fiction of Virginia Woolf: Second Edition*. New York: Harvest, 1989.

WORKS CITED

Baudelaire, Charles. *Modern Poets of France: A Bilingual Anthology*, Louis Simpson ed. Ashland, OR: Story Line Press, 1997.

Carson, Anne. *Autobiography of Red*. New York: Vintage, 1999.

Dillard, Annie. *The Writing Life*. New York: Harper Perennial, 1990.

Gutkind, Lee (ed.). *The Best Creative Nonfiction Vol. 1*. New York: W.W. Norton, 2007.

Kitchen, Judith. *Short Takes: A Brief Encounter with Contemporary Nonfiction*. New York: W.W. Norton, 2005.

Kitchen, Judith and Mary Paumier Jones (eds). *In Brief: Short Takes on the Personal*. New York: W.W. Norton, 1999.

Lanham, Richard. *Analyzing Prose*. New York: Scribner, 1983.

Pinsky, Robert. *The Situation of Poetry*. Princeton: Princeton University Press, 1976.

Purpura, Lia. 'On Miniatures'. *Brevity: A Journal of Concise Literary Nonfiction*. Fall 2007, last accessed on 14 January 2008 www.creativenonfiction.org/brevity/index/htm

Stafford, William. *Poets on Poetry: Views on the Writer's Vocation*. Ann Arbor: University of Michigan Press, 1984.

Thomas, Francis-Noel and Mark Turner. *Clear and Simple as the Truth*. Princeton: Princeton University Press, 1996.

Thomas, James and Robert Shapard (eds). *Flash Fiction Forward*. New York: W.W. Norton, 2006.

Williams, Joseph M. *Style: Toward Clarity and Grace*. Chicago: University of Chicago Press, 1995.

Chapter 11

Voice, Form and Point of View

Graeme Harper

1. WELCOME TO THE WORKSHOP

A recent edition of *The Literary Press and Magazine Directory,* published by the Council of Literary Magazines and Presses (CLMP) lists approximately three hundred and thirty places where creative writers might publish their work. The vast majority of these listings relate to fiction and poetry, and the vast majority of these listings are from North America. *The Literary Press and Magazine Directory* includes listings noted as being from 'independent literary publishers'. *The Literary Press and Magazine Directory* is an extensive and substantial publication, but its publishers wouldn't claim, of course, to include in it ever single opportunity for dissemination of creative writing, worldwide.

However, for 1 minute let's ignore 'the market'! Instead, let's ask the question: Is there something that draws together creative writers, regardless of the form or genre in which they work? Is there something they share, irrespective of whether they publish here or there; in fact, whether they publish at all.

Creative Writing is, in its essence, a way of viewing, approaching and responding to the world. Being a creative writer is a choice bound up in an attitude and outlook. There are a myriad of *other* ways that someone could choose to respond. Other creative responses are, of course, possible. Thus: Do creative writers share something fundamental with musicians, fine artists, film directors or dancers? Do they have affinities with computer games designers, architects, potters and graphic artists? And, naturally, there are other responses to the world that are not very often considered as 'creative': responses – those founded equally in the servicing of human, societal or industrial need; responses that involve very little that we might call 'creation'.

In all this, identifying what is distinctive about the act of Creative Writing does not seem overly difficult. To start simply: creative writers are largely concerned with words. This is obvious. However, the ways in which creative writers use words are not as simply stated. Can this use be compared to the ways in which a fine artist – say, a painter – uses paints? Can we compare the creative writer's use of pattern and movement with the way in which a dancer uses these things? It is easy to be lulled into thinking entirely comparatively here, without perhaps allowing for diversity of usage. So, for example, it would be ham-fisted to suggest that a biologist didn't ever use words in the same way as a playwright; or that a deep-sea diver didn't ever use ideas of pattern and movement in the way a poet uses these ideas. So what is distinctive about a creative writer's interest in, and use, of words?

It could be said that Creative Writing is hogtied – to use an unfamiliar critical idiom! – because, at its core, it cannot avoid the tyranny of words. Despite some notable experiments – Laurence Sterne's *Tristram Shandy*, for example, some of Donald Barthelme's short stories, Diane Schoemperlen's *Forms or Devotion*, the poetry of the members of the Electronic Literature Association, the work of Fluxus[1] – Creative Writing largely relies on words set out on a page, a screen or some other material mounting. Sound and image, while occasionally incorporated into works of Creative Writing, are almost exclusively secondary to the aspect and approach of materially bound words.

Now to take an alternative viewpoint. That is: that Creative Writing is advantaged because, at its core, it is privileged with access to the commonly used, and considerably revered, world of words. Despite some deviations from this core, Creative Writers are, thus, recognized as the primary proponents, and possessors of knowledge, involved in the understanding and use of words, set out on the page or screen or elsewhere. It is to creative writers that the world turns to see how words can inform, affect, alert, alarm and comfort; that is, how words can empower us all.

Returning to the market, then: whether hogtied or advantaged, who is it that forms the market for the work of creative writers? General readers. Educational readers: teachers and learners. Other creative writers. There's little doubt that a publication such as *The Literary Press and Magazine Directory* raises a primary question: if creative writers seek to *produce* who is that seeks to *consume*? Certainly other creative writers form a substantial proportion of the market for what is often called 'literary fiction' and a notable proportion of the market for poetry. Likewise, it is reasonably safe to state that general readers form a considerable proportion of the market for what is often called 'popular fiction' and a reasonably large portion of the market for creative non-fiction. It is unlikely the general reader forms much of the market for printed plays or screenplays; however, if we extend our exploration of Creative Writing product out into the computer games industry, it is highly likely the general 'reader' forms a large part of the market for these games. But, would we call these consumers readers? And if educationalists use works of Creative Writing for various purposes of knowledge exploration and knowledge acquisition in what sense is their reading produced by, and tied to, other forms of consumption slightly askew from the independent motivations of the majority of creative writers?

If Creative Writing is a way of viewing, approaching and responding to the world, understanding how do different readers or, indeed, new kinds of readers, respond to the voices and forms and points of view employed in Creative Writing?

Enter the workshop here, and leave behind the notion that you are a short story writer, a poet, a novelist, a screenplay writer, a creative non-fiction writer. Begin with the proposition that you are a creative writer. Begin with the idea that this involves certain attitudes and approaches to the material and ideas contained in the world and, that, with this in mind, the marshalling and organization of these things responds to your own needs and feelings. Imagine, then, that your reader is defined by the kinds of writing you are undertaking, and by the notions your chosen genre and your style project. Set out, if only informally, some sense of how these things define the actions you will undertake.

2. WRITERS AND READERS

There are many books that explore the nature of reading, and of the reader. Alberto Manguel's *A History of Reading* is one of the most notable. Manguel writes:

> Coming together to be read to also became necessary and common practice in the lay world of the Middle Ages. Up to the invention of printing, literacy was not widespread and books remained the property of the wealthy, the privilege of a handful of readers.[1]

The notion of there being privilege connected to reading is worthy of exploration. If – taking into account the history of printing and bookselling, considering the role of language (or, indeed, languages) and variations in regional and national access to avenues of communication – there is a history that can be discussed 'generically', how can creative writers today, and their readers, benefit from considering it?

Creative Writing was, at its origins, an activity largely confined to a few people. Its offerings were, again in the larger part, associated with acts of ceremony and celebration. Consider the role of writing in the liturgies of Christianity to place such a comment in Western context. Creative Writing was, at the time before the emergence of the modern reader, something devoted to acts of patronage. The creative writer, set forth into their activities by formal requirement and request, offered work bound to hierarchies that both separated this work from the average man or woman but also gave to it something of its cultural significance. Like the building of cathedrals or the passing on of stories by elders, the act of Creative Writing had value because of its relative remoteness from those who might encounter it, but never cause it to occur.

These, of course, are generalizations. Individual cultures reveal variations on this history. Sticking here to the Western and, in this first instance, the European, we can see throughout the period until the eighteenth century a general spread of the activity and consumption of Creative Writing, based on acts of limitation, privilege and control. Medieval European universities – not, it must be said, that these were only universities in the World, because we can look at the same time towards China and other non-Western cultures for notable emerging institutions of higher learning – medieval European universities housed a variety of individuals who would, today, be considered 'creative writers', individuals most often associated with the subjects of religion and theology.

It is a huge leap of time from the medieval period, over the Renaissance, to that of the modern literary arts market, commencing in the eighteenth century. But the logic of making such a leap here is straightforward. The Renaissance and, indeed, the periods of the sixteenth and seventeenth centuries, brought about developments in the role and place of Creative Writing – for example, the use of Creative Writing in articulating the modes of discovery brought about by global exploration by Europeans or, at least, as much 'global' exploration as could be accomplished with the transportation available at the time. Likewise, the role of Creative Writing in articulating ideas of novelty and discovery made in the burgeoning sciences. But it is the emergence of the modern writing marketplace, founded on the evolution of printing technologies, the birth of such Creative Writing forms as the novel, the emergence of the notion of copyright (even if, in the first instance, largely for the benefit of booksellers not writers) and the slow but important spread of the ability to read.

The eighteenth century, thus, is key to how we consider the modes and methods of Creative Writing as we undertake and understand them today. It is so because, particularly as the century moved on, Creative Writing formed a new relationship with its readers, with its disseminators and, therefore, with its writers. Where as previously Creative Writing was determined almost exclusively by acts of elitest selection and privilege; the eighteenth century saw the emergence of Creative Writing as determined by preferences of general consumption and by the demand for Creative Writing that could address a wider range of issues, determined not solely by religious and political concerns. In addition, once copyright law was applied, modes of dissemination began to change; for example:

> The compiler of the Renaissance commonplace book composed, transcribed, commented on, and reworked the writings of others – all in apparent indifference to the identity of the originators and without regard to ownership . . . one of the most powerful vehicles of the modern authorship construct was provided by laws which regulate our writing practices.[2]

Of course, this story is not entirely clear, entirely linear or spread entirely evenly across countries, years or genre. Nor is the discussion here focused on a literary critical analysis of the works that emerged during the period. Rather, what emerges in examining the changes in the marketplace, the changes in published works, the changes in consumption practices – the coffee-house consumption of novels, the public house consumption of biographies, to offer one shorthand version of the developments – is the modern sense of creative writers and their readers and the earliest evidence that, far from being defined by the notion of selection by the few Creative Writing became a mode of discovery, articulation and communication that soon could be accessed by the many.

3. BACKGROUND AND CONTEXT

Voice, Form and Point of View are some tools of the creative writer. Were they always thus? Perhaps not, or at least not in the same way: there's room here for some interpretation. It could be said that all forms of writing, throughout time, have used styles of voice, choice of form and aspects of point of view, to enhance the way they have delivered subject and theme. However, prior to the eighteenth century the notion of using these things in order to build a bridge between creative writer and general reader was not as significant and, indeed, the choices of method were curtailed by the demands of patronage and privilege. It would be ridiculous to suggest these things changed overnight; however, the fact that they were changing, and changing radically as the availability, and demand, for works of Creative Writing changed is significant.

Alternatively, it therefore could be said that a modern sense of Voice, Form and Point of View began in the eighteenth century and evolved according to the requirements of the modern market for Creative Writing works, a set of requirements that owed something to an increased secularization, an increased ability to read, and a wider spread of writers and readers whose relationships, both market-driven and aesthetically informed, became more cultural complex, if less overtly hierarchical. To put this in a simple fashion: what could be said, how it could be said, and who might say it, changed.

Again, it is important to shift away here from thinking about this only from the angle of literary criticism. There's enough evidence, certainly in the early part of this modern period, to argue from such a literary critical perspective that not much was different at all. However, from the perspective of Creative Writing, and its focus on the aspects of process, act and action, the development of the means (e.g. printing technologies), the motivations (e.g. emergence of copyright; highlighting of the human act of discovery through travel and/or through the machinations of science) and the methods (e.g. a new form such as the novel embracing the desegregating of creative writer and general reader) to support the argument that dealing with notions of Voice, Form and Point of View had begun to change.

Of course, history manifests itself in one of three ways: as long, slow movement; as cyclical rises and falls; and as event or incident. The motivations above might, in many ways, be considered as event – the passing of the Statute of Anne, in 1710, for example, that established copyright and set in motion circumstances by which individuals could claim ownership of a piece of Creative Writing for reasons other than patronage. The means, above, might be considered within the longer context of emerging dissemination strategies that continues today with the relatively recent impact of the worldwide web on the ways in which creative writers alert readers to their work; even to the way in which they write – which leads, of course, to a consideration of methods, some of which are founded as if overnight (e.g. the relatively swift development of the hypertext novel) and some of which persist against the impact of events or cycles of interest and action (e.g. the use of characters in fiction or the role of omniscience).

Voice, then, is a tool best understood in historical as well as creative context. The choice of voice – today a wide and varied choice – reflects the condition of culture around both creative writer and reader, and the choices employed reflect an interpretation by the creative writer of what will achieve the desired effect given the cultural moment at hand. The truth of this statement can be readily supported by anecdotal evidence from Creative Writing classes where perfectly able writers fall foul of thinking the voice of their fiction or poetry or even their screenplay must be that of something they read that was published a hundred years earlier! Most often this mistake comes about because of a desire to address some canonical literary critical notion of 'great writing' – though it is rarely the intention of the literary critic or of the Creative Writing teacher to give the impression that great contemporary writing is defined this way.

Creative Writing Form encapsulates many contextual considerations. Paul Horgan's memorable book, *Approaches to Writing*, touches on some of these. Horgan writes:

> Experiments in form, new vessels for each generation, renewed insights, must always be hoped for. The novel at its best is no more static and fixed in a mold than any expressive procedure.[3]

And this:

> The artist should look for form in everything – nature's forms, those of all the arts, those of the performing athlete, in which energy precisely meets need. The bodily tension we see in the great athletic act, even in its brevity, is a good analogy for the need for utmost coordination of all the faculties available to the writer when he is at work.[4]

While Diane Johnson in the *New York Times* collection *Writers on Writing* adds:

> On the other hand there are covert operations of your own character – your personal obsessions, perhaps – that ordain that, however you start out, you end up with the sort of novel that only you would write.[5]

And Jonathan Raban, writing in *The Writing Life: Writers on How They Think and Work*, a collection from the *Washington Post*, says:

> A book is strictly a subordinated world. Its logic, of symbol and metaphor, is at once tantalizingly suggestive and ruthlessly exclusive. From the moment a narrative begins to develop its momentum, it insists on what it needs and what it has no time for.[6]

Form in Creative Writing might, thus, best be understood in context in the same way form is generally understood in its broadest human context, as 'due to the action of force'.[7] That is, form comes about not simply because *it is*; rather, it comes about *because something, or someone, makes it so*. Form has an intimate relationship with the way in which individual writers view the world, the genre in which they are working and with ideas that might even be connected with body image, the physiology of sight, or the spatial sense of the writer brought about by cultural influences. Creative Writing Form, therefore, is the natural result of being in the world, and of being a writer faced with choices that are only in part defined by traditions or genre or canons of literary works.

Finally to 'point of view', a term most often associated with prose but, in fact, applicable to all kinds of writing. From whose perspective does any particular piece of Creative Writing proceed? How much authority does this point of view carry? How close to that of the perceived reader might it be? How much of a bridge between writer and reader does it create – a complete, empathetic arch from writer's experience to reader's interest; or, at the other extreme, barely a hint of outreach between them: instead, a clash, the kind of viewpoint that is at odds with the majority? Talking about point of view also initiates discussion about writing tone and tempo; it brings up questions about organization of ideas, about the veracity of facts presented, about the invoking of, or appeal to, emotions, and about the readership for different styles or packaged Creative Writing products (by which we might understand the ways in which contemporary publishing and bookselling often labels certain forms and genre).

4. THE WORKSHOP EXERCISES

Exercise 1: Voice

Voice doesn't only mean vocal qualities – however, perhaps even as much so as the idea of voice connected to dialogue in the screenplay, voice in poetry relates to how words 'sound', in the broadest possible meaning of sound.

Today, we can in some ways think of sound as a visual quality. This might appear to be a ridiculous comment. But wait! There is a connection with the cultural and historical changes we have experienced, particularly over the past century, and an important way in which the concept of a soundscape has changed over time. Increasingly, because of the impact of visual media such as film and television and, today, the digital imagery provided via the computer, we have come to associate sound not only with that which appears in front of us, or with detached, 'unseen' sound, but also with sound created or manipulated to support a visual artefact. More so than ever, then, sound has a quality of 'appearance'. Thinking about this in metaphorical terms is useful in understanding how sound has been used in Creative Writing throughout history.

Voice, or the combination of sounds as if spoken by someone or, occasionally, some thing, relates to personality. Imagine a poem as a personality and it is possible, almost immediately, to imagine the voice this poem might make. This is the case because we tend to think in terms of personalities we know, people we associate with our definitions of personality, and how they sound. To create this personality/poem it is possible to imagine how the arrangement of words, the use of diction, the manipulation of tempo, the use of syllable, punctuation and syntax, and the physical appearance of the poem on the page and screen, all contribute to a poem's voice.

Of course, a poem might not have only one voice. In fact, the idea of juxtaposing and contrasting, combining or paralleling voices can be a key part of a creative writer's strategy. Think of the ways in which a playwright uses word choice in dialogue to highlight the cultural or social background of a character; imagine, equally, the ways in which creative non-fiction must most often maintain a voice of considerable authority in order to convince a reader that they are dealing, largely, in facts. Voice is almost always a human-centred comparative idea – we understand voices by swiftly analysing in relation to other voices we have heard. So, for example, if someone speaks in a high voice, combined with the use of a limited vocabulary, we might describe that voice as 'child-like'. A shaky and soft voice might be described, alternatively, as 'old'. A very deep, slow voice could be said to be 'creepy' or 'ominous'. Some of this is largely subjective, of course; but this is only *largely* not entirely the case. The idea is simple: we make comparisons and endeavour to define voice according to a metaphorical leap away from the idea of sound to the idea of personality, attitude, aspect, possible action. Sound heralds, and sound informs, and voice is the most human manifestation of sound.

For this exercise, therefore, begin with the idea of a poem having a voice; list how this voice relates to the personality of the poem, to its subject and to its theme.

Complete a first draft of a poem, based on the definition you have established, and then ask whether the voice you have chosen – or the voices – give strength to the personality you had envisaged. If so, how? If not, why not? If not, start again: what do you need to do to imbue your poem with the personality of your choice?

Now consider an alternative poem, a poem you expect will have a contrasting voice to your first poem. Explain why: write these reasons down so that you can examine them. Juxtapose poem 1 and poem 2 and look at the word choice, structural approaches, and patterns of form, that have helped to create the shape of these poems.

A third poem might challenge the approaches of 1 and 2. You now have – and this might take some time as there is no limitation in terms of length or style of poem – you now have poems in conversation, quite literally perhaps. You could even begin to consider whether this evolving 'collection' represents the kind of conversation you might hear among friends or whether it is much more like an argument you've stumbled on at the counter of a supermarket! How these poems converse might metaphorically define whether they can form the basis of a publication in which they all might live.

Exercise 2: Form

The screenplay is one of the most 'formatted' of works in contemporary Creative Writing. It is therefore very concerned with aspects of form, though it could be considered that its concern with form is often in a narrowly defined fashion. This is for a number of reasons, not least because screenplay structure and appearance – if not also its style and relationship with its reader – relates to its existence almost entirely as a template for another art form (i.e. a film).

One rule of thumb for approaching screenplay writing is to let go of any literary notions, to not attempt to use the kinds of formal considerations that might often anchor a work of prose fiction or poetry. There are exceptions to this rule; but the premise of the screenplay is, fundamentally, that it seeks to be at the core of an art form that does not rely on writing presented on a page. There's a danger, of course, that this can be misinterpreted as 'the screenplay is never very good Creative Writing'. Nothing could be further from the truth. The screenplay is not often very good *literature*, in the narrow definition of that term – however, nor does it ever seek to be! In fact, there's some firm evidence that a screenplay that reads like a good novel or poem, on the page, produces the least successful film.

So here is a type of Creative Writing that concerns itself with form in order to communicate between individuals who need clear instructions on how to deliver the final results. Here is a type of Creative Writing that seeks to use form to *lift itself off the page*. And here is a type of Creative Writing that seeks to use the macro elements of format, if not necessarily the micro elements of form to make itself internationally comprehensible. In other words, a screenplay in any language seeks to appear similar and has the same purpose.

In this exercise, begin with a page of screenplay. This is one taken from the 1967 film, *The Graduate*:

INT. VERANDA ROOM
In the door to the lobby in the b.g. is Mrs Robinson. She pauses, looks into the room, sees Ben and starts toward him. Ben is looking out the window. He does not see her approach.

MRS ROBINSON
Hello, Benjamin

BEN
Oh. Hello. Hello.

He rises quickly.

MRS ROBINSON
May I sit down?
BEN
Of course.

He pulls out a chair, for her . . .

MRS ROBINSON

May I have a drink?

Ben looks toward a passing WAITER and raises his hand. The waiter pays no attention. Ben looks back at Mrs Robinson apologetically.

BEN

He didn't see me.

MRS ROBINSON

Waiter!

. . . The waiter stops in his tracks.

MRS ROBINSON

I will have a martini.

The waiter moves away.

MRS ROBINSON

You don't have to be so nervous, you know.

BEN

Nervous. Well, I am a bit nervous. I mean it's – it's
pretty hard to be suave when you're –

He shakes his head.

MRS ROBINSON

Did you get a room?[8]

Two aspects of form are immediately observable in this extract. First, here the screenplay can be seen very clearly in its formatted guise, a piece of Creative Writing that must address seriously the positioning of its elements on the page, and use this physical appearance as a call sign to identify its role as template for film-makers. Slug Line (description of location, time) is positioned above the scene. Action description follows. The character's name is positioned towards the centre of the page, and the dialogue offset from this name. There are many books that explain this structural appearance and thousands of available examples.

Secondly, this section of *The Graduate* leaves some room for interpretation of form. For example, the style and tone and pace of the action of description in this extract is relatively neutral. That is, the personality or character of the film is not overly idiosyncratic; the screenwriter doesn't use obscure words, a lot of jargon, or a syntax that suggests a strong cultural or linguistic bias. The action description is, thus, simple and direct, and therefore places a lot of the qualities of the film (certainly in this extract) in the interaction found in the dialogue. The dialogue, too, is relatively simple. However, even if we don't know the story of *The Graduate* we can see and, indeed, hear here in the dialogue of the screenplay the nature of the developing relationship between Mrs Robinson and Ben.

Imagine this section of *The Graduate* composed differently. Imagine, for example, an opening action description that used a number of paragraphs (a new paragraph often represents a new camera angle or shot). Imagine these paragraphs described the surroundings in detail and that they described Mrs Robinson and Ben and their actions. Imagine the waiter was described thoroughly. Now consider the dialogue and, rather than the pared down tension we see/hear in the original, imagine that Ben articulates in spoken word his feeling about the situation. Imagine Mrs Robinson responds in equal measure. Now think on a new order for the information, so that while the scene is largely the same

Mrs Robinson gets to her seat more slowly and the waiter responds, in the description, more effusively. This extract is also taken not directly from the screenplay but as it is quoted in Kenneth Portnoy's book *Screen Adaptation: A Scriptwriting Handbook* to emphasize that interpretative tools are often at play in considering screenplay form – while formats are relatively fixed (have a look at the Peter Howitt screenplay and film *Sliding Doors*, to see something slightly different) the internal dimensions of the screenplay can be adjusted, weighted, positioned to create the style of film the screenwriter intends. Other things then contribute: the director's input, the actors, the film's budget, and so on, but the screenplay can at very least suggest the end-product, if not always determine it entirely.

Having considered the questions above, try writing three pages of a screenplay of your own. List the characteristics you wish it to carry forth to a film production. When you've tried this once, create a second, contrasting list of characteristics. Write the three pages again. Now think on the subject and theme of your screenplay – whether it is just a wild idea or a fully developed concept – and ask yourself what aspects of form will best accomplish the task of creating a template for the film you imagine.

These kinds of considerations of form in the screenplay can be carried over to other works of Creative Writing. Though in the case of poetry or prose fiction, for example, the notion of being a template for another art form is mostly secondary, a lot can still be learnt from thinking about how a piece of Creative Writing sends interpretative signals to its reader/s, not least through its representation of form.

Exercise 3: Point of view

A standard way to explore point of view would be to consider the viewpoint of a piece of fiction – emphasizing First versus Third Person viewpoints, mostly, and perhaps commenting on the infrequent occurrence of the Second Person. This would give us an entirely reasonable background to viewpoint, and allow further exploration of such things as alternating viewpoints, multiple viewpoints, omniscience, limited viewpoints, writer–reader empathy, unreliable narration, and other things that reflect back on the ways in which viewpoint choice establishes a relationship both with the material at hand and with the potential readers or audience.

But viewpoint is both an easier *and* a harder concept than the discussion of First or Third person reveals. For instance, while the perspective from which a piece of Creative Writing is written is straightforward enough – for example, is it presented by a created narrator internal to the piece of Creative Writing, or by the author adopting a persona, or by a persona external to the Creative Writing – while thinking about this is simple enough, the question of how that perspective might assist or detract from the intentions of the *actual* writer is complex. The methods of understanding and exploring point of view are, fortunately, reasonably graspable – and this is the case whether the Creative Writing is prose, poetry, script.

Begin this exercise by identifying a scene. Perhaps this scene is reasonably multidimensional (e.g. a cityscape or a room containing a number of artefacts, people or a variety of acts and actions). Describe this scene as if you have entered through a certain street or door – say, to the left, with your entrance point now behind you – and say that you have entered this scene for some specific reason or reasons. Write this. Now, enter the scene again, but from an alternative street or door, and with contrasting intentions or reasons. How does the scene change? In what ways does viewpoint alter how the scene might be played out? How does reasons and intention impact on choice of viewpoint? How does it change the sense of the Creative Writing that must occur to articulate your ideas? These kinds of questions can be asked of any piece of Creative Writing – even the most intentionally 'neutral' will have a point of view.

5. FOLLOW UP

Voice, Form and Point of View are substantial topics in the field of Creative Writing. To suggest that they can be entirely wrestled into shape here, against the general rush of other things going on all around, would be over-optimistic. However, there are a number of important things that can be followed up.

First, as the condition of these Creative Writing techniques is related to the prevailing historical conditions, a personal survey of how these things are represented in the contemporary writing arts will no doubt yield considerable results. To add to this, if only anecdotally, the penchant for first-person novels, with fairly idiosyncratic voices, was plainly evident in English language fiction, worldwide, not so many years back; similarly, shifts in the use of traditional poetic forms has been notably impacted upon, historically, by changes in cultural tastes. A visit to the bookstore reveals a great deal.

Secondly, and taking on board the nature of historical change, it would be inaccurate not to point to the impact of late twentieth century digital media technologies on the modes and methods of creative writers. Much as the opening up of the book market in the eighteenth century brought about attitudinal changes, so the role of the internet, the wide distribution of visual and aural artefacts, via the web, and the increased opportunities for the domestic intersection of writer and reader, sound and vision, past texts and present works, has at very least asked creative writers to consider their techniques. Not everyone has been immediately affected! But the air of these changes is breathed by the vast majority, and looking at how Creative Writing is evolving, in conjunction with, or even alongside, these new methods of communication and entertainment is a worthwhile exercise.

Thirdly, this discussion has endeavoured to 'reach across the workshops', and the reasons for this are significant: though many writers favour one genre or style or form over another what can be gained from slipping outside of a chosen genre is considerable. It is, of course, a rare sight to find a creative writer who can reach levels of excellence in all Creative Writing areas; so examining the work of those do achieve genre-specific excellence seems universally useful. But reaching across the workshops also has another, deeper purpose, in that it asks for some consideration of whether creative writers in general approach the world with a certain perspective, the perspective of those who creatively use words to explore and, perhaps even to explain the things that they find.

Finally, following up on this chapter most obviously will entail comparing and contrasting the instructions of various 'How To' Creative Writing books, of considering whether one or other of these provides useful additional information on Voice, Form and Point of View. It will entail thinking more broadly about Voice, Form and Point of View, too, in that these are terms that carry a great deal of literal and metaphoric meaning. We frequently use them to describe angles of interest, ways of reporting, shapes and attitudes. D'Arcy Thompson, writing about the biological sciences in his book, *On Growth and Form*, first published in 1917, supplies a wonderful analogical conclusion:

> Some lofty concepts, like space and number, involve truths remote from the category of causation; and here we must be content, as Aristotle says, if the mere facts are known. But natural history deals with ephemeral and accidental, not eternal nor universal things; their causes and effects thrust themselves on our curiosity, and become the ultimate relations to which our contemplation extends.[9]

No doubt there are many who will defend the eternal or universal contributions of certain works of Creative Writing; but the nature of cause and effect – how we write and how this impacts on the reader or audience – is indeed a matter of considerable curiosity and contemplation.

Notes

Chapter 1: Short Fiction

1. Lorrie Moore, 'People Like That Are the Only People Here: Canonical Babbling in Peed Onk', *Birds of America* (New York: Picador, 1998) 212.
2. Gabriel Garcia Marquez, interview with Peter Stone, *Writers at Work: The Paris Review Interviews, Sixth Series* (New York: Viking, 1984) 324.
3. Moore, 212.
4. Edgar Allan Poe, rev. of *Twice-Told Tales*, by Nathaniel Hawthorne, *Graham's Magazine* May, 1842: 298.
5. Poe, 299.
6. James Baldwin, 'Sonny's Blues', *Going to Meet the Man* (New York: Dial Press, 1965) 140.
7. James Joyce, *Stephen Hero*, ed. John J. Slocum and Herbert Cahoon (Norfolk, CT: New Directions Books, 1944) 213.
8. James Joyce, 'The Dead', *Dubliners* (New York: Signet, 1991) 236.
9. Baldwin, 141.
10. I. A. Richards, *The Philosophy of Rhetoric* (New York: Oxford University Press, 1965) 125.
11. Edgar Allen Poe, 'The Poetic Principle', *Home Journal* 31 August, 1850: 1.
12. Donald Barthelme, 'The School', *60 Stories* (New York: Penguin, 1993) 312.

Chapter 3: Novel

1. Mario Vargas Llosa, *A Writer's Reality* (London: Faber, 1991) 39.
2. Darth Vader, *Star Wars*, 1977.
3. Anthony Trollope, *An Autobiography* (1883), chapter xv, in Miriam Allott, Novelists on the Novel, 148.
4. Carolyn Chute, 'How Can You Create Fiction When Reality Comes to Call' in *Writers on Writing: Collected Essays from the New York Times* (New York: Times, 2001) 35.
5. Vladimir Nabokov, *Strong Opinions* (London: Weidenfeld and Nicolson, 1974) 29.
6. Michael Korda, *Making the List: a Cultural History of the American Bestseller 1900–1999* (New York: Barnes & Noble, 2001) xxvi.
7. Joseph T. Shipley (ed.) *Dictionary of World Literature: Criticism, Forms, Technique* (New York: Philosophical Library, 1943) 405.
8. Vladimir Nabokov, *Lectures on Literature* (New York: Harcourt Brace, 1980) 5.
9. Vladimir Nabokov, *The Enchanter* (New York: Vintage, 1991; written in 1939, but unpublished).
10. Vladimir Nabokov, *Lolita* (London: Weidenfeld and Nicolson, 1959) 122.
11. Paul J. Hunter, *Before Novels, the Cultural Contexts of Eighteen Century English Fiction* (New York: Norton, 1990) 35.
12. Hunter, 354.
13. Burton Pike, 'The City as Image' in *The City Reader*, ed. Richard T. LeGates and Frederic Stout (London: Routledge, 1996) 243.

14. Lewis Mumford, 'What Is a City?' in *The City Reader*, ed. Richard T. LeGates and Frederic Stout (London: Routledge, 1996) 185.

15. Joyce Carol Oates, 'To Invigorate Literary Mind, Start Moving Literary Feet' in *Writers on Writing: Collected Essays from the New York Times* (New York: Times, 2001) 171.

Chapter 4: Playwriting

1. Cummings, ee. *Poems 1923–1954*, 332.

2. Edgar, David. MFA Dramatic Writing Workshop Course Notes, USC School of Theatre, 1 November, 2007.

3. Levitin, Daniel J. *This Is Your Brain on Music*, 127–128.

4. Zulu maxim umuntu ngumuntu ngabantu (A person is a person through other persons).

Chapter 7: New Media Writing

1. Jitter comes with the programming platform Max/MSP, which is for real-time musical and interactive applications. See http://forumnet.ircam.fr/366.html?&L=1 for more information.

2. A Quicktime movie of *soundAFFECTs* is embedded in Hazel Smith, *SoundAFFECTs*: Transcoding, Writing, New Media, Affect, *Scan: A Journal of Media Arts Culture* 4.1 (2007).

3. In Flash, a keyframe is a frame in which you establish exactly what will appear in that frame. It can be an image or a word or it can be blank. A keyframe is a way for you to specify that you want the image or word which is on the stage (the working area) to change.

4. In Flash you will only be able to do a small amount of work in one scene, and you will need to add scenes to extend the timeline. A movie of any length will be composed of many scenes in succession.

Chapter 10: Structure, Style and Theme

1. Robet Pinsky. *The Situation of Poetry* (Princeton: University Press, 1976) 162.

2. Charles Baudelaire. *Modern Poets of France: A Bilingual Anthology*, ed. Louis Simpson (Ashland, Oregon: Story Line Press, 1997) 73.

3. Richard Lanham. *Analyzing Prose* (New York: Scribner, 1983) 54.

4. J. D. Schraffenberger. *The Best Creative Nonfiction Vol. 1*, ed. Lee Gutkind (New York: W.W. Norton, 2007) 85–87.

5. Lia Purpura, 'On Miniatures'. *Brevity: A Journal of Concise Literary Nonfiction*. Fall 2007, last accessed on 14 January 2008 www.creativenonfiction.org/brevity/index.htm

6. Ismail Kadare, 'Before the Bath' in *Flash Fiction Forward*, ed. James Thomas and Robert Shapard (New York: W.W. Norton, 2006) 28–30.

7. William Stafford, *Poets on Poetry: Views on the Writer's Vocation* (Ann Arbor: University of Michigan Press, 1984) 20.

Chapter 11: Voice, Form and Point of View

1. Alberto Manguel, *The History of Reading* (London: Harper Collins, 1996) 116.

2. Martha Woodmansee, 'On the Author Effect: Recovering Collectivity' in *The Construction of Authorship*, ed. Martha Woodmansee and Peter Jaszi (Durham: Duke University Press, 1994) 27.

3. Paul Horgan, *Approaches to Writing* (London: Bodley Head, 1973) 88–89.

4. Horgan, 31.

5. Diane Johnson, 'Pesky Themes Will Emerge When You're Not Looking' in *Writers on Writing: Collected Essays from the New York Times* (New York: Times, 2001) 114.

6. Jonathan Raban, 'Notes from the Road' in *The Writing Life: Writers on How They Think and Work* ed. Marie Arana (New York: Public Affairs, 2003) 348–349.

7. D'Arcy Wentworth Thompson, *On Growth and Form*, first pub. 1917 (Cambridge: Cambridge University Press, 1995) 11.

8. Buck Henry and Calder Willingham, 'The Graduate' in Kenneth Portnoy, *Screen Adaptation: A Scriptwriting Handbook* (Boston: Focal, 1998) 42–43.

9. Thompson, 3.

Index

adaptation 74
Albee, Edward 47
Alien 57
alter ego *see* pen name
American Beauty 60
Andrews, Jim 80
Anglo-Saxon 26
animation 79–80, 83
Antigone 46
Aristotle 25
Arlington Road 57
Arteroids 79
Atlantic Monthly, The 9
Atwood, Margaret 26
Auden, W. H. 26
audiences 20
Austin, Jane 95
austraLYSIS 79, 83
authenticity 22

Bachelard, Gaston 20, 22, 23
Baldwin, James 7, 10–11
   Sonny's Blues 10–11
Ball, Duncan 104
   Selby Shattered 104
Barr, John 21
Barrett, Andrea 8
Barthelme, Donald 16, 93
Barthes, Roland 20
Beat-influence 15
Beehive 83
Bellow, Saul 38
Bender, Aimee 8
Berk, Laura 108
Black, Lewis 91
Black, Molly 101
Blume, Judy 99, 101
Blyton, Enid 99
   Famous Five series 99
Books for Keeps 108
Born Magazine 84
Brewster, Anne 80
Bulletin magazine 27
Bullets over Broadway 56
Burgess, Melvin 101

Campbell, Joseph 101
Cann, Kate 101
Carousel 108
Carver, Raymond 91, 95
Catholic Church 90
Cayley, John 78, 80, 83
   riversisland 80
   windsound 80
character 13–14
Chopin 67, 95
Chute, Carolyn 32
Cole, Joanna 105
   The Magic School Bus 105
Coleridge, Samuel Taylor 20–1
Collins, Billy 22–3
computer 79
convention 16–17
Cool Reads 108
Coover, Robert 16
Coverley, M. D. 80
   Afterimage 80
cummings, e.e. 41
cyberwriting 76, 79
cyborg 77

Daly, Niki 98
   Ruby Sings the Blues 98
Davis, Lydia 8, 16
Dean, Roger 79, 80
Degan, Bruce *see* Cole, Joanna
dialogue 13–15, 73–4, 93
Dickens, Charles 13
digital poetry 76
Dr Jekyll and Mr Hyde 47
Donaldson, Julia 98
   The Gruffalo 98
dramaturgy 43
Drunken Boat 84

East/West 54
Edgar, David 42
Electronic Literature Organization 84
Eliot, T. S. 26
energy 60
epic 15